"In clear-eyed and gorgeous prose, *Toy Medium* moves the question of Art's encounter with Science to an utterly original point of conflagration: where matter is mostly not matter. . . . Going to the bottom of the Imagination, where it still truly involves images, Tiffany explores how we have learned to see the inscrutable via our imagistic grasp of materiality. . . . This book is daring, brilliant, and deeply clever."

> JORIE GRAHAM, Boylston Professor of English,
> Harvard University, author of *Materialism* and winner
> of the Pulitzer Prize

"In this bold, speculative, and immensely learned study . . . Tiffany['s concept of] lyric substance—the 'sense' of materiality supplied to us by poets like Wallace Stevens and Marianne Moore—constitutes a world whose inaccessibility is legitimized by the principles of scientific materialism. Thus lyric, too long on the periphery of materialist discourse, emerges as being squarely in its center."

> MARJORIE PERLOFF, Stanford University, author of
> *The Futurist Moment* and *Wittgenstein's Ladder*

"Daniel Tiffany's *Toy Medium* is a lyrical inquiry into the circle of ideas: materialism, science, poetics. Winding through the whole is a fascinating exploration of toys—children's toys, physicists' toy models, philosophers' robots, nuclear weaponeers' toy towns. . . . My hope is that this book will contribute to a growing interest not in cleaving science from the arts but rather in exploring, poetically, the language, images and things that illuminate both."

PETER GALISON, Mallinckrodt Professor of the
History of Science and Physics, Harvard University

"*Toy Medium* is a brilliant achievement, synthesizing the history of science and poetics, technology and the arts, in an iconology of materialism. . . . All that is solid melts into air in this book, but just as quickly the airy poems of our climate condense into material, objective forms, weird gadgets, and objects of scientific research. . . . A wonderful feast of learning and wit."

W. J. T. MITCHELL, University of Chicago, author of
Picture Theory and *Iconology*

Toy Medium

Toy Medium

Materialism and Modern Lyric

Daniel Tiffany

UNIVERSITY OF CALIFORNIA PRESS

Berkeley   Los Angeles   London

Title page illustration: Drawing of Eros in a chariot pulled by a
butterfly, Jaquet-Droz automaton (Switzerland, late eighteenth
century). Courtesy Musée de Neuchâtel.

University of California Press
Berkeley and Los Angeles, California

University of California Press, Ltd.
London, England

Library of Congress Cataloging-in-Publication Data

Tiffany, Daniel Newton,
    Toy medium : science, materialism, and modern lyric /
Daniel Tiffany.
      p.   cm.
    Includes bibliographical references and index.
    ISBN 0-520-21920-1 (alk. paper).—ISBN 0-520-21922-8
(pbk. : alk. paper)
      1. Poetry, Modern—20th century—History and criticism—
Theory, etc.   2. Lyric poetry—History and criticism—
Theory, etc.   3. Literature and science—History—20th
century.   4. Materialism in literature.   I. Title.
PN1271.T54   2000
809.1'4—dc21   99-20033

                                  CIP

Manufactured in the United States of America
08   07   06   05   04   03   02   01   00
10 9 8 7 6 5 4 3 2 1
The paper used in this publication meets the minimum require-
ments of ANSI/NISO Z39.48-1992 (R 1997) (*Permanence of Paper*).

Λάθε βιώσας

Epicurus

CONTENTS

ILLUSTRATIONS

Materia Poetica

If a modern poet maintains that for each individual there exists an image which engulfs the world, how often does that image not arise out of an old toy chest?

Walter Benjamin, "Toys and Games"

Air is air,
Its vacancy glitters round us everywhere.
Its sounds are not angelic syllables
But our unfashioned spirits realized
More sharply in more furious selves.

Wallace Stevens, "Evening without Angels"

To give sense and passion to insensible things
is the most sublime task of poetry.

Giambattista Vico, The New Science *(1714)*

What does a mechanical Orpheus in the royal gardens of Saint-Germain-en-Laye in the seventeenth century have in common with the physical explanation of a rainbow? Or, to use more contemporary examples, what does a surrealist mannequin, or the practice of automatic writing, have in common with a theory of radiation? One might begin to respond to these questions, which sound like riddles, by examining the way ideas about toys and the weather have informed modern poetics. Yet a discussion of the literary significance of these analogies would hardly make a ripple in the expanse of cultural studies today, in part because so little appears to be at stake in contemplating an affinity between modern lyric poetry and a philosophy of toys or meteors. Another line of response, however, which speaks more directly to the way pictures inform our conceptions of matter and corporeality, engages larger issues, if only because it pertains to real bodies: mechanical dolls and meteorological phenomena have served as important models of corporeality in the history of physics.

To historians of science, these analogies are common knowledge, even if such expertise is not always sufficiently curious or critical. By contrast, the vigorous but often narrow defense of "materiality" now under way in literary studies lacks the conceptual vocabulary (and perhaps the imagination) to make sense of analogies or hypotheses generally regarded as milestones in natural philosophy and modern physics: the idea, for example, that a material body may be like a rainbow, or that its substance can best be described as a mechanism of radiation. In addition, literary scholars and theorists persist in equating materialism with realism, despite the literary evidence: what matters about the world in a poem often defies intuition. Physical events, combined with the materials of literature, frequently escape the horizon of experience—though not the limits of materialism. Equally puzzling, in light of the growing scholarly attention to material culture (not to mention the ethical and epistemological priority frequently assigned to materialist criticism), the question of materiality—what is material substance?—is largely absent from contemporary criticism. Even scholars and critics whose work rests, more or less directly, on the premises of materialism, or who purport to take up explicitly the question of materiality, often overlook altogether the history of philosophical materialism.[1] Matter, the very substance of bodies and artifacts, remains hostage to simple intuition or to scientific understanding. Most important, literary criticism has failed to address—though it is ideally suited to do so—the intrinsic role of pictures and elaborate analogies in shaping our knowledge of material substance, starting with the classical notion of the atom.

The iconography of materialism consists not only of analogies and tropes, of course, but also of material images in a variety of media produced as tools, models, or illustrations of material phenomena and materialist hypotheses. Natural philosophers of the seventeenth century liked to compare bodies to ingenious toys, and material substance to the weather, but they also crafted physical models of these analogies. They designed and built automata, for example, and made notes for elaborate fireworks displays that would approximate the meteoric bodies of nature. Some of these icons of corporeality referred to observable phenomena; some did not. Increasingly, however, with the development of more powerful technical media, the visual culture of modern physics came to assume that no phenomenon is intrinsically obscure, or immune to verification, unless it is unreal. The equation of materiality and visibility thus ruled out the possibility of phenomena that are, by nature, inscrutable. In principle, then, the idea of a material occult—a realm of phenomena that can be grasped only through the imagination—is anathema to modern science. In practice, however, this imaginary, material domain is an inescapable feature of the history of physics.

Inquiries into the nature of material substance rely fundamentally on images that do not bear witness to empirical entities, but rather serve as models of unobservable phenomena. Indeed, the *realism* of modern physics (in contrast to its mathematical foundation) relies, by necessity, on a framework of vivid analogies and tropes, sometimes realized in visual practice. That is to say, the foundation of material substance is intelligible to us, and therefore appears to be real, only if we credit the imaginary pictures we have composed of it. My concern, I should emphasize, is not whether atoms actually exist (a fierce point of debate in modern physics), or whether new electronic devices (such as the scanning tunneling microscope) can truly visualize the foundation of material substance. Rather, even if we now possess machines that can take pictures of atoms, the history of philosophical material-ism—and its many popular manifestations—is nevertheless condi-tioned by the invisibility of material substance and by the regime of analogy associated with it. Even more perplexing, the laws (and pic-tures) of material substance do not always coincide with the laws of intuitive bodies. At present we have no way of reconciling the nature of quantum materiality (the physics of subatomic matter) with the experience of ordinary bodies. Real objects appear to be made of unreal substance. At least for the foreseeable future, it is unlikely that we will overcome what Ian Hacking calls "the persistence of the image" in philosophical materialism. And beyond this impasse, we might ask: what if the image were to become law and we knew how to revise the laws of ordinary bodies to conform to our pictures of material sub-stance? With this question in mind, the visual illustrations in this book should be viewed not only as pictures of material substance but also, potentially, as images of the laws of ordinary bodies.

A book such as *Toy Medium*, which lingers over the transactions of materialism and lyric poetry, with the aim of reassessing the discursive import of poetry in contemporary culture, bears a complementary re-lation to certain recent developments in the history and philosophy of science. Bruno Latour, summarizing these momentous changes, writes: "The active locus of science, portrayed in the past by stressing its two extremities, the Mind and the World, has shifted to the middle, to the humble instruments, tools, visualization skills, writing practices, fo-cusing techniques, and what has been called 're-representation.' Through all these efforts, the mediation has eaten up the two extrem-ities: the representing Mind and the represented World."[2] In the latest thinking about science, a preoccupation with subject and object has given way to a concern with mediation and representation, with the agency of *pictures* (and various other "mediators")—an orientation that Latour calls "iconophilic." As a result, the conventional view that art invents and science discovers has begun to lose its hold on popular and scholarly opinion, permitting a revision, however tentative, of the capacities of art and science. At this historic juncture, Latour contends, "Science becomes rich in visualizing skills and art gains many entries into the object. Fiction is no longer free under the pretext that it would be subjective or impotent, and science is no longer merely 'accurate,' because to be so it would also need to be unmediated, unsituated, and ahistorical" (428). To historicize and aestheticize science, then, is to grant reciprocally to art and literature a deterministic role in the construction of the real. In this light, the forms of mediation and imagination proper to lyric poetry begin to resemble the tools and practices of science—especially, as in physics, when it is a question of depicting unobservable phenomena.

Certain plausible correspondences between science and poetry can therefore be traced to shared forms of material and imaginative practice, but also to the basic inclination of materialism: to make the intangible tangible. Both science and poetry proceed, in part, by making pictures of what we cannot see (or what merely escapes our notice), by attributing corporeal qualities to inscrutable events. Thinking about the relation of poetry to science inevitably calls to mind the genetic theory of poetry proposed by Giambattista Vico in his book *Nuova Scienza* (published in 1714). Vico, formulating a "new science of history and myth" amid the birth of the physical sciences, argues that the scientific imaginary (in all its branches) descends from the "wholly corporeal imagination" of poetry.[3] That is, basic scientific concepts (such as the atom) derive from what Vico calls "poetic characters" (32). Not only does science (like poetry) give tangible expression to the unseen or the imponderable, it imagines bodies to be "divine substances," thereby giving life and "passion" to insensible things. The origins of poetry (in divination and idolatry) are confirmed, Vico believes, by the "eternal property" it shares with science: "Its proper material is the credible impossibility. It is impossible that bodies should be minds, yet it was believed that the thundering sky was Jove" (78). Vico's insistence on the "credible impossibility" of science and poetry anticipates Latour's point about the "iconophilic" disposition of science.

Indeed, one of the aims of the present study is to mount a defense of poetry that does not shrink from the Vichian implications of the changing status of scientific knowledge and which therefore advances the prospect of viewing lyric poetry as a model for materialist criticism in the humanities.

Generally, I want to address the problem of materiality by developing a dialogue between poetics and philosophical materialism, and by elaborating a conception of lyric substance based on correspondences between scientific models of corporeality and a doctrine of materiality proper to lyric poetry. Because physics and poetics have historically shared the iconography of toys and meteors—the twin axes of materialist rhetoric—poetry's vision of the corporeal can help to elucidate the sometimes paradoxical bodies conjured by scientific materialism. I approach the concept of matter through the category of the aesthetic, but I also seek to articulate the aesthetic through the vocabulary of materialism. With these ends in mind, I develop a critique of the iconography of materialism, analyzing the kinds of pictures and analogies we have devised to represent the nature of matter and material bodies. At the same time, reviewing the constitutive role of the image in lyric poetry, I argue that the history of philosophical materialism coincides with modern poetics in its reliance on analogy (or pictures) and in its persistent equation of material and invisible phenomena. In this sense, one could say that the toy medium of material substance is never entirely distinct from the toy medium of lyric poetry.

To elaborate fully the historical and theoretical correspondences between poetics and materialism, and to make available to literary and cultural studies a more productive sense of the ambiguity of material substance, *Toy Medium* presents a wide range of popular and theoretical views pertaining to the history of materialism, coupled with an evolving theory of modern lyric. Chapter 1 reviews the modern polarization of science and poetry and introduces the idea of lyric substance—a doctrine of materiality proper to lyric poetry but also congruent with the philosophical problems intrinsic to scientific materialism. At the threshold of my discussion of lyric substance, Yeats's trope of the mechanical bird makes an emblematic (though contrary) appearance, followed by a summary and critique of the corporeal qualities attributed to lyric by the dominant figures of modern aesthetic philosophy: Lessing, Kant, and Heidegger. Chapter 2 initiates the book's critique of the iconography of materialism by surveying the doctrine of atomism in relation to the history of automata and mechanical dolls, the chief emblems of corpuscular philosophy, and to La Mettrie's conception of the "man-machine." Chapter 3 examines how the reliance of materialism on the figure of the automaton carries over into modern poetics through the "aesthetic of the toy," developed by Kleist, Baudelaire, Rilke, and Yeats, and by the surrealists (Hans Bellmer and Roger Caillois in particular).

Chapter 4 introduces the other main problematic of the book (after the toy): meteorology. How does the "mechanical philosophy" of materialism come to terms with the weather, and how does a "philosophy of meteors" relate to the phenomenon of lyric substance? In what respect is a cloud, or a snowflake, or a rainbow—all meteorologic phenomena—a body that can be regarded as an automaton? I address these questions by examining Johannes Kepler's elegant treatise on the snowflake and by drawing comparisons between the Baroque philosophy of meteors and Wallace Stevens's poetic meteorology (poems that yield some surprising observations on the synthesis of meteoric and racial identities). On the basis of these readings, Stevens emerges as a central figure in the modern formulation of lyric substance, the poetic materialist par excellence. More broadly speaking, I trace the conundrum of the meteoric body—the imponderable body—as it evolves through the doctrines of mesmerism and animal magnetism, through modern dance and performance at the Dada Cabaret Voltaire, and through the fascist collaboration of Mary Wigman and Leni Riefenstahl at the 1936 Berlin Olympics. Chapter 5 extends my critique of materialism to modern physics, with particular attention to the figure of the atom, which often marks, or lies beyond, the limits of sensation and analysis, and to the way its abstract nature affects our sense of what stone is, or flesh, or water, or fire. In this chapter, I also examine Karl Marx's rarely cited Ph.D. dissertation on Democritus and Epicurus (the founders of atomism in antiquity), in which Marx establishes the terms of dialectical materialism, including the ambiguous corporeality of the fetish. In addition, the final segment of chapter 5 examines the Baroque invention of the microscope and its bearing on the evolving relation between materialism and spectacular culture, as well as the genealogy of the "virtuoso" (as the early microscopist was called).

The final two chapters return to the question of lyric substance, that is, to the elaboration of material substance in modern lyric. Chapter 6 begins by examining the optical thesis of "radiant species," a model of vision fusing ethereal bodies and "atomic idols," and uniting this conception of vision, descended from atomism, with the regime of analogy in scientific materialism. Through the doctrine of radiant species, I outline a cultural poetics of radiation by documenting the instability of material substance—and its apparition in popular culture—in the 1950s, the heyday of the atomic age. I monitor, for instance, the strange birth of the radioactive body (borrowed from animal magnetism and the philosophy of meteors) in poems about the atomic bomb by Allen Ginsberg, Gregory Corso, and others, and in the apocalyptic rhetoric of the National Civil Defense films of the era. I also recount the strange coupling of the Beat poet and the physicist and examine the curious (and lethal) substance whose secrets they alone are said to possess. Chapter 7 ponders the rupture of materialism and realism in quantum mechanics and in the allegorical lyric of Marianne Moore. Specifically, as a way of evoking the political unconscious of material substance, I consider what bearing the ideological climate of Weimar may have had on the impossible pictures of material substance yielded by quantum mechanics. I make a final attempt to characterize the nature of lyric substance (and the fate of the animal machine) by assembling the bodies (and toys) in Moore's animal fables as if they had escaped from Erwin Schrödinger's "cat paradox." In the conclusion of my study, I address the implications for literary theory of the growing debate about mediation in science and the premises (and precedents) for greater lyricism in critical discourse.

These diverse materials are linked by the prospect of viewing corporeality, and material substance itself, as a medium that is inescapably informed by the pictures we compose of it. We are confronted with the idea that a material body, insofar as its substance can be defined, is composed of pictures, and that the conventional equation of materialism and realism depends on the viability of the pictures we use to represent an invisible material world. Indeed, to abandon pictures in the context of materialism means, as quantum theorists discovered in the 1920s, that material substance may be nothing more than a series of discrete events, without continuity or intuitive coherence. If modern lyric yields a *provisional* nature inevitably masking a world of tropes—an allegorical mode of understanding—then we must ask if the knowledge produced by lyric poetry does not coincide in fundamental ways with the realism of modern physics and with the inherently figurative character of Western materialism. To view the "engine" of lyric as essential to the configuration of scientific knowledge inevitably raises questions that have, until recently, escaped the purview of philosophy, not to mention the arena of public debate: Does poetics have a place in the history of materialism? Does poetry really "matter"?

CHAPTER 1

Poetics and Materialism

It is a curious fact that the Atomists, who are commonly regarded
as the great materialists of antiquity, were actually the first to say
that a thing might be real without having a body.

John Burnet, Early Greek Philosophy *(1892)*

Thou seest a hectic fever hath got hold
Of the whole substance, not to be controlled,
And that thou hast but one way, not to admit
The world's infection, to be none of it.
For the world's subtlest immaterial parts
Feel this consuming wound.

John Donne, "The First Anniversary"

LYRIC SUBSTANCE

Only a fool reads poetry for facts. Precise observation contributes, of
course, to the effects of poetry, and sometimes, in the absence of other
texts, poetry plays a substantial role in our knowledge of a world—as
in the case of Homer or John Clare (who writes about a way of life
that is scarcely documented). All the same, a modern reader does not
generally consider poetry to be a reliable source of knowledge about
the nature or substance of material things. Indeed, when it comes to

objective representations of corporeal phenomena, poetry appears to have no say in determining what matters and what does not. To be honest, I'm not sure what a poem could tell me about things as they really are—physically speaking—cleansed of thought and feeling, memory and dream. My reluctance to grant poetry any authority in these matters stems, in part, from a certain conception of poetry but also, and more importantly, from certain assumptions prevalent in the humanities about the unequivocal nature of matter and material phenomena.

Few ideas are more deeply entrenched in Western society than the assumption that poetry and scientific materialism are antithetical modes of knowledge, having produced two disparate—and perhaps incommensurable—cultures. In the twentieth century, a number of influential modernists (often associated with the avant-garde) sought to mitigate the effects of the increasingly polarized relation between art and science, or to subvert altogether its hierarchical nature, especially the priority of scientific reasoning. In the Anglo-American tradition, T. S. Eliot developed a complex literary and historical analysis of relations between science and poetry, acknowledging that poetry is fully implicated in what he calls the "dissociation of sensibility" prevalent in modern culture since the mid-seventeenth century.[1] In response, he calls for a poetry that would incorporate and revise—but not entirely abandon—the rationalism of modern physics. This strategy, like his diagnosis of the problem, acknowledges the historical imbrication of science and poetry, even if it does not fully grasp the Baroque consonance of Metaphysical poetry and corpuscularian philosophy. He contends that a modernist revival of Metaphysical poetry—which he regards as "the direct current of English poetry" (66)—would help allay the dualism of modern experience. According to Eliot's analysis, the conjunction of poetry and materialism achieves its most significant form in the Metaphysical lyric.

In continental philosophy, Martin Heidegger's diagnosis of the problem—and his response to it—reflects his view of the relation between science and art as antithetical and immutable. He proposes a new mode of thinking—a radical alternative to science—modeled after poetry and recalling the prescientific mentality of the Greeks. His attack on scientific method presumes that atomic physics and the "age of the world picture" are both rooted in a mode of representation that possesses the object—and indeed determines its essential nature—through "calculation" (the essence, in his view, of the scientific mind).[2] From this perspective, the world of objects, and indeed the material substance of all bodies, is merely an effect of calculation, which Heidegger regards as a kind of picture—a "subjective" picture—but also as the root of modern technology. In contrast to scientific reasoning and the fatality of the world picture, Heidegger turns to what he calls the "open place" of poetry—a trope he borrows from Rilke's *Duino Elegies*—which he associates with modes of being and knowing that invert the relation, integral to science, between mind and world. Although Heidegger's conception suffers in comparison with Eliot's, since Heidegger fails to historicize "poetry," or to see it as implicated in the regime of calculation, both Eliot and Heidegger overlook the many forms of mediation shared—and wielded to divergent effects—by poetry and science. In both cases, the view that poetry and scientific materialism are essentially at odds rests on a superficial knowledge of the history of materialism. This view is not only mistaken, I want to insist; it is dangerously misleading, because it implies that poetry can recover a place in public discourse only as a radical alternative to science, a position inevitably construed as anti-realist—and unrealistic.

Even the best poets are not immune from assumptions about poetry and materiality that lead to an absolute distinction between scientific and lyrical modes of knowledge. This distinction often coincides with an antipathy to poetry—and not only on the part of readers who are unfamiliar with poetry. Marianne Moore, for example, once declared about poetry: "I, too, dislike it."[3] The context of her complaint makes it all the more provocative: these are the first words of a poem, and hence what remains of the poem oscillates in light of this antithetical statement. In addition, the complaint is troubling because the reader can't be entirely sure that Moore's confession actually refers to poetry. The poem skirts the object of the poet's displeasure, withholding its name, banishing it to a place—the title—outside the proper boundaries of the poem. Through this displacement, Moore sentences poetry to a kind of internal exile, a medium sequestered in a world of its own making. She reads poetry, she says, with "perfect contempt." And her disclosure alludes, in complicity, to the reader's disaffection: the great poet is not alone in her antipathy to lyric.

Perhaps, though, I'm jumping to conclusions about what Moore dislikes about poetry, since the short (and final) version of "Poetry" never spells it out. She names, or describes, the object of her "contempt" only in segments of the poem that she deleted from the final version—though even in these variations she is far from explicit about what she dislikes. In its first published version (from 1919), "Poetry" begins: "I, too, dislike it. There are things that are important beyond all this fiddle." If we assume "it" to be poetry, then "all this fiddle" refers to poetry in general but also to Moore's own poem. "Fiddle," of course, implies equivocation and uncertainty but also perhaps, in this context, what Yeats called the "sensual music" of lyric. A later version of "Poetry" (published in the second edition of *Observations* in 1925) proscribes what Moore views as the poet's greatest temptation: "Enigmas are not for poetry." Hence, though Moore's own poetry is hardly free of enigmas (as this poem demonstrates), she appears to regret poetry's inability to be completely literal and explicit about things. "Beyond all this fiddle," beyond poetry, are things precisely as they are physically in the world, and poetry, in Moore's opinion, generally gets things wrong.

Still, Moore concludes her denunciation of lyric in the short version of "Poetry" by claiming that it somehow remains "a place for the genuine." In so doing, she reserves a place for poetry's version of things. But is poetry merely a "place" in which real things might appear? Or could it be that bodies possess, or are possessed by, something called *lyric* substance, a consistent and perhaps even systematic doctrine of corporeality proper to the devices of lyric poetry? And I wonder what this lyrical matter might have in common with the materials of poetry itself—the substance of words and pictures—or even with scientific explanations of matter. Is it possible for lyric to maintain a kind of objectivity, to conceive a substance apart from its own body? Further, if we could produce a model—a picture—of lyric substance, might it not, despite its illegitimacy, have a place in current debates about material culture and the nature of corporeality? More specifically, is it possible that the "soul" of lyric—the technical apparatus proper to its effects—plays a more substantial role than we suspect in the *institution* of material substance?

To pursue the question of the nature of lyric substance would require close attention to the kind of body produced by lyric; to the nature of its material substance, whether continuous or discontinuous, palpable or impalpable; to its modes of appearance and disappearance; to its limits, its temporal nature, and its modes of relation. Is lyric substance commensurable with intuitive experience, either wholly or partially? Is it susceptible to historical analysis, to lawful prediction, and hence to domination? Because lyric substance is inherently qualitative—at once performative and representational—these questions concerning the nature of the lyric body can never be entirely distinct from questions about the intelligibility and corporeality of the lyric image and about the pneumatic substance—the breath—of the poem. Thus to inquire into the nature of lyric substance inevitably requires attention to poetics, to the apparatus of image, analogy, and trope that forms the productive matrix of the lyric body, and also, of course, to metrics, to the body of air that constitutes the poem. From a broader perspective, aesthetic philosophy suggests that the ephemeral nature of the lyric apparatus gives it a crucial position in the genealogy of the so-called disembodied images of the modern technical media. Hence any consideration of the lyric apparatus (already a topic with a distinguished critical history) could be enlarged by framing it in terms of the materiality of pictures in contemporary visual culture.

To determine the place of lyric in a genealogy of the aesthetic therefore requires that we come to terms, both historically and philosophically, with the principle of materiality. If the idea of lyric substance possesses any significance beyond the sphere of literary criticism, that significance lies in its relation to the iconography of materialism, to the kinds of pictures we have devised to represent the nature of matter and corporeality. A critical assessment of the materiality of pictures cannot proceed without, as it were, conducting an archaeology of matter. To grasp the nature and significance of lyric substance, we must refrain from granting any sort of critical immunity to the principle of materiality. To this end, the chapters that follow attempt not only to address the problem of materiality through the category of the aesthetic but also to view the nature of the aesthetic through the history of materiality. And it is the former problem—the aesthetic foundation of materialism—that, because it is more controversial, requires closer inspection.

We must also ask, however, whether poetry may be inherently materialist in its orientation (as Vico believed), or whether the conjunction of materialism and poetry might be traced to a specific historical matrix and therefore identified with a particular school of poetry. The answers to these questions depend in part on one's definition of materialism, yet one can also discern certain persuasive historical alignments. In Anglo-American literary history, the possible conjunction of materialism and lyric poetry cannot be isolated from the example of Metaphysical poetry and its critical reception. Eliot revives this controversy for twentieth-century poetry, yet his basic understanding of the Metaphysical lyric (not to say his evaluation of its qualities) rarely departs from Samuel Johnson's essay on Cowley's poetry, which Johnson regards as typical of Metaphysical verse. Eliot ignores, however, the degree to which the *"discordia concors"* of Metaphysical poetry, in Johnson's view, derives its radical premises, and its style, from the "new science" of materialism in the seventeenth century.[4]

Johnson makes it perfectly clear that he regards the Metaphysical poets as counterparts to the Epicurean philosophers (known as "virtuosos") promoting the "mechanical hypothesis" of atomism. He reminds the reader that Cowley was made "Doctor of Physic" in 1757 at Oxford, becoming a member of the Royal Society in 1761. Further, consulting Birch's *History of the Royal Society,* Johnson notes that "he appears busy among the experimental philosophers with the title Dr. Cowley" (343). And, more generally, Johnson compares the Metaphysical poets in their scientific demeanor to "Epicurean deities making remarks on the actions of men, and the vicissitudes of life, without interest and without emotion" (348). It is only in reference to statements such as this that one can grasp the true import of Johnson's attack on the "subtility," fragmentation, and "perversity" of Metaphysical verse. For we must bear in mind Johnson's conjugation of the poet and the scientist (both compelled by "violence" and "novelty") when we read: "Their attempts were always analytic; they broke every image into fragments, and could no more represent, by their slender conceits and labored peculiarities, the prospects of nature or the scenes of life, than he who dissects a sunbeam with a prism can exhibit the wide effulgence of a summer noon" (348–49). In Johnson's view, "analytic"—or prismatic—verse pulverizes experience: metaphysics in poetry becomes a branch of physics.

The legacy of Metaphysical poetry sometimes survives in an emblem of mechanical philosophy that is inherited, in turn, by a modern poet. And sometimes a poem supplies an image that functions both as an emblem of corporeality and as a reflection of the lyric apparatus, thereby allowing us to consider the relation between poetics and materialism through the medium of a picture. Students of modern poetry are familiar with the mechanical singing bird that appears in two of Yeats's most famous poems, "Sailing to Byzantium" and "Byzantium." The bird in these poems, an automaton, revises the Romantic topos of the bird, which functions in the poetry of Keats, Coleridge, and Shelley as an emblem of lyric poetry. Yeats's lyric automaton represents a body "out of nature" inhabited by the poet, but also a body that is distinguished, in the end, by its immateriality. The prospect of analyzing the toy as a figure of lyric substance can only be enhanced by taking into account the philosophical connotations hovering about the metal bird—specifically, the role of the automaton in mechanical philosophy, the Baroque foundation of atomic physics. For the automaton is the most prominent emblem of corporeality in early modern science. Thus the lyric automaton of Yeats's poems evokes, at least implicitly, the divergence—and the possible concurrence—of poetic and scientific conceptions of materiality.

What can we learn from this figure? In the first stanza of "Sailing to Byzantium," the poet surveys

> the young
> In one another's arms, birds in the trees,
> —Those dying generations—at their song . . .

He continues:

> Whatever is begotten, born and dies.
> Caught in that sensual music all neglect
> Monuments of unageing intellect.[5]

Here the poet anticipates the antithetical character of the mechanical bird by emphasizing the mortality of its natural counterparts: "Those dying generations—at their song." Further, this scornful description of the bird in nature and its "sensual music" prepares the reader to align the mechanical bird, when it appears in the poem's final stanza, with the "monuments of unageing intellect":

> Once out of nature I shall never take
> My bodily form from any natural thing,
> But such a form as Grecian goldsmiths make

Of hammered gold and gold enamelling
To keep a drowsy emperor awake;
Or set upon a golden bough to sing
To lords and ladies of Byzantium
Of what is past, or passing, or to come.

In this passage, the poet, "out of nature," transforms himself into a mechanical bird, an automaton clearly opposed to any conception of the natural body—a symbol instead of what he calls "the artifice of eternity." The poet therefore assumes a body that is first and foremost a representation, a work of art. The speaker refrains from calling the device a bird, referring to it instead as a "form," to emphasize its dissociation from mere sensuality and nature and to insinuate the automaton into the realm of "unageing intellect."

The poem, however, resists converting the artificial bird into an immaterial form, since the automaton, like the bird in nature and the lyric genre it represents, is inevitably caught in its own "sensual music." Because the "sensual music" the poet wants to disavow is at once the song produced by the poet and the rhythm of mortal life ensnaring the poet and the bird in nature, he cannot reject one without rejecting the other. In addition, insofar as "sensual music" refers to physical vitality, the mechanical bird comes to life when it sings and is transformed into a kind of living picture. Thus, signifying both the lyric medium and the corporeal fate of the poet, the trope of "sensual music" illustrates the dual nature of lyric substance. Yeats confirmed the basic ambiguity of lyric substance in comments he made about fashioning a "soul" in this poem: "It is right for an old man to *make his soul,* and some of my thoughts on that subject I have put into a poem called 'Sailing to Byzantium'."[6] The crucial point here is that the soul, conventionally opposed to corporeal existence, is something the poet *makes:* the soul is an artifact. We can thus regard the lyric automaton in the poem as an image of the material soul, as well as an emblem of immateriality. At the same time, the lyric automaton by implication confronts its double, the automaton of mechanical philosophy, which depicts the body of scientific materialism.

At first glance, then, "Sailing to Byzantium" sets up a rather simplistic contrast between the bird in nature and the bird of artifice and immateriality. Yet the poem's final stanza makes it clear that the automaton, ostensibly an emblem of "unageing intellect," comes perilously close, in the context of the luxurious court, to the condition of a mere toy or plaything for the "drowsy emperor." Indeed, the automaton is a deeply sensual and precious object made of "gold and gold enamelling." The mechanical bird, then, is not merely the antithetical foil to its natural counterpart, but rather an antithetical object that sustains within itself a dialectic of sensuality and intellect, matter and immateriality. The lyric automaton mediates between two divergent visions of Byzantium: a realm "out of nature," faithful to "unageing intellect" and its mechanical forms, and the setting for the hedonistic tastes and habits of the Byzantine court. These two dimensions of Byzantium, which coalesce in the figure of the luxurious and ingenious mechanical bird, represent the two dominant (and historically intertwined) aspects of philosophical materialism: speculation and observation, that is, the mechanical—and purely intellectual—method of hypothesis (or deduction), on which modern theoretical physics is based; and empiricism, which has its roots in the Epicurean correlation of knowledge, perception, and pleasure. It is entirely plausible therefore to regard the mechanical singing bird of "Sailing to Byzantium" not (as it is conventionally interpreted) as an expression of idealism, but rather as an articulate emblem of philosophical materialism.[7]

In "Byzantium," written three years later, in 1930, Yeats once again explores the figure of the mechanical singing bird, revising significantly its position in the dialectic of materialism:

Before me floats an image, man or shade,
Shade more than man, more image than a shade . . .

Miracle, bird or golden handiwork,
More miracle than bird or handiwork,
Planted on the starlit golden bough,
Can like the cocks of Hades crow,
Or, by the moon embittered, scorn aloud
In glory of changeless metal
Common bird or petal
And all complexities of mire or blood.[8]

In these later reflections on the poet's specular body (and, by impli-
cation, on the mechanical bird), now characterized as an "image," Yeats
retains the contrast between "common bird" and "changeless metal,"
yet all trace of the epicurean court has vanished.[9] Isolated from its
hedonic aspect, the automaton now completes the stalled pageant of
dematerialization, advancing from "bird" to "handiwork" to "mira-
cle"—a rhapsodic progression toward incorporeality that reiterates the
spectrum of man, shade, and image. Through the figure of the autom-
aton, then, both of Yeats's poems offer a puzzling—and sometimes
paradoxical—picture of materiality, as well as a complex meditation
on the materiality of pictures. The idea of lyric substance emerges at
the point where these corresponding representations of corporeality
and the lyric medium intersect, which is also the point where the
automaton becomes a *living* picture.

THE ICON WEEPS

The personification of lyric and the material soul by an animated toy
in Yeats's poems suggests that the idea of lyric substance may have
something to tell us about the nature of images in contemporary cul-
ture—as long as we bear in mind that a toy, animated or not, is a kind
of picture. But what could lyric poetry, a mere plaything among the
arts, possibly tell us about the burgeoning empire of visual culture?
Poetry, for the most part, plays no role in the mechanism of institu-
tional power or in the great public debates that determine what's real

and what's not; whereas pictures always seem to be in the thick of things, competing with reality and influencing it profoundly. Indeed, given the ubiquity and allure of pictures in public discourse, some people insist that the old distinctions between reality and representation must on occasion be abandoned, or at least inverted. The latest generation of pictures (and machines) continues to erode our sense of the limits of being, undermining the difference between beings and "picture-flesh" (to use Merleau-Ponty's phrase) and distinctions between matter and immateriality.

All right, then, some say pictures are more fun than the real thing, and some say you can't tell the difference between the two anymore; but nobody would dream of calling a picture a thing with a mind of its own, or a mind without a body. Since almost no one wants to say pictures are alive, it's hard to know what to make of certain kinds of pictures, often associated with the modern technical media, which appear to be possessed of the desire to cross the border between animate and inanimate, material and immaterial. The material ghosts emanating from contemporary media have a number of historical precedents, ranging from the medieval topos of the miraculated icon (which bleeds, weeps, or even accosts an observer) to the discourse of automata and mechanized toys (which finds belated expression in Yeats's emblem of the mechanical singing bird).[10] As usual, it's the iconoclasts who take most seriously the secret life of pictures, brooding over the old dynasties of intelligence and countersurveillance until a new layer of deception comes to light, and pictures begin to look like spies to the anxious spectator. Paul Virilio, for example, writes about "swarms of image-beings," and Jean Baudrillard's notion of the simulacrum appears to have been conceived with some of the requisite features of a new reality.[11] All the same, despite Virilio's marvelous detective work on the metaphysics of the new image, we still tend to draw a firm line between pictures and "life" (however that may be conceived). And because we do, pictures that show signs of "life" should, by definition, be regarded not as ordinary pictures but rather as phenomena (with or without bodies) that share certain properties with what we call pictures.

I suspect that a more palpable, and certainly more plausible, scandal remains submerged in the romance of the ontology of pictures. Indeed, if we are to grasp its true significance (that is, what it can tell us about our own bodies), then we must understand the problem of the animate image as an allegory—a theatrical rendering of the enigma of corporeal substance. For the iconoclastic vision of eidetic "life" (as well as the anxiety it arouses) invariably seizes on the uncertain *materiality* of images. Thus questions about the ontology of pictures can often be traced to certain paradoxical implications concerning their corporeality. Furthermore, the impulse to revive (and revise) Erwin Panofsky's concept of *Kunstwollen,* to ascribe to pictures a kind of will, appears to coincide with their disembodiment. Thus if we are to reach the core of the problem of the aesthetic in contemporary culture, we must choose a path that leads through the province of materialism.

A paradoxical notion of incorporeal images also appears to be closely linked to the emerging disciplinary formation of "visual studies," viewed by some as a successor to art history. A recent "visual culture questionnaire" (sent to "a range of art and architecture historians, film theorists, literary critics, and artists") asked its respondents to comment on several propositions, including the following statement: "It has been suggested that the precondition for visual studies as an interdisciplinary rubric is a newly wrought conception of the visual as disembodied image, re-created in the virtual spaces of sign-exchange."[12] According to this view, the so-called "new paradigm of the image" (the "precondition" of the emerging discipline of visual studies) rests on a paradoxical notion of corporeality that equates the anomalous materiality of the mediated image (the precondition of the new *Kunstwollen*) with the *absence* of a body. When this paradox (that a material image is not a body) is aligned with questions concerning the material substance of natural bodies, we can begin to glimpse the scandalous implications of a doctrine of incorporeal images. It is not altogether surprising that a thesis regarding images (and machines) as a singular order of being might emerge from a vision of the immaterial body, as if the material substance of a picture were commensurable only with the anomalous body of an angel.

We need not abandon or discount what W. J. T. Mitchell calls "the constitutive fiction of pictures as 'animated' beings" to examine more carefully the materiality of pictures.[13] Indeed, we can reach the province of materialism by following an ancient, if somewhat treacherous, path through the discourse of aesthetics. For the Greek term *aisthēsis* means, generally, "sense perception, sensation," as well as the "sensual apprehension of a thing"; the substantive, *aisthēton,* denotes "the sensible, the object of the senses."[14] The problem of aesthetics bears directly on the discourse of poetics, a term that functions, in its broadest sense, as a synonym for *technē* but also, in its proper sense, as the "productive science" *(poiētikē episteme)* of representation—pertaining both to making and to judging imitations.[15] More specifically, in Aristotle's conception, poetics treats the material and technical properties of an artifact *as if it possessed a soul.* Thus Aristotle is less concerned with existing drama than he is with its form *(eidos)* or "species," which constitutes the "soul" of the artifact.[16] What Aristotle calls the soul of tragedy—or any imitation—pertains to the form of sensible things without matter. The soul of an imitation is therefore a kind of formal picture (the *eidos* or species) that borrows its substance from the medium at hand. If we compare Aristotle's conceptions of rhetoric and poetics, we find, as Richard McKeon observes, that "in rhetoric, Aristotle's chief emphasis is on determining the 'body' of that which is essential to art"; by contrast, in poetics, "the analysis of the objects of the fine arts . . . turns not merely on the powers or habits of artists, nor on consideration of the materials susceptible of treatment or the 'body' of art, but it is concerned with the examination of the form or 'soul' of poetic production."[17] Thus, whatever the discourse of poetics may reveal about the technics and the corporeity of the artifact always reflects the "constitutive fiction" that the material artifact possesses a "soul."

Viewed from this standpoint, poetics obviously poses a significant problem, related in the context of modernity to fetishism, concerning the erotic and spiritual "life" of material objects. Indeed, historically speaking, the emergence of modern aesthetic philosophy in England and Germany in the early eighteenth century cannot be isolated from the role of the fetish in Enlightenment thought. Shaftesbury and, later, Kant (in his essay on the sublime) acknowledge the relevance of fetishism to the experience of art, yet they seek, for obvious ideological reasons, to distinguish it from "higher" forms of "interest" and pleasure in aesthetic experience. The distinction, however, remains ambiguous and unstable, even in Kant's *Critique of Judgment*. Despite the historical convergence of poetics and fetishism around the question of value (which supplies the principle of animation), the two discourses fashion the secret "life" of the artifact in very different ways. What distinguishes poetics from fetishism in this respect is the particular conception of materiality inherent in its assumption regarding the "soul" of an artifact (as well as the relative insignificance of the principle of exchange in poetics).

Clearly, the "problem" of poetics begins, for the modern reader, with the word *soul:* what does Aristotle mean by *soul,* and how does the soul of an artifact become evident through its material and technical features? What is the relation between soul and *technē*? Although McKeon contrasts the "body" and the "soul" of poetic production, we should be wary, in this context, of any firm distinction between corporeal and incorporeal elements. For the soul is a property not of the mind, or of some other impalpable entity, but of the body. It is a natural phenomenon: humans and animals have souls, according to Aristotle, and so do plants.[18] The soul, a "habit" or "power" possessed only by bodies—though not by all bodies—is a formal picture of animation. The analogous "soul" of poetic production is its form, *eidos,* or species:

not its immediate sensual existence, but a shape lacking a body, a picture without matter. Hence to argue that pictures have souls implies that the power of art to captivate the mind derives in part from its ambiguous materiality, which is a countersign of animation. The problematic body of art survives in the *Critique of Judgment*, where Kant argues that aesthetic pleasure derives from the apprehension of *form,* an ideal material phenomenon divorced from the sensuality of the artifact. The idea of a body that is not a body calls to mind the "form" of the lyric automaton, which Yeats regards as a soul fashioned by the poet. Modern formalism in this respect can be described as a poetics of the material soul, a formulation that accounts for the fetishistic qualities of art—its latent animation—in terms of artifice and bodies that subscribe to a principle of nonsensuous similarity. Generally speaking, then, we can refer the problem of live pictures to the poetic principle of a material soul (even if we don't yet fully understand what *soul* means).

As the term *poetics* indicates, Aristotle initiated a tradition that views poetry as the paradigm of all aesthetic production, a tradition sustained and elaborated by the dominant texts of modern aesthetic philosophy. Privileging poetry in this manner has distinct implications not only for our thinking about the body of art, but also for our assumptions about the materiality of natural bodies. For if lyric substance is only breath—a pneumatic form—or traces of writing, then the body of lyric lacks the unambiguous physical presence of sculpture, painting, or architecture. Lyric poetry, of course, possesses a body, but the materials of the voice are fleeting and its substance in print all but inscrutable. Aristotle, and those who follow him by maintaining the primacy of lyric, therefore imply, or contend overtly, that the effects of aesthetic production are heightened by the ephemerality of the medium, by pictures and artifacts that are, to some degree, disembodied. Thus, to grasp the meaning of formalism in the context of poetics, we must be prepared to assimilate the art *object* (and material artifacts in general) to what I want to call the "meteoric" body of lyric. Indeed, as Yeats suggests by depicting the soul as a mechanical toy, the lyric poem itself—its body—is the primordial image of the material soul. Clearly the discourse of poetics, which maintains that sensuous imitation is enhanced by the incorporeality of the medium, also has a great deal to say about the "soul" of the electronic image.[19] Poetics therefore provides the basic terms for a genealogy of the aesthetic extending from lyric to the so-called disembodied pictures of contemporary media.

By placing poetry at the top of the hierarchy of the fine arts, modern aesthetic philosophy privileges the immaterial body of lyric in a way that decisively affects our sense of the corporeality of pictures in general. According to Lessing and Kant, the arbitrariness and the temporality of the linguistic sign, along with its ambiguous corporeality, place poetry at a distinct remove from the sensuality of nature. And it is precisely this alienation of lyric from the material world that enables it to represent visible (and invisible) worlds with greater freedom and ingenuity than any other medium. Thus the most effective medium of sensuous imitation (or invention) is the medium barred by its physical properties from directly imitating the material world. Lessing concludes that poetry, as a temporal medium, has no business describing things, or making pictures of bodies at rest. Further, the language of poetry, as a medium, is distinct from language as a means of communication—a thesis that modern poetics has found all but irresistible. Concerning the impression of reality conveyed by a poem, Lessing contends, "I am a long way from seeing the object itself.... I do not deny to language altogether the power of depicting the corporeal whole according to its parts.... But I do deny it to language as a medium of poetry, because the illusion, which is the principal object of poetry, is wanting in such verbal description of bodies."[20] Poetry is therefore adept at producing illusions, some of which (such as the "cloud" of invisibility that envelops the Homeric warrior) have no basis in intuitive experience.[21] There is a distinct correlation, moreover, between the amorphous and illusory bodies conjured so effectively by lyric and the ephemeral device of the poem itself. The principle of lyric substance comes into play inasmuch as the Homeric cloud of invisibility reflects the meteoric body of lyric.

Kant, even more explicitly than Lessing, asserts the priority of poetry in his *Critique of Judgment:* "Among all the arts, *poetry* holds the highest rank."[22] In addition, Lessing's thesis that the language of poetry is not suitable for describing things (and should not therefore be judged as a means of communication) becomes more articulate, and more emphatic, in Kant's aesthetic philosophy. For, in Kant's view, poetry's superiority as a medium coincides with its independence from nature and with the unreality of the imagery it produces.

> Poetry fortifies the mind: for it lets the mind feel its ability—free, spontaneous, and independent of natural determination—to contemplate and judge phenomenal nature as having aspects that nature does not on its own offer in experience either to sense or to the understanding, and hence poetry lets the mind feel its ability to use nature on behalf of and, as it were, as a schema of the suprasensible. Poetry plays with illusion, which it produces at will, and yet without using illusion to deceive us.[23]

Poetry therefore apprehends sensuous nature by inventing it, by producing "illusions" or *impossible* pictures that exceed the qualities of intuitive experience or understanding. Thus, Kant explains, to things "exemplified in experience" the poet "gives sensible expression in a way that goes beyond the limits of experience, namely with a completeness for which no example can be found in nature. And it is actually in the art of poetry that the faculty of aesthetic ideas can manifest itself to full extent."[24] Poetry dissembles nature, so that nature, disfigured, becomes the body of an invisible ("suprasensible") world. And this invisible material world is truer than the nature depicted by the other, more palpable arts (which produce "mere imitations") precisely because it is unconstrained by nature, because it is produced by a medium, poetry, that does not share the unambiguous physical presence of natural objects. Hence the subtle body of lyric reflects the mind's independence from nature even as it evokes the sensuality of nature with supreme ingenuity.

Heidegger's lectures on the nature of art and poetry, perhaps the most probing philosophical essays on art in the twentieth century, preserve the idea of poetry's preeminence in the arts as well as the doctrine of poetic incommensurability advanced by Lessing and Kant. In "The Origin of the Work of Art," Heidegger maintains, "The nature of art is poetry"; and, further, "The linguistic work, the poem in the narrower sense, has a privileged position in the domain of the arts. To see this, only the right concept of language is needed. In the current view, language is held to be a kind of communication. It serves for verbal exchange and agreement, and in general for communicating. But language is not only and not primarily an audible and written expression of what is to be communicated."[25] And it is poetry, in Heidegger's view, that preserves the essential, noncommunicative function of language, thereby linking it, for example, to architecture. Thus the reason for the superiority of poetry, as Heidegger explains it, echoes Lessing's thesis of poetic incommensurability. Further, in the language of poetry, "Everything ordinary and usual becomes unbeing. The ordinary and usual have lost the capacity to give and preserve being as measure" (72). Thus poetry's resistance to communication coincides with its disfigurement (or dematerialization) of nature. In this respect, Heidegger's philosophy of art adds little to the views of Lessing and Kant.

Heidegger's thinking about poetry departs significantly, however, from traditional aesthetics in his elaboration of the concept of "the Open" and its relation to lyric. As I understand it, his treatment of "the Open" pertains essentially to the *matter* of lyric, to its peculiar substance, which ensures the freedom and independence of poetry from nature emphasized by Lessing and Kant. Heidegger declares, "Due to the poetically inventive essence of art, an open place turns up in the midst of what *is,* in the openness of which everything is other than usual."[26] Hence the lyric artifact, the material opus, coincides with, or indeed is identical to, an "open place" (a conception related to Moore's sense of poetry as "a place for the genuine"). The body of lyric appears to comprise a latent body—a form of *nothing*. Yet the concept of "the Open" in poetry can be understood, according to Heidegger, only in relation to *naming* and *lighting*: "Language brings what *is* as something that *is* into the open for the first time. . . . Language, by naming beings for the first time, first brings beings to word and to appearance. . . . Such saying is a projecting of lighting" (73). The "open place" of lyric, which is at once the body of lyric and its power to name things, is to be associated not with vacancy but rather with a form of *illumination* that makes it possible for things to appear in the world. Lyric substance can then be regarded as analogous to the physical properties of light, as long as we recall that lighting is equivalent to naming.

Heidegger confirms the strange corporeality of lighting and naming, which constitutes the "open place" of lyric, when he probes the material medium of the artifact. He asks, "What does the work set forth? . . . What is the nature of that in the work which is usually called the work-material?" (45–46). To answer this question, he contrasts the nature of what he calls "equipment" to "temple-work"—the dwelling, the artifact, which "portrays nothing." On one hand, the matter of equipment "vanishes into usefulness"; "By contrast, the temple-work, in setting up a world, does not let the matter disappear, but rather lets it come forth for the very first time and to come into the Open of the world of the work" (46). Here we find the topology of the Open coinciding with the emphatic materialism of "temple-work." In addition, Heidegger explains, "All this comes forth as the work sets itself back into the massiveness and heaviness of stone, into the firmness and flexibility of wood, into the hardness and luster of metal, into the clang of tone and into the naming power of the word" (46). Remarkably, this evocation of the material media of the fine arts ends by revealing that the substance of lyric consists in "the naming power of the word." This disclosure suggests that the corporeality of lyric is unlike the material dimension of other art forms in that its body possesses a kind of agency, like naming or lighting. Lyric substance, as Heidegger conceives it, therefore comprises what poetry brings to light in a name.

CRITICAL MASS

This talk about lyric substance is tolerable, of course, only so long as it's confined to the sphere of poetics. But what about the real stuff, or at least about the stuff that is judged to be real by disciplines with a say in these matters? Can there be any relation between the provisional formulation of lyric substance I have outlined here and the substance of philosophical or scientific materialism? Almost a hundred years ago, Bertrand Russell observed, "The word matter is, in philosophy, the name of a problem."[27] Today we have only to reflect on the astounding plasticity of imageric substance, and the corporeal theater of "substance abuse," to realize that popular culture has superseded philosophy as the critical laboratory of material substance. Yet the current explosion of materialist criticism, or scholarship devoted to material culture, in the humanities appears to rest on the assumption that materiality is not so much a "problem" as a principle taken on faith, at once the unavoidable medium of social realism and a countersign of ethical consciousness. Although one might expect to find some uncertainty about the difference between bodies and figures of speech, since literature professors are now almost as likely to study material culture as the text of a poem, it appears that the distinction between corporeal and incorporeal phenomena is secure, at least intuitively, in the emerging curriculum of cultural studies. Further, this distinction appears to be the basis of an ethical priority increasingly associated with the study of bodies and material artifacts—not including literary texts, unless they happen to document an episode in the history of corporeality. No one, I think, would dispute that academic scholarship, even when it pertains to ordinary bodies, rests on more than perceptual or intuitive experience; yet the objectivity of material substance in academic discourse (as opposed to popular culture) appears to be largely an effect of something resembling intuition—a kind of faith, if you like.

Russell made his statement two decades before he recognized in the new postulates of quantum theory a scientific "problem" adequate to his philosophy of logical atomism. Thus for Russell, but also generally speaking, the problem of materiality in philosophy, or in literary and culture studies, need not be contingent on scientific models. We may wonder, however, what significance the epistemological crisis of quantum physics in the 1920s possesses for materialist criticism in the humanities. How would the work of cultural studies (and its preoccupation with material culture) be affected by the idea that the "substance" of things does not always observe the laws of causality or ordinary intuition that appear to govern the things themselves—the idea that material substance may not be compatible with the phenomenology of bodies? It's not clear that we are willing to inquire about the materiality of material culture, or the corporeal substance of bodies, despite—or perhaps because of—the enormous political stakes associated with these critical paradigms. Perhaps we should leave all that to science. Indeed, as Gianni Vattimo contends, "in contemporary philosophy, matter—the concept, the problem of materiality—has no role; it is simply absent!"[28] We should not, however, misunderstand Vattimo's point; the absence of a problematic does not imply uncertainty. On the contrary, this lacuna implies stable and reductive conceptions of materiality. Ironically, in his view, only science preserves the essential ambiguity of matter: "It is only in the scientific and positivistic disciplines, prior to philosophy, that the concept of matter has lost its proper consistency and definite contours" (49). By implication, therefore, it is only in philosophy, or in humanistic disciplines increasingly dependent on the authority of historical evidence, that one finds stable and functional definitions of materiality.

To be fair, it is clear that Vattimo's charge is not entirely accurate; for questions pertaining to the historical construction of bodies animate some of the most valuable studies emerging from the humanities today.

Even so, the very substance of all these bodies (alive or dead) is too often left—with misgivings, of course—in the hands of science. If not left to science, "the materiality of matter" (in Vattimo's phrase) emerges as the "other" of language, a thing inimical to reflection or representation, which we overlook even when we mean to confront it, or else abandon—with a clear conscience—to "trauma," or to some lifeless notion of "pleasure." When we do suffer to entertain the stuff, or to think about which bodies "matter," we tend either to trivialize "substance," as if it were a toy, or to endure it, as if it were a climate. And if we find ourselves inside the picture—the phenomenology of the weather comes to mind—we find it difficult to describe the difference between its material and ideal dimensions. So what are we to make of these pictures of material substance, fashioned by familiar hands, yet which return to us as ciphers? Although it may be the case that matter is nothing more than a constellation of events, intelligible only to mathematicians, we cannot yet be absolved of the phenomenology of pictures dwelling about us and dwelling in matter.

CHAPTER 2

The Natural Philosophy of Toys

Each organized body of a living being is a kind of divine machine
or natural automaton, which infinitely surpasses all other automata.
Gottfried Leibniz, Monadology *(1714)*

DOLLS AND DIVINATION

To develop more fully the idea of lyric substance, we must start by
examining the kinds of pictures, such as automata, that have close
historical ties to authoritative doctrines of materialism. An investiga-
tion of this sort participates in the growing body of research by art
historians, philosophers, and historians of science into the writing and
visual practices of science, and especially into the ways in which these
practices affect the gathering and analysis of evidence. Lorraine Daston
and Peter Galison, for example, have studied the role of visual atlases
in the formulation of objectivity, and Daston has more recently ex-
amined the relation between collecting and the genealogy of "facts."[1]
A great deal of the work now being done on the material "culture" of
science concerns the formalization of intuitive phenomena through
experiment, inscription, and representational practice. By contrast, I

am interested in scientific images or artifacts depicting material phenomena that are beyond the limits of sensation—a kind of image directly related to literary tropes, and to allegory in particular.[2] In his account of scientific "iconophilia," Bruno Latour examines assumptions about the use of images that "point at remote phenomena and absent features," gestures that "help us to see the invisible."[3] At the foundation of the iconology of materialism is the invisible figure of the atom, an image whose durability stems from its extreme simplicity. Indeed, the intuitive features of the atom are so tenuous—so abstract—that the history of materialism has consistently found it necessary to supplement the figure of the atom with analogies that render material substance in a more plausible and concrete way. For example, in the context of Baroque natural philosophy, the automaton served as a model not only of the visible mechanism of the body but also of the invisible foundation of material substance—the realm of atoms. The "reality" of material substance almost always depends, therefore, on a double layer of imagery: the abstract figure of the atom requires translation into a more lyrical repertoire of scientific "models." Images or tropes of invisible phenomena, insofar as they produce (one could even say "invent") intuitive features of the phenomena they depict, demonstrate in an absolute sense the critical thesis that scientific evidence *produces* the phenomena it depicts. This thesis is reminiscent of Vico's genetic theory of poetry—"genetic" in the sense that poetry is said to produce what it depicts.

Evidence of the dialogue between physics and poetics has been largely effaced from scientific discourse in the three hundred years since the birth of the "mechanical hypothesis." Vico's writing on the "new science" gives the most substantial account of this dialogue. For example, in his essay *On the Study Methods of Our Time,* published in 1709, he writes,

Modern physics, too, I would be inclined to think, is conducive to poetic craft. Poets, today, employ expressions describing the natural

causes of phenomena because they intend to vindicate their an-
cient claim, the earliest poets having been singers of physical phe-
nomena. . . . In conclusion, inasmuch as modern physics borrows
its most sensuous images, expressive of natural causes, from me-
chanics, which it uses as its instrument, it endows poets with a
treasure of new expressions both striking and novel.[4]

The legacy of this lost discourse can be recovered from a variety of
historical and literary sources. To begin with, the special significance
of the relation between scientific materialism and mechanical simu-
lacra remains embedded in the cultural history of the automaton as a
mechanical device and as a philosophical or literary topos. In the lit-
erary imagination of popular narrative, for example, traces of the sev-
enteenth-century dialogue between physics and poetics survive in two
of E. T. A. Hoffmann's tales on the subject of automata. In "The Sand-
man" of 1816, the character Spalanzani, who creates a female autom-
aton named Olympia (whom he calls his daughter), is described as "the
clever mechanician and automaton-maker," and also as a "famous sci-
entist" and "professor of physics."[5] In "The Automaton," a story writ-
ten two years before "The Sandman" that is in many ways a model
for the later story, the clairvoyant and automated "Talking Turk" is
the work of a Professor X, a philosopher of aesthetics and a physicist
who maintains a laboratory where he constructs his automata (includ-
ing an orchestra of automated musicians and, ostensibly, the anony-
mous woman who is the object of the main protagonist's affection).[6]
The precise correlation between physics, aesthetics, and dollmaking is
never spelled out in either of Hoffmann's stories, though the reader
might plausibly assume that the ability to construct a lifelike autom-
aton is linked, in some fashion, to an understanding of the material
substance of objects and bodies (the special precinct of the physicist).
Still, given the nature of the task, it would seem more appropriate for
the dollmaker to be a biologist or physiologist.

Several qualities ascribed to the automata in Hoffmann's stories do,
however, call to mind the technical as well as the cultural origins of

the automaton, thereby offering a clue to the riddle of the priority of physics in the fashioning of animated dolls. Olympia, the automaton in "The Sandman," is a singer and musician who at one point performs "a bravura aria in an almost piercingly clear, bell-like voice."[7] Similarly, though to greater effect, music and automation converge in the narrative of "The Automaton." When Professor X reveals to Ferdinand his orchestra of musical automata, he provokes a philosophical and sometimes technical discussion of the possibility of reproducing "nature's music."[8] In addition, Ferdinand's attraction to his beloved, whom he suspects to be an automaton, is precipitated by the sound of her singing voice, which he hears coming from behind the walls of the Professor's garden. The mixture of dread and wonder that Ferdinand feels over this mysterious woman is compounded by the fact that the Talking Turk, the fortune-telling automaton of the narrative, repeats to him a dream that he (Ferdinand) had about his beloved prior to meeting her. Thus the function of the principal automaton in the story (the Talking Turk) is divinatory and oracular, though the townspeople suspect it of being a false automaton (a figure manipulated surreptitiously by human hands).[9]

The automata in Hoffmann's stories are associated either with music or divination, qualities that recall the most ancient, and the most persistent, applications and mythical themes associated with mechanized figures. The first complex, self-activating machines in antiquity were not tools but toys, and, more precisely, *singing birds* and other *parerga* (ornamental devices), including moving or talking statues employed at the sites of oracles.[10] Indeed, the mechanical singing bird has remained a popular and enduring motif. In these correspondences between song, divination, and the mechanized toy, we can discern the basic features of the automaton as a mythical figure; yet if we are to explain the allusion to physics in Hoffmann's tales about automata, we must also examine in some detail the role of the mechanized toy in the history of materialism. We might, for example, ask why the physicist of the seventeenth century, an adherent of "corpuscular

Figure 1.   Engraving of Von Kempelen's chess player, showing its false mechanism and space for human accomplice (Austria, eighteenth century). See note 9.

philosophy," granted special significance in his scientific training to the techniques and intuitions of the dollmaker. For the leading figures of seventeenth-century scientific materialism, following a strong medieval tradition that regarded the construction of automata as standard scientific practice, were not only natural philosophers but also technicians involved in the fabrication of clocks, toys, and automata.[11] Descartes, to take the most salient example, expressed a keen interest in the construction of mechanical figures; according to one of his correspondents, he planned to build "a dancing man, a flying pigeon, and a spaniel that chased a pheasant." In addition, he "toyed with the notion of constructing a human automaton activated by magnets."[12]

Figure 2.   Mechanical birds (with view of interior mechanism). Private collection (France).

Leibniz, a generation younger than Descartes, in addition to constructing one of the first calculating machines (in 1673), presented to the Paris Académie des Sciences in 1675 a new spring design for a clock mechanism.[13] It is therefore hardly surprising that, in Georges Canguilhem's observation (citing a letter from Leibniz to the Duke of Hanover in 1676), "Leibniz exalts the superiority of German art, which has always strived to produce works that move (watches, clocks, hydraulic machines and so on) over Italian art, which has always attached itself exclusively to the fabrication of lifeless objects made to be contemplated from without."[14]

The seventeenth-century natural philosopher's interest in automata cannot be understood without reference to the origins of technology in antiquity and, more specifically, to the Alexandrian phenomenon of the mechanized toy. The first recorded automata are the singing blackbirds of Ktesibios (third century B.C.E.), sometimes found in conjunction with the earliest examples of the water-clock (also developed by Ktesibios) and refined by Philo of Byzantium (second century B.C.E.).[15] Although the natural philosophers of antiquity characterized automata as *parerga,* the clockwork and the singing birds in these devices shared the same pneumatic technology, making it impossible, as Derek Price suggests, to distinguish between the two mechanisms on the basis of technical or functional criteria: "The deepest complementarity exists between the clepsydra principles used in astronomical models and clocks and the almost identical workings of the Heronic signing birds and other *parerga.*"[16] Further, as Price emphasizes, the characterization of automata as *parerga* contradicts what he discerns to be the primacy of the aesthetic function in the development of pneumatic technology: "The most ingenious mechanical devices of antiquity were not useful machines but trivial toys. Only slowly do the machines of every-day life take up the scientific advances and principles used long before in despicable playthings and overly-ingenious, impracticable scientific models and instruments."[17] Clearly, the ambiguity of the *parergon* in the development of clocks and automata coincides with a question regarding the role of the aesthetic. A fundamental confusion emerges between what appears to be intrinsic to the device (in this case the clockwork) and the toys or figures that animate it and move by the same mechanism as the inscrutable clock.[18]

To argue that the ambiguity of the *parergon* implies the primacy of the aesthetic function in the early development of automation depends largely on a critical evaluation of the machines that we presume to be

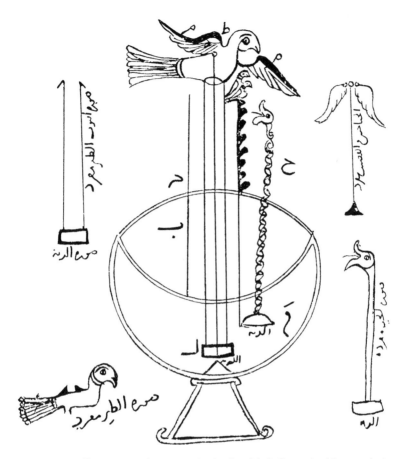

Figure 3. Illustration of pneumatic singing bird, from Arabic translation (c. 1350) of Philo of Byzantium, *Pneumatica*. Ms. 3713, Aya Sofya Museum, Istanbul. The mechanical singing bird to which Yeats refers in his Byzantium poems would have been made with the help of technical drawings such as this one.

useful in these circumstances—that is, the *clocks* associated with the mechanical singing birds (and other automata) of antiquity. The clocks described by Ktesibios, Philo, and Hero had no scale of hours, no hands or pointer, nor any kind of legible face.[19] With no constant means of indicating the time to an observer, the ancient water-clock does not so much tell time as possess it, or embody it in its mechanical "movement" and technical configuration. Thus, the first clock, like the mechanical singing birds and *parerga* built in conjunction with it, is essentially a simulacrum of nature—though perhaps more abstract in its topographical features than the mechanized puppet or bird. Even if such a machine does tell time through the routine but enchanting gestures of its automata, the essential fascination must lie with the mechanism itself: absent the "signals" of the automaton, one simply observes the clockwork, wondering at its abstract yet material possession of time. This is precisely the conclusion that Price draws from the enigmatic appeal of a clock without hands or face: "It would be a mistake to suppose that water-clocks, or the sun-dials to which they are closely related, had the primary utilitarian purpose of telling time. . . . On the whole, their design and intention seems to have been aesthetic or religious satisfaction. . . . The designing is a mathematical *tour-de-force* in elegantly mapping the heavenly vault on a sphere, a cone, a cylinder, or on specially placed planes."[20] The ambiguity of the *parergon* in these devices makes it impossible to isolate the mechanical singing bird or puppet from the idea of a mathematical picture or a topographical "mapping" of time and nature. Further, insofar as the automaton is a kind of picture, it is a picture that is also a timepiece. The relation of the automaton to time, which derives from its identity as a clock without hands or face, pertains not only to the incorporation of time, and to an image of the body in time, but also to implacable laws that exceed the body's mortal span.

The key to the correlation between materialism and the automaton lies in the fact that ancient clocks, mechanical singing birds, and other automata were all regarded, as the titles of Philo's and Hero's treatises indicate, as *pneumatica*—instances of pneumatic technology. Pneumatics is the branch of physics that deals with the mechanical properties of air and other elastic fluids or gases (such as water).[21] With its theoretical assumptions about the nature of matter, pneumatics in antiquity was essentially a specialized application of atomist theory. Indeed, it was arguably the *only* successful application of atomist physics, and it later constituted the principal framework for the revival of atomism in the seventeenth century. Although the texts written by philosophers in the Heronic tradition were dominated by technical descriptions of automata and other pneumatic devices, they also contained substantial *theoretical* discussions of the atomic foundations of pneumatic technology. Thus the writings of Ktesibios, Philo, and Hero have always been regarded as expressions of the school of Democritus and Epicurus, the founders of ancient atomism. The precise correlation in these texts between philosophical materialism and the mechanized figure or toy is therefore fundamental to their historical significance. It would hardly be legitimate to claim that the mechanical singing birds of Hero's treatise stand for the principles of atomism that underlie their construction; in these texts the automaton is clearly not yet an emblem or symbol of materialism and corporeality. It would be more accurate to describe the automata as demonstrations of the authenticity of atomist theory, as proofs that are at once rigorous and lyrical in their persuasive power. All the same, despite the fact that these texts do not equate materialism and mechanism, the Heronic tradition clearly implicates technology in the particular features of atomism, just as one may draw from these texts, by implication, a disquieting correlation between materialism and the origins of illusionism and spectacular culture, between the specific principles of atomism and the mechanized figures that are the most cogent demonstration of its scientific authority. None of these correspondences, however, are yet explicit in these ancient texts.

A few preliminary comments are in order about the features of atomism that have special relevance to the discourse of automated (and therefore animated) figures. Atomism, the preeminent discourse of Western materialism (at least in antiquity and, more convincingly, since the seventeenth century) contends that the authentic material existence of any body (as opposed to its merely phenomenal appearance) consists of infinitesimal and irreducible particles called atoms.[22] As a school of physics, then, atomism purports to explain the various properties of physical bodies. But atomism is also a metaphysical doctrine: it holds that *only* material bodies exist and that knowledge of real things necessarily derives from our senses. In addition, since the writings of Epicurus (341–271 B.C.E.), atomism has been prominently and controversially associated with an ethical doctrine centered on the principle of pleasure: hedonism. Based in part on its materialist orientation, which proscribes the possibility of immaterial gods or the concept of a disembodied afterlife, Epicurean atomism developed the notion of a material soul oriented along the axis of intellectual and corporeal pleasure. Since antiquity, then, philosophical atomism has comprised a physical doctrine of invisible corpuscles, an ethical doctrine of hedonism, a metaphysical and polemical materialism, and a discourse of automated—and spectacular—"proofs."

The history of materiality is thus largely a history of the peculiar affinities of the divergent—and often incommensurable—discourses of atomism. Philosophical and scientific critiques of atomism, from antiquity to modern positivism, have focused on the paradoxical nature of its physical doctrine. The metaphysical thrust of atomism maintains that nothing we do not perceive can be real, yet the essential component of its physical doctrine—the atom—is infinitesimally small and hence imperceptible. This, the basic element of Western materialism, is perceptible only to the intellect: an atom is a being of reason, and hence unreal according to the metaphysics of atomism. Western materialism therefore depends, paradoxically and irremediably, on the equation of materiality and invisibility (insofar as atoms are permanently beyond the reach of our natural senses). Further, the invisibility of matter in atomist doctrine explains the dependence of atomic physics on the regime of analogy. Because the atomic microcosm is at once the sole reality and wholly undetectable, it can be evoked only by analogy with the phenomenalistic and therefore specious qualities of the world at large. The only intuitive knowledge that we can possess of the inscrutable reality of material existence comes in the form of insubstantial *pictures*—though to be fair to the rigor of its materialist perspective, I should note that atomism regards mental pictures as the physical residue of perception. Nevertheless, critics from Aristotle to Werner Heisenberg have attacked atomism for its fatal dependence on hypothetical models and pictures. In the mid-nineteenth century, Ernst Mach charged atomism, and by implication physics, with intellectual "fetishism."[23] This charge finds its ultimate target in Marx's theory of dialectical materialism, which evolved from a critique of ancient atomism.[24] In any case, given its abject dependence on pictures, and its persistent correlation with hedonism and libertinism, it is perhaps not surprising that ancient atomism should become associated through pneumatic philosophy with a retinue of wondrous, mechanized figures—with the discourse of automata.

Questions about the nature of what I want to call lyric substance, as well as its relation to modern conceptions of materiality and to the fate of the automaton in the twentieth century, cannot be adequately addressed without first probing in some detail the convergence of "corpuscular" and "mechanical" philosophies in the seventeenth century. At the very instant of its modern revival, philosophical atomism (which became known as "mechanical philosophy") seized on the figure of the automaton as a symbol of its emerging conception of corporeality and of the very constitution of matter. And it was precisely at this moment, when the discourses of materiality (that is, physics) and mechanical simulacra became explicitly intertwined, that materialism and its symbolic counterparts, the toy and the machine, both became associated with realism.

The interest in pneumatics and philosophical atomism that arose suddenly at the end of the sixteenth century has never been adequately explained.[25] We simply do not know why, and to what purpose, people began to read the texts of Epicurus and Hero of Alexandria. We can be sure, however, that it was works by these authors in particular (or by authors who cite them) that served as the textual matrix for the revival of modern atomism. Thus, depending on the emphasis you wish to place, the philosophical basis of modern materialism derives either from Epicurean or from Heronic inflections of atomism. The Epicurean legacy is generally viewed as the more significant, in part because the relevant texts were published earlier and in part because of the influence of Pierre Gassendi (1592–1655), the leading exponent of the Epicurean school.[26] The hedonic and atheistic features of Epicurean philosophy were, however, condemned by the Catholic church (and by Gassendi as well), so it was not always easy for the adherent of corpuscular philosophy, who often regarded his scientific activities as a kind of "natural theology," to publicly dissociate his interest in the largely Democritean physics of Epicurean philosophy from a scandalous doctrine of hedonism and atheism.[27]

A very different inflection of seventeenth-century materialism emerges if we view the Epicurean legacy, afflicted by the tension between physics and ethics, as significant but not necessarily dominant or primary. In an important article published in 1949, Marie Boas argues that we should regard "Hero's atomism, a simple non-Lucretian, non-philosophic particulate theory of matter" as "a hitherto unsuspected source of that non-Epicurean corpuscularianism of the seventeenth century, by no means exclusively derived from Descartes, which reached its culmination in the 'corpuscular hypothesis' of Robert Boyle."[28] Boas is referring not merely to Hero's technical descriptions of automata but also to a short theoretical treatise on the principles of atomism that serves as the preface to the *Pneumatics*.

Several factors lend obvious support to Boas's thesis. First, the widespread correlation of atomism and mechanism in the seventeenth century (which I will examine in a moment) can derive only from the Heronic corpus (or from some derivation of its Democritean principles), since neither Epicurus nor Lucretius draws any significant analogies between automata or machines and the nature of atoms. In addition, Hero's short treatise on pneumatic "philosophy" restricts itself solely to physics, ignoring entirely the more problematic ethical and theological implications of materialism. Second, the widespread use of the term *corpuscular* to designate the doctrine of atomism can be traced directly to translations of Hero's text that sought to distinguish his orientation from Epicureanism. Boas observes, "The word used to describe Hero's particles varied, but they were never called atoms, a word too closely associated with Epicureanism"; the preferred term for the Heronic atom, Boas notes, was *corpuscle.*[29] This preference for the Heronic "corpuscle," shorn of its Epicurean ethics, is not, however, a rejection of the essential doctrine of atomism but rather an ideological preference for the more narrowly physical theories of Democritus (a thesis first advanced by Marin Mersenne).

It is symptomatic of the greater dialectic of atomism that Hero's neglect of the philosophical dimension of materialism should be marked by calling the atom a "corpuscle." Only by disavowing the doctrines of pleasure and the material soul can he construe the atom as a body—a little body. Although Boas emphasizes the ideological appeal of science without pleasure (such as can be derived from Hero's treatise on pneumatics), she is careful not to obscure the dual legacy of the Heronic tradition. For Hero's text, taken in its entirety, does not eliminate the question of pleasure from materialism so much as it projects it into the discourse of mechanized figures that serve as demonstrations of atomic theory. Thus, on one hand, Boas explains, "Hero's *Pneumatics* is essentially a treatise on natural magic, as later centuries called the study of unexplained properties of nature, in which are described various contrivances worked by air, water, and steam."[30] On the other hand, she sees the *Pneumatics* as providing early modern science with an ethically viable *theory* of atomism: "The *Pneumatics* is of interest in the history of scientific theory no less than in the history of technology."[31] Thus Hero's text elicited two types of responses: a debate within the emerging community of physicists (including Gassendi and Robert Boyle) over his theory of corpuscles and *vacua;* and a legacy of technical treatises on automata and natural magic (including phenomena such as "magnetism, change of state, and optical illusion").[32] This bifurcation of the reception of Hero's *Pneumatics* (into the spheres of physical theory and the technology of illusion) continues to haunt the discourses of scientific materialism and modern spectacular culture. Clearly, in the Heronic variation of atomism, the question of pleasure and the material soul had not been eliminated but displaced—without explicit formulation—into a burgeoning discourse of machines.

Hero's *Pneumatics* offers yet another advantage over the Epicurean legacy because it provides a clear and pragmatic motivation for the revival of atomism. From the standpoint of the history of technology, one could argue that people in the seventeenth century became interested in atomism (and more precisely pneumatics) not so much for its explanation of natural phenomena as for its practical bearing on the design and construction of new *machines.* In essence, people read Hero for his knowledge of machines, which required, more or less, that one accept his theory of matter. Indeed, one could not understand the mechanics of his automated devices without taking into account his theory of corpuscles. Since, moreover, atomism, as a physical theory, had proved successful at explaining only the pneumatic properties of mechanical bodies, one was obliged, if one wished to adopt a more encompassing theory of atomic physics, to regard all of nature as a machine. Atomism then, at the moment of its historical translation into modernity, served primarily to explain the physics of automata and other illusionistic devices. Only by bringing natural phenomena within the sphere of mechanism and magic could atomism be regarded as a general theory of matter and corporeality.

Although Boas suggests that the twin legacies of the Heronic tradition (corpuscular theory and the technology of illusion) remained separate and distinct, the historical evidence indicates quite the opposite. Indeed the automaton, which some writers early in the seventeenth century characterized as a "vice," became the ubiquitous symbol of early scientific materialism.[33] Virtually all the major theoreticians of the new physics regarded "corpuscular philosophy" as indistinguishable from what Robert Boyle called the "mechanical hypothesis." According to "mechanical philosophy" (as the new theory of materialism was called in the seventeenth century), "the manifest properties of bodies are to be explained in terms of the size, shape, and motion of tiny corpuscles which, it is claimed, make up the bodies of every-day experience."[34] The explicit thesis of mechanical philosophy is that the movement and aggregation of tiny "corpuscles" are characterized above all by geometrical and mechanical properties. Thus all bodies, and indeed the very constitution of matter, are to be understood as machines (and, more precisely, as automata). In addition, as Catherine Wilson has pointed out, mechanical philosophy referred to "studies that could be undertaken of, or with the help of, machines."[35] Thus, mechanical philosophy, which arose as an interpretation of "corpuscular" philosophy, pertains to knowledge produced with the help of machines and, more fundamentally, to knowledge derived from reflection on the nature—at once physical and metaphysical—of machines. We must not forget, however, that the automaton, as an emblem of mechanical philosophy, stands for a conception of matter (atomism) that is irremediably hypothetical in its dependence on unsubstantiated pictures. In the hands of science, the automaton—little more than an ingenious toy—symbolizes a conception of materiality founded on immateriality, a discourse of bodies whose sole reality is the invisible corpuscles of which they are composed.

When we turn to the writings of Descartes, Leibniz, Boyle, and other seventeenth-century natural philosophers for evidence of the machine analogy, the first thing we notice is that the complementarity of clock and automaton that characterized the Heronic tradition reappears in the Baroque revival of materialism. In the famous opening statement of his *Treatise on Man* (1662), Descartes declares:

> I suppose the body to be nothing but a statue or machine. . . . We
> see clocks, artificial fountains, mills, and other such machines
> which, although only man-made, have the power to move of their
> own accord in many different ways. But I am supposing this ma-
> chine [the body] to be made by the hands of God and so I think
> you may reasonably think it capable of a greater variety of move-
> ments than I could possibly imagine in it, and of exhibiting more
> artistry than I could possibly ascribe to it.[36]

More specifically, in his treatise *Passions of the Soul*, Descartes compared
"the body of a living man" to "a watch or other automaton (that is, a
self-moving machine) when it is wound up and contains in itself the
corporeal principle of the movements for which it is designed."[37] It is
not, however, only the human body but all of nature that Descartes
compares to a machine: "I have described this earth and indeed the
whole visible universe as if it were a machine."[38] Furthermore, as the
earlier reference to the automata of the royal gardens suggests, Des-
cartes appears to have been fully cognizant of the manner in which
the figure of the automaton in corpuscular philosophy functioned as
a medium between the emerging discourses of scientific materialism
and modern spectacular culture. In "The Search for Truth," Descartes
declares, "I shall lay before your eyes the works of men involving
corporeal things. After causing you to wonder at the most powerful
machines, the most unusual automaton, the most impressive illusion,
and the most subtle tricks that human ingenuity can devise, I shall
reveal to you the secrets behind them."[39] In this passage, Descartes
suggests that knowledge of "corporeal things" follows from an ex-
amination of the technology of illusion.

Leibniz extends the analogy of the corporeal machine to the level
of the atom itself; in "Principles of Nature and Grace" (1714), a sum-
mation of his physical and metaphysical theories, he writes that a "body
is organic when it forms a kind of automaton or natural machine,
which is not only a machine as a whole, but also in its smallest distin-
guishable parts."[40] By pushing the machine analogy to its irreducible

limit, Leibniz simply confirms the essential correspondence between atomism, as a theory of matter, and the mechanized toy figure. The analogy, moreover, is reciprocal: just as the corpuscle—the body in miniature—reveals itself to be an automaton, so the automaton, at the level of the infinitesimal, becomes imperceptible and immaterial.[41] Summarizing the mechanical philosophy of Leibniz, Michel Serres writes, "One cannot conceive the organic except by reiterating to infinity the mechanical; there is no void in the mechanical constitution of the living, which one can therefore call the *complete automaton*."[42]

Indeed, the fundamental assumptions of materialism require that mechanical philosophy extend beyond the level of the organic to include the soul. In an explanation of his doctrine of preestablished harmony, Leibniz offers the following analogy: "Suppose two clocks or two watches which perfectly keep time together. . . . Now put the soul and the body in the place of the two clocks."[43] In this instance, the incorporeal soul becomes a machine, thereby illustrating the essential role of the immaterial in conceptions of material substance derived from atomism. Although the clock/automaton functions here, and in the other examples I have given, as a metaphor, and although the automaton itself may generally be conceived as a simulacrum of nature, the automaton clearly becomes something more than a mere image or representation when it is situated at the convergence of mechanical and corpuscular philosophies. Indeed, in this context, the automaton no longer functions as a picture of anything; rather, the organic body depicts and confirms the ontology of the mechanized figure. The toy becomes the metaphysical ground of the organic body, which nevertheless exceeds, in its infinite mechanicity, any man-made machine.

The metaphysical priority of the machine in corpuscular philosophy suggests that the automaton, as a figure of speech, is not exhausted by its reference to corporeality. Indeed, as Catherine Wilson notes, the clock/automaton functioned as an emblem of two distinct (but related) theses in the development of modern materialism: "The real contributions of the seventeenth century were its image of nature as a machine, or (a different matter entirely) its image of nature as something related to a machine as a clock face is related to the clock mechanism."[44] Focusing more precisely on the Cartesian sense of the clock metaphor, Laurens Laudan contends, "I am not maintaining that Descartes was the first to liken nature to a clock-like mechanism; on the contrary, this was a common metaphor among mechanistic philosophers throughout the sixteenth and early seventeenth centuries. . . . However, Descartes *was* (so far as I can tell) the first to use the analogy to justify a hypothetical view of knowledge and science."[45] In antiquity, and in its revival as corpuscular philosophy, atomism was characterized, and indeed constituted, by "free and Democritean speculation": any claim about the nature of atoms—the foundation of material existence—was unavoidably hypothetical (since atoms could not be substantiated by observation). To conjure the world of atoms, by analogy, from the world at large, and to extrapolate reliably from this analogy the details of atomic reality, it is necessary to attribute to this inscrutable domain an inherent lawfulness and regularity. In other words, the hypothetical discourse of atomism, and the deductive method it entails, can be guaranteed only by positing the *mechanicity* of atoms and bodies. The automaton, as an emblem of mechanical philosophy, thus gives expression to the overriding determinism of Democritean physics. It reveals itself, in the context of corpuscular philosophy, to be a figure of necessity and fatality. At the same time, however, the mechanical doll symbolizes the hypothetical modeling of invisible matter: it becomes an emblem of the rational divination of science, thereby recalling its mythical origin as an oracular device. The toy divines the invisible substance of things.

The basic assumption of mechanical philosophy therefore serves as the foundation of probabilism (the Cartesian framework of modern theoretical physics) and the divinatory method of science. Mechanicism does not, however, provide assurance of the empirical truth of atomic doctrine, but demonstrates only that such conjectures are logically consistent. Thus, according to probabilism, "Theories describe only the mechanisms whereby nature might conceivably produce the effects we observe, not necessarily the mechanisms which nature in fact uses."[46] From an empirical standpoint, therefore, atomic substance must remain eternally conjectural and uncertain.

If the principle of mechanicity enables the creation of a hypothetical material world, then what relation does the figure of the mechanized toy bear to the method of hypothesis? In what manner does the automaton function as an emblem not only of the corpuscular machine, but of the method that deduces this invisible machine from the world at large? First of all, the clock or automaton commands attention as an emblem of the hypothetical method because its mechanism is *internal*, hidden from view. What distinguishes the automaton from other types of pictures (sculpture or painting, for example) is its interiority—the fact that it possesses an inside, an inscrutable interior. Thus the automaton stands readily for a method obliged to deduce from external features the hidden corpuscular mechanisms of natural bodies. (The particular cogency of this metaphor depends on the fundamental inscrutability of the body at a molecular level in the seventeenth century.) Laudan explains, "The scientist thus resembles the skilled watchmaker of the analogy who is given a watch but cannot see its internal mechanisms. Like the watchmaker, he knows the general principles which govern his subject matter, but he is uncertain about the way they exhibit themselves in any particular case. Equally like the watchmaker, the scientist can only offer conjectures about internal construction and mechanisms."[47] The clock metaphor articulates the *method* of corpuscular philosophy in such a way that hypothesis is at once possible (because of the lawful and mechanical nature of things); obligatory (because this basic mechanism is invisible); and contingent (because it is impossible to verify conjectures about the hidden mechanism). The mechanized toy figure therefore symbolizes at once a conception of the body that is wholly externalized (the corpuscular machine)[48] and a conception of method that yields only the imagined interior of things. This tension between exteriority and interiority in the figure of the automaton reiterates the dialectical substance of the atom.

For Leibniz, the toy of method appears in the guise of an angel, a transformation that realizes fully the sublimation of the automaton implicit in Cartesian method. In his brief essay "On the Method of Arriving at a True Analysis of Bodies and the Causes of Natural Things" (1677), Leibniz initiates his discussion of method by referring to an angel: "All things come about through certain intelligible causes, or causes which we could perceive if some angel wished to reveal them to us."[49] Aside from the thematic correspondence between the mechanical doll (or clock) and the angel as figures of methodology, another, more precise historical affinity helps to explain Leibniz's analogy. For the figure of an angel is probably the earliest prototype for the *jacquemart*—the mechanical figure that announces the hours, by striking a bell with a hammer or blowing a trumpet, in the first monumental public clocks (such as the famous mechanized angel on the cathedral of St. Mark's in Venice).[50] There is thus a strong historical reason for examining the correlation between the Cartesian automaton and the methodological angel. Leibniz continues:

> Let us imagine, therefore, that some angel comes to explain to me
> the true cause of magnetic declination and the periods observed in
> it. He will surely not satisfy me by saying that this is the nature of
> the magnet or that there is a kind of sympathy or a kind of soul
> in the magnet by which it happens. Rather, he must explain some
> cause to me, such that, if I understand it, I can see that the phe-
> nomena follow from it as necessarily as the cause of the hammer
> stroke when a given time has elapsed follows from my knowledge
> of the clock.[51]

The angel in this passage affords insight into the "natural magic" of magnetism not by applying the old Scholastic doctrines of form and substance but by deploying the new deterministic method of science, which explains things according to mechanistic causality and, as Leibniz asserts in another example, finds its purest expression in mathematical physics.[52] Thus, as Robert Butts explains, "To think as an angel thinks—or would have to think if he had our kind of body—is to reduce body to number by means of a methodology Leibniz calls 'mechanical' "; that is to say, "The 'intelligible causes' that the angel would reveal to us if we listened are all mechanical, mathematically expressible, causes."[53]

Although Leibniz doesn't make much of the correlation between the angel and the clock, they both function explicitly as emblems of probabilism (the hypothetical method), and also, more subtly, as figures of corporeality. The clock/automaton can be regarded as an embodiment, or materialization, of the angel's mechanical mind, whereas the angel, inversely, appears to us as the immaterial automaton of lawful speculation (hypothesis). The particular phenomena explained by the angel—magnetism and color—should not be regarded as incidental to the formulation of corporeality issuing from the dialectic of angel and automaton. The Heronic tradition, as I indicated earlier, regarded both magnetism and automata as demonstrations of "natural magic." More specifically, according to Derek Price, "The corpus of knowledge about clockwork and automata . . . became entwined with concepts of perpetual motion (an idea apparently unknown in classical antiquity) and of magnetism and the mystery of magnetic force."[54] These historical affinities inform Leibniz's juxtaposition of the angel and the automaton as well as the angel's hypothetical explanation of phenomena known as *incorporeals* or *effluvia* (invisible substances or forces, such as magnetism, that blurred the distinction between material and immaterial phenomena). By disclosing the material cause of immaterial effluvia, the angel alludes to the mystery of its own incorporeal body. The substance of the angelic body thus becomes equivalent to the magnetic effluvium, so that the angel, like the mechanized toy in Descartes, functions as an emblem both of corpuscularity and of the hypothetical method that divines the immaterial body. Moreover, the force of the angel's magnetic body can be understood as the material

Figure 4.   The writer/draftsman of Henri Maillardet (Switzerland, eigh-
teenth century). Courtesy Franklin Institute, Philadelphia.

soul, or engine, that brings to life the automaton of corpuscular philosophy.

PHILOSOPHICAL TOYS

If the seventeenth century witnessed the emergence of the automaton as a device poised between science and spectacular culture, the eighteenth century was the golden age of the mechanical toy, estranged from science yet still charged with philosophical implication. In the 1730s, Jacques Vaucanson (1709–1782) created two of the most intricate automata ever made: an android musician—a flautist—that could move its fingers and play eleven tunes by blowing through its lips; and a duck that could walk, swim, and flap its wings (and came complete with functional digestive system). Both devices captured the popular and intellectual imagination of the time. In the latter part of the century, the father-and-son team of Pierre and Henri Jaquet-Droz (of Geneva) created a remarkable series of androids, including a female harpsichord player. (Mary Shelley paid a visit to the Jaquet-Droz collection before writing *Frankenstein*.) In addition, near the end of the eighteenth century, Jaquet-Droz and Henri Maillardet built several automated writers and draftsmen, which toured Europe with great success. Among the texts composed by the Jaquet-Droz draftsman is an epigram that inverts the Cartesian dictum, "Je pense, donc je suis," thereby capturing the essential polemic of materialism: "Je ne pense pas ... ne serais-je donc point?" (I do not think ... do I therefore not exist?) Maillardet's automaton, perhaps the most complex writer-draftsman ever built, could sketch six different images, including a ship and Eros in a chariot pulled by a butterfly (an image also in the repertoire of the Jaquet-Droz draftsman). The Maillardet automaton could also compose three poems in English and French, including the following "autogram":

> Un jeune enfant que le zàle dirige,
> De vos faveurs sollicit le prix,

Qu'il l'obtient ne'en soyez point surpris.
Le désir de vous plaire enfanta ce prodige.[55]

Not only is this "autogram" the first example, quite literally, of "automatic writing," but the Maillardet automaton continues to this day to produce these artifacts (at the Franklin Institute in Philadelphia). The history of automation and inscription took another turn in the nineteenth century, when Johann Maelzel (inventor of the metronome) patented the first talking doll in 1823: it said "Mama" and "Papa." Later, Thomas Edison incorporated the new technology of the phonograph into dolls that could recite "Mary had a little lamb." In addition, the historical relation between automation and "natural magic" is preserved in the name "Houdini"—the great magician who took his name from the nineteenth-century French maker of automata, Jean Robert-Houdin.

These technical marvels were not isolated from the philosophical trends I have been discussing; the eighteenth century also saw the publication in 1747 (ten years after the exhibition of Vaucanson's duck) of a work that revitalized and transformed the principles of mechanical philosophy in the popular imagination: Julien Offray de La Mettrie's *L'homme-machine*. La Mettrie, who published his book anonymously in Leyden to avoid censure, sustained and elaborated mechanical philosophy's dominant idea, the corporeal machine. The text of *L'homme-machine* repeatedly invokes this idea: "Man is a machine so complicated that it is impossible at first to form a clear idea of it."[56] La Mettrie is moreover entirely faithful to the dominant tropes of mechanical philosophy, the clock and the automaton. He declares, "The human body is an immense clock," and, more specifically, "The human body is a self-winding machine, a living representation of perpetual motion."[57] In addition, he calls man "a well-enlightened machine" with "a few more cogwheels and springs than in the most perfect animals" (50).

Although La Mettrie acknowledges the Cartesian origin of his central idea, the man-machine, he differs from Descartes in viewing the mind as a material entity; he belongs, from our perspective, to the eighteenth-century school of English and French sensationalism (dominated by the ideas of John Locke and Étienne de Condillac). La Mettrie revives the metaphysical premises of ancient materialism (atomism) by insisting that matter is the only reality and that purely mental or spiritual entities are therefore inconceivable. Moreover, in the opening paragraphs of his treatise, he seeks to link the implication of materialism to the clock metaphor of mechanical philosophy: "Strictly speaking, to ask if matter sheerly in itself can think is like asking if matter can tell time" (27). The central task of his book is therefore to materialize the mind, to fashion a discourse of the *material soul*—a point he illustrates as graphically as possible, insisting that metaphysical materialism requires "unravelling the soul as one pulls out the guts of the body" (30). More precisely, in keeping with the tenets of mechanical philosophy, he seeks to adumbrate a *mechanics* of the soul: "The soul is only a principle of movement,—a sensible, material part of the brain, which one can regard as the machine's principal spring" (65). In the end, taking up Locke's suggestion that "thinking may also be material,"[58] La Mettrie contends, "Thought is so far from being incompatible with organized matter that it seems to me to be just another of its properties, such as electricity" (72). Here the trope of electricity (a phenomenon belonging, at the time, to the discourse of "incorporeals" and "effluvia") rehearses the dialectical materiality of a body situated at the convergence of mechanical and corpuscular philosophies.

Although La Mettrie in this respect fully realizes the implications of orthodox materialism, he does not characterize his ideas as solely, or even directly, pertinent to physics. Instead, he calls his treatise "a *philosophy* of the human body" (my emphasis, 76). This subtle yet unmistakable dissociation from physics is symptomatic of the emerging disciplinary fragmentation of natural philosophy (which, in the seventeenth century, served as the matrix of modern physics). The key to the "philosophical" aspect of La Mettrie's text, and to its influence on modern, popular conceptions of corporeality, is its explicit and utterly persuasive assimilation of Epicurean hedonism to the Democritean framework of mechanical philosophy. The dogmatic yet precarious separation of corpuscularian physics and ethics simply collapses in La Mettrie's text; he grafts onto the fatality of Democritean physics an eroticized phenomenology that encompasses both physical and intellectual experience. In a lengthy preface, La Mettrie declares,

> Sensual pleasure has only one climax, which is the tomb. . . . How different are the resourceful pleasures of the mind! . . . This pleasure comes in a rush faster than lightning strikes, yet it lasts for a long time. Should we be astonished that the pleasure of the mind is as superior to sensual pleasure as the body is to the mind? Is not the mind the first of the senses, that meeting place of all sensations, on which they converge like rays returning to the center that produces them? (21)

In the essay proper, La Mettrie roots the "cataleptic" pleasures of the mind in the imagination, which he regards as the faculty of intellectual plasticity (from which reason derives). He writes, "Only the imagination perceives. . . . Just as it cannot enjoy the pleasures of the senses without experiencing their voluptuous perfection, the imagination could not reflect on its mechanically conceived ideas unless it were identical with judgement itself" (44). Critics of course have noted the Epicurean flair of La Mettrie's mechanics. Aram Vartanian, for example, observes, "There is evident in La Mettrie's entire method of thought an underlying interaction between *volupté* and materialism, with the result that scientific and erotic curiosity seem to him to function together in a sort of alliance, each serving to strengthen and stimulate the other."[59] One is nevertheless always astonished at the exuberance and outright abandon with which La Mettrie yokes sexuality and determinism: "Who would have ever divined *a priori* that shooting off a gob of sperm during copulation would make one feel such divine pleasure, and that from it would be born a tiny creature one day, following certain laws, who would enjoy the same delights?" (71–72). In this passage, one discerns the unholy alliance of eroticism, mechanism, and spermaticism from which the modern man-machine was born.[60]

The corporeal machine, after La Mettrie, is distinguished above all by its capacity for wonder and pleasure, which are in turn enhanced by the complete mechanicity of the organism. However, La Mettrie's hybrid materialism is distinct both from Epicureanism, since Epicurus makes no mention of machines, and from the Heronic tradition, whose mechanistic rendering of pneumatic principles proscribes any explicit reference to pleasure. The themes of eros and blind necessity collide in the figure of the man-machine, concocting for modernity a catastrophic vision of mechanized sexuality. La Mettrie reinvents the corpuscular machine as a toy ruled unequivocally by pleasure and founded, as in the past, on a discourse of "incorporeals." What's more, his synthesis of libertinage and physics gives new meaning to the fundamental contradiction of the automaton, involving at once spontaneity of movement and its mechanization—a significant formulation and reference point, by the way, for the emerging discourse of the uncanny.

Unlike Mary Shelley's *Frankenstein, L'homme-machine* fully embraces the prospect of a human machine or automaton (which in the mind of the materialist are the same thing). Indeed, La Mettrie's text can be regarded as a kind of political *manifesto* of atheism, popular mechanics, and libertinage, whose central figure, the android, emerges as a harbinger of revolution and sexual license (a prefiguring of the Sadean implications of Jacobin terror). The invincibility (and paradoxical immateriality) of the revolutionary man inscribes itself in the figure of the automaton fueled by erotic desire and lapsing into compulsion or "delirium" (21). La Mettrie's *L'homme-machine* is therefore the archetype of twentieth-century, machine-age manifestos, including Marinetti's Futurism and English vorticism. More recently, Donna

Haraway's "Manifesto for Cyborgs" recapitulates the basic principles, the vanguard politics, and the exuberant tone of La Mettrie's essay— though the central figure is now a woman-machine. Haraway writes, "By the late twentieth century, our time, a mythic time, we are all chimeras, theorized and fabricated hybrids of machine and organism; in short, we are cyborgs. The cyborg is our ontology; it gives us our politics. The cyborg is a condensed image of both imagination and material reality."[61] Haraway, moreover, makes it clear that the cyborg is essentially an automaton, "self-moving, self-designing, autonomous" (60). In addition, the Epicurean thrust of the cyborg doctrine is unmistakable: "This essay is an argument for *pleasure* in the confusion of boundaries and for *responsibility* in their construction" (66). Thus, in the ethics of Haraway's corporeal machine, pleasure itself is mechanistic, since it is always calculated. Unlike La Mettrie, however, Haraway draws not on science but on science fiction for her understanding of materiality. Though she might well have done so, Haraway fails to draw any correlation (except for an allusion to quantum mechanics) between the corporeal machine and corpuscular philosophy. She does, however, evoke in lyrical terms the ambiguous materiality of the cyborg, emphasizing, in the manner of philosophical atomism, the essential *immateriality* of the automaton: "Our best machines are made of sunshine. . . . Cyborgs are ether, quintessence. . . . They are as hard to see politically as materially" (70–71).

CHAPTER 3

The Lyric Automaton

A poet might succumb to the domination of a marionette, for the marionette has only imagination. The doll has none, and is precisely so much less than a thing as the marionette is more. But this being less than a thing, a condition without remedy, is the secret of its superiority.

> *Rainer Maria Rilke, "Some Reflections on Dolls"*

you in the view and no real walls
you in the view and no real walls
express flow   black-whi
express flow   black-whi
    firm shiny terror
    firm shiny terror
express flow   black-whi
express flow   black-whi
you in the view and no real walls
you in the view and no real walls

> *Kenward Elmslie, "Girl Machine"*

The eyes are wide. They cannot address
the helplessness which has lingered
in the airless peace of each glass case:
to have survived. To have been stronger than

a moment. To be the hostages ignorance
takes from time and ornament from destiny. Both.
To be the present of the past. To infer the difference
with a terrible stare. But not feel it. And not know it.

> *Eavan Boland, "The Doll's Museum in Dublin"*

The prominence of the pleasure principle in La Mettrie's man-machine signals a decisive shift in the discourse of automata from natural philosophy to the domain of aesthetics, combined with a revival of the technological disposition of the Heronic tradition in antiquity (though its emphasis on hedonism is far more explicit). Moreover, the effort to coordinate the automaton with a *philosophy* of pleasure signals the demise of mechanical philosophy as a viable matrix for theoretical physics, a failure precipitated in part by the emerging scientific authority and disciplinary specificity of modern physics. The new aesthetic disposition of the automaton did not come at the expense of philosophical atomism, however, but rather through a realignment of its principal components, the discourses of fatality and wonder (Democritean physics and Epicurean hedonism). At the same time, in the context of late eighteenth-century philosophy, the concept of aesthetic pleasure was undergoing a formalization or, more aptly speaking, mechanization. Thus, as the figure of the automaton, no longer at home in the discourse of the exact sciences, exercised anew its lyric affinity, the philosophy of pleasure, culminating in Kant's *Critique of Judgment*, sought to assimilate aesthetic experience to the purest expression of mechanical philosophy—to mathematics. In its drive toward universality and tautology, then, Kant's aesthetic philosophy aimed, in certain fundamental respects, to revise pleasure in a manner that transformed it into a relic of mechanical philosophy. And, indeed, the shades of materiality issuing from the new aesthetic disposition of the automaton only confirm the corpuscularian rigor of modern pleasures.

The chiasmic exchange between the automaton and the discourse of aesthetic pleasure emerges in distilled form in Kleist's classic text "On the Marionette Theater" (1810), published four years before E. T. A. Hoffmann's tales about automata. Kleist's brief narrative explores in some detail, through the figure of the marionette, the eccentric conjugation of physics and aesthetics personified in figures such as Spalanzani and Professor X in Hoffmann's stories. The first crucial

observation to make about Kleist's philosophical tale is that a mario-
nette is not, strictly speaking, an automaton. Yet this displacement
from automaton to puppet or doll is, as we shall discover, an essential
feature of the evolving modernity of the automaton figure. Indeed, as
Roman Paska observes, Kleist's narrative advances "the Romantic view
of the puppet as a representational figure intent on acquiring mechan-
ical autonomy."[1] Evidence from this period of the fundamental insta-
bility of the automaton can also be found in "The Sandman," where
the automaton, Olympia, is described interchangeably as "a machine,"
"a lifeless doll," "an automaton," and a "lovely puppet."[2] Although
many questions arise about the displacement of the classical automaton
by the doll, it is apparent in the texts of Kleist and others that this
transaction pertains to the demechanization of the automaton, in a
manner that, paradoxically, only enhances the autonomy of the device
as a simulacrum. That is to say, it pertains to an evolving ontology of
pictures in modern culture and to the enduring interdependence of
pictures and bodies.

Kleist's narrative (actually a series of anecdotes) occurs as a dialogue
between the narrator and an acquaintance of his, a certain "Herr
C——, who had recently been engaged as the principal dancer at the
opera."[3] By chance, on a walk, they happen on "a puppet theater that
had been set up in the marketplace" (415), which occupies their con-
versation for a time. The limbs of the marionettes are said to move
"in a mechanical way," yet "the whole figure, shaken at random, often
assumed a kind of rhythmical movement that was similar to dance"
(415). Indeed, their comments focus generally on "the line that the
center of gravity had to describe," characterized as "the path of the
dancer's soul" (416), and on the mechanicity of the figures "described"
by the puppet's dance. The operator of the puppets is called a "me-
chanic" (416), and the marionette itself appears to the narrator to re-
semble an automaton: "Its dance could take place totally in the realm
of mechanical forces" (416). Ultimately, however, it is analytical ge-
ometry that, in Herr C's view, subsumes the "line" issuing from the

mechanic's deliverance of the puppet to the force of gravity: "The movements of his fingers are related to the movements of the puppets attached to them somewhat like numbers to their logarithms or the asymptote to the parabola" (416). Although Kleist's deployment of mathematical terms may not be altogether reliable (note the qualifier "somewhat"), the correlation of rhetoric and mathematics remains fundamental to his understanding of the automaton.

In a critique of Kleist's essay, Paul de Man focuses precisely on "Kleist's notion of the 'mathematical' as a model for aesthetic formalization," on "the articulation between trope and epistemology," carried to its limit in "mathematical language."[4] He draws attention to the fact that the *line* of the "dancer's soul" (described by the puppet's movement) is at once a trope and a geometrical curve (or formula). Hence, the line of the puppet's soul is, as Kleist puts it, a "logarithm"—a word combining "word" and "number." Assimilated to the "random" dance of the marionette, "tropes certainly acquire," according to de Man, "a machinelike, mechanical predictability" (288), thereby disclosing "the formal laws of tropes" (286). Further, Kleist's anatomy of the marionette turns on "the anamorphosis of the line as it twists and turns into the tropes of ellipses, parabola, and hyperbola. Tropes are quantified systems of motion" (285–86). Here de Man makes his point about the convergence of aesthetic and mechanical "laws" in Kleist's marionette by exploiting certain figures (ellipses, parabola, hyperbola) that function both in geometry and rhetoric. The reference to anamorphosis (a distortion of representational reality) is essential to de Man's reading of the automaton, since mimesis can never be more than a contingent figure in the tautology of the geometrical formula and the figure of speech (embodied by the puppet's movement). Hence, in de Man's view, the formal (that is to say, figurative or mathematical) character of the marionette involves not so much a flight from realism as a *provisional* realism that refers, on closer inspection, to a state of "grace" unattainable by any human being.

In addition, we discover, the anamorphic character of the marionette comprises not only the geometric formality of tropes but also the utter weightlessness of its frame: "These puppets have the advantage of being *antigravitational [antigrav]*. They know nothing of the inertia of matter."[5] The marionette thus appears to defy the first principle of its physical being: mass. Although the puppet's movement follows mechanically from "the line that the center of gravity had to describe" (416), the puppet's body is somehow, paradoxically, immune to the effects of gravitation. "Herr C" pursues this paradox to its limit, observing, "There could be more grace in a mechanical puppet than in the structure of the human body"; further, he insists, "It was absolutely impossible for man even to equal the puppet in this. Only a god could compete with matter in this field" (418). The idea that the paradoxical materiality of the puppet is commensurable only with the incorporeality of a god spurs de Man to invoke the figure of the angel[6] and Paska to observe that Kleist emphasizes "the puppet's innate 'otherness,' granting it its own ontological status distinct from man."[7] Thus, Paska concludes, Kleist's marionette is "something mysterious, immaterial, and pure—like an idea, a spirit, or god" (411).

Given, however, the materialist orientation of Kleist's equation of puppet and god (which implies a theological materialism), we should perhaps emphasize a correspondence between the dialectical materiality of atomism and the anomalous corporeality of the gods in antiquity. That is to say, we should understand the immateriality of the marionette, a degenerate emblem of mechanical philosophy, in relation to what Jean-Pierre Vernant calls "a body of the gods"—"a body that is not a body."[8] In antiquity, Vernant explains, "in order to think of the divine life and body, the required reference point of departure for the Greeks is this defective body—this mortal life which they experienced each day" (26). Despite its derivation from the palpable and ephemeral body of man, a god's body is "a body invisible in its radiance, a face that cannot be seen directly: the apparition" (38). Thus, in substance, the god's dialectical body simply inverts the premises of atomism (matter founded on the invisible). Moreover, Vernant observes,

"In many ways, the divine super-body evolves and touches upon the non-body. It points to it; it never merges with it" (43). This last point, that the god's body is never identical to the non-body, is essential in grasping the paradoxical materiality of the doll and its historical relation to corpuscular philosophy.

Implicit in Kleist's anatomy of the marionette is, as de Man reminds us, an equation between mechanical gestures and figurative language. The line described by the automaton is a geometrical figure but also a trope, that is, an image, a device essential to poetry and poetics. The specifically lyric connotation of Kleist's marionette emerges more explicitly, as we shall discover, in essays by Baudelaire, Rilke, and the surrealists—texts that allude to Kleist's narrative. Yet, even in the context of modern poetics, as with Yeats's elaboration of the mechanical singing bird, the correlation between lyric and the automaton (or doll) is at once obvious and perplexing. Baudelaire, for example, in "The Philosophy of Toys," a short essay published in 1853, equates what he calls "the barbaric toy, the primitive toy" with "childhood poetry" and "poetic means."[9] Yet the meaning of the correspondence between poetry and toys depends, in part, on how we construe the relation between childhood and barbarism. Baudelaire's text encourages the reader in certain respects to equate the two, but it also furnishes good reason to contrast them. Indeed, without some consideration of how lyric has historically been distinguished from other modes of poetry, it is difficult to know whether (or how) to introduce the question of primitivism into the more obvious association of childhood and toys (which pertains, according to Baudelaire, to a certain kind of poetry).

Eighteenth-century speculation about the origins of language (by Vico, Herder, Rousseau, and others) generally held that poetry was the first form of language, and that lyric verse in particular possessed an archaic and even primordial aspect. The equation of lyric poetry and archaic language can be understood in diverse ways. Theodor Adorno, for example, in his essay "On Lyric Poetry and Society," warns his reader that a materialist approach to lyric "will seem especially distressing to you in the case of lyric poetry," since lyric is conventionally viewed as "the most fragile thing in the world."[10] From Adorno's description, we might conclude that lyric poetry is a toy genre and indeed that literature itself, in the lyric mode, is a *toy medium*. Elaborating further on what he calls "the lyric's substance," Adorno calls "invisibility" the "criterion of the lyric."[11]

One traditional way of construing the immateriality of lyric substance, which nevertheless retains its authority as primordial language, stems from the equation of song and breath in the term lyric "air." In addition, the tenuousness or invisibility of lyric substance can be ascribed to poetry's reliance on imagery and figurative language. For, as W. R. Johnson observes, "It goes without saying that images are the essence of poetry . . . the image, most particularly in lyric, has enjoyed a secure and necessary centrality."[12] The immaterial yet primordial substance of lyric, which coincides with the ephemerality of breath and image, should not, however, be associated—at least not by necessity—with realism. On the contrary, as the most prominent European theorist of lyric, Hugo Friedrich, observes, "No one would think of evaluating any poetry, especially lyrical verse, according to how accurate and complete the imagery is with regard to external reality."[13] Indeed, according to Friedrich, the imagery of modern lyric in particular participates in "an aimless destruction of reality" (a thesis recalling Samuel Johnson's description of Metaphysical lyric), accompanied by a relentless and complete disintegration of self.[14] Furthermore, the violent antirealism of modern lyric should not, according to the tradition that associates lyric poetry with the origins of language, be regarded as a departure from the essential qualities of lyric but rather as the culmination of its primitive, nondiscursive character.

Paul de Man, in an essay titled "Lyric and Modernity," disputes the fundamental assumptions of Friedrich's argument. "It would be an absurdity to speak of the modernity of lyric poetry since the lyric is precisely the antithesis of modernity"; and, further, "To claim, with

Friedrich, that modernity is a form of obscurity is to call the oldest, most ingrained characteristics of poetry modern."[15] More precisely, de Man portrays modern lyric poetry as a distinct development in the history of lyric, as a departure from the traditional correlation of lyric and linguistic primitivism; he thereby avoids the faulty logic of equating modernity with what are ostensibly archaic features of literary language. In addition, he makes allusion—never fully developed in the essay—to a broader correspondence between modernity as a general, theoretical principle (applicable to any historical period) and the general features of lyric. Essentially, de Man argues that the lyric mode is inherently modern because the basic instability of the lyric object conveys a sense of modernity long before the modern era of history. In addition, he contends that the "irrealization" of the object is not, as Friedrich contends of modern lyric, a fait accompli, but a problem intrinsic to language. Lyric poetry stages this problem exquisitely, though always imperfectly, with the result that one can never be sure of the substance, or "reality," of the object as it appears in a poem. De Man's theory of modern lyric is therefore fundamentally at odds with Eliot's famous thesis concerning the "dissociation of sensibility" evident in lyric poetry after the seventeenth century.[16] Modern lyric, from de Man's perspective, is not so much a symptom of dissociation as the *agent* of a more specialized—and incomplete—linguistic "irrealization" of the object (which has its roots in seventeenth-century poetry and physics). Eliot, indeed, finds the Metaphysical poets laudable precisely for their ability to translate sensation into a "state of mind." Yet his thesis about the subsequent schism between poetry and science, proves, on closer inspection, to be unreliable because he misunderstands, or disregards, the implications of Baroque materialism. Lyric poetry should not be understood as a casualty of modernity but rather as an enduring witness—and figurative key—to the partial "disappearance" of things (that is, the atomization of things) associated with the revival of corpuscular philosophy in the seventeenth century.

The key to de Man's attack on Friedrich's definition of modern lyric as a complete "loss of representational reality" is his insistence on "levels of meaning that remain representational."[17] In this respect, de Man's attempt to recover the literal, or mimetic, dimension of lyric resembles Adorno's "materialist approach" to lyric "immateriality." The poetry de Man regards as modern embodies "a conflict between poetry of representation and a poetry that would no longer be mimetic" (170). Drawing on Yeats's introduction to the 1936 *Oxford Anthology of English Poetry*, de Man contends that modern lyric exploits

> the ambivalence of a language that is representational and non-representational at the same time. All representation is always also allegorical, whether it be aware of it or not, and the allegorical power of language undermines and obscures the specific literal meaning of a representation open to understanding. But all allegorical poetry must contain a representational element that invites and allows for understanding, only to discover that the understanding it reaches is necessarily in error (185).

Thus conferring on Yeats, along with Baudelaire and Rilke, the garlands of lyric modernity, de Man proceeds to unveil the crucial affinity between lyric and what he calls "allegorical poetry." Allegory, in de Man's view, is characterized not by an absence of representational realism but by a provisional realism that defers, on closer inspection, to a world based on the constitutive power of tropes. Thus the allegorical object, like the substance of the corpuscular "machine," is founded on the curious matter of tropes. This does not imply that lyric substance, or the world it comprises, is essentially unreal, but rather that things under the spell of lyric oscillate between the literal and the immaterial, real and unreal. If we recall de Man's reference in the Kleist essay to the marionette's simultaneous compliance with "mechanical" laws and its infidelity to mimetic structures,[18] we must regard the automaton, in its uncanny effects, as an emblem of allegory. For the automaton, like the allegorical object, appears at first sight to be "real," only to recede irrevocably into metaphysical uncertainty. The doomed male

suitors of Hoffmann's tales are haunted by the dreadful, but also tit-
illating, ambiguity of the automaton (is it real or not?), and it is pre-
cisely this ambiguity that de Man regards as the principal effect of
modern lyric—and of modernity in general.

Given the controversy over the equation of lyric poetry and lin-
guistic primitivism, Baudelaire's treatise on "the barbaric toy" demands
closer scrutiny. For, although Baudelaire's reflections on the toy are
informed by memories of his own childhood and by observations—
often scornful—of other children, it is clear that the "barbaric toy"
can be associated with childhood only insofar as the discovery of art
(and poetry) take place in childhood: "The toy is the child's earliest
initiation into art, or rather it is the first concrete example of art."[19]
Further, Baudelaire states, "The toy can sometimes act upon the
child—above all in cases of literary or artistic predestination" (20).
Specifically, he confesses, "I have moreover retained an abiding affec-
tion and reasoned admiration for that singular statuary which . . . so
well answers to childhood notions of beauty" (15). Thus Baudelaire
represents the toy not only as the emblem of an individual's first (and
therefore, in some sense, archaic) experience of art but also as an abid-
ing influence on his own mature sense of *beauty*—and, by implication,
on his *poetic* inclinations. Indeed, a sentence deleted by Baudelaire
from the manuscript indicates that "he dreamed of developing the
contents of this essay into a full-fledged *aesthetic of the toy*."[20] The
subtlety, as well as the strong emotional coloring, of Baudelaire's anal-
ysis of the toy encourage us therefore to read this essay as touching on
the core of his own poetic values, as a *formulation of modern lyric*.
Baudelaire's elaboration of a "philosophy" of the toy, in addition to
recalling the status of the toy in mechanical philosophy, indicates the
unexpectedly broad horizon of the doll in modern poetics.[21]

Baudelaire, like Kleist, emphasizes the toy's defiance of simple re-
alism; he contrasts the "impotent imagination of our blasé public which
demands of its theaters physical perfection" to the aesthetic of the toy,
"a machinery of barbaric simplicity."[22] He regards the toy as an "im-

age," but one that is physically impoverished. Indeed, the toy is next to nothing: "The maker's problem consists in constructing an image as approximate as possible out of materials as simple and economical as possible. For example, the cardboard pulcinello, worked by a single thread" (18). As an image possessing only the most tenuous physical presence, the toy provokes in the child a longing for the immaterial and the immortal: "The overriding desire of most little brats, on the other hand, is to get at and *see the soul* of their toys. . . . I cannot find it in me to blame this infantile mania: it is the first metaphysical stirring" (24). Thus the toy awakens in the child the sense of a "metaphysical" world, of material things founded on the immateriality of "the soul"—the allegorical object, in effect.

Baudelaire elaborates his notion of the "barbaric toy" in a brief narrative embedded in his essay, which depicts the meeting of two boys, one wealthy, the other poor, and their toys.[23] He contrasts the rich boy, reared in "luxury" and the "daily spectacle of wealth" (10) to "another boy, dirty, somewhat rickety," a child "born and bred in mediocrity and poverty" (20). The boys' dolls reflect their differences: beside the rich boy, "a magnificent doll lay on the ground, looking as neat and clean as its master, varnished and gilded, dressed in a beautiful tunic, covered with feathers and glass beads" (20). By contrast, "the poor boy's toy" is what Baudelaire calls a "living toy" (10); in fact, the poor boy's toy, which entirely claims the rich boy's attention, is "a live rat" in a cage—"a toy drawn from life itself" (20). Thus the archetype of the "primitive toy" in Baudelaire's essay is *animate,* a kind of automaton whose alarming vitality fulfills (though it also inverts) the uncanny properties of the allegorical image. As the central figure in Baudelaire's "philosophy of toys," and hence in his formulation of modern poetics, the *living toy* illustrates nicely de Man's conception of lyric indeterminacy as well as the metaphysics of the lyrical body.

One might suppose that the extravagance of the rich boy's doll is to be contrasted to the abject spectacle of the "living toy," yet the rich boy covets the hideous rat for his own collection, "examining it greedily as if it were some rare and unknown object" (20). The abject "doll" is easily converted into a marvelous possession prized by the dandy, its resistance to material plenitude transformed into the very sign of "the daily spectacle of wealth." Thus, as Yeats reminds us by placing the mechanical bird in the opulence of the Byzantine court, the extravagance and ingenuity of the toy is yet another mark of its archaic identity.

In one of the most surprising developments in the essay, Baudelaire underscores the correlation of primitivism and Epicurean values by displacing the reader's attention from the "living toy" to what he calls the "scientific toy" (21–22). The examples that Baudelaire gives of the scientific toy, the stereoscope and the phenakistoscope, are important precursors of the modern technical media, especially the cinematic apparatus. These new "toys," according to Baudelaire, "develop in the mind of a child the taste for marvelous and unexpected effects" (21). Indeed, from a remark made earlier in the essay, it appears that these devices should be regarded as an exteriorization of the child's image-making faculty and its relation to the doll: "All children talk to their toys; the toys become actors in the great drama of life, scaled down inside the *camera obscura* of the childish brain" (16). Thus, if we understand these "scientific toys" to be the social and industrial counterparts of the "primitive toy," then the imagistic character of the barbaric toy must clearly be implicated in the "toys" of modern visual culture (particularly in light of the reference here to the "camera obscura"). Baudelaire confirms this correspondence when he comments on the child's "considerable faculty of abstraction and high imaginative powers; they play without playthings" (16). Indeed, the evolution from the "living toy" to the uncanny realism of the phenakistoscope recalls not only the allegorical criteria of lyric modernity, but also the conjunction of scientific materialism and spectacular culture that we have observed to be characteristic of the discourse of automata since antiquity. The incorporeality of the cinematic image simply reconstitutes, by means of modern technical media the "pneumatic" materiality associated with the automaton and, by implication, the lyric substance of Baudelaire's poetry.

If Baudelaire shrewdly abducts the toy from the sphere of childhood (appropriating it for the uncertain fate of poetry), Rilke's great essay on dolls seeks (but fails) to wrench the doll more forcibly from the world of childhood, thereby placing the poet in a more ambiguous and more traumatic relation to the strange muse of the doll. Indeed, he infers that the doll, as an idea or figure, is not a possession of childhood but rather its subject. For, in his estimation, it is not children but their dolls that grow up and become independent: "There are no children in their lives; this would be, in a certain sense, the conditions of their origin. . . . In these figures the doll has at last outgrown the understanding, the sympathy, the pleasure, and the sorrow of the child, it has become grown-up, prematurely old, it has entered upon all the unrealities of its own life."[24] From this passage, we understand that the doll's departure from childhood pertains at once to its origins and to the dream of autonomy. Though the frequent animation of the doll in Rilke's essay is highly ambiguous, there can be little doubt that the doll, as an emblem of modern lyric, is essentially an automaton. The doll's fundamental alienation from childhood signals a return to its place in the history of technology and in mechanical philosophy. In the context of Rilke's essay, however, the revolution of the doll constitutes a return to a place it has never been, to a crypt prepared for it long ago, in the trope of the mechanical bird.

Although Rilke never explicitly associates the doll with lyric, the doll appears in Rilke's oeuvre as a belated, though not entirely unexpected, permutation of the *angel,* the most persistent and fully developed figure of the poet in all of Rilke's work. The immediate chronology of the essay's composition is revealing. The first two Duino elegies, in which angels figure prominently, were composed in 1912; the doll essay was written in 1914 and the fourth Duino elegy, in which dolls and angels both appear, in 1915. Angels appear in Rilke's work as early as 1902 in the *Book of Images*, where they are described as "bright souls without a seam":

> They wander each and each alike,
> in God's garden silently,
> as many, many intervals
> in his might and melody.[25]

Here angels appear as "souls" and are associated both with lyric (as "intervals" of "melody") and with a model of seriality ("each and each alike") that evokes the soullessness, the pure exteriority, of the automaton. As an "interval," moreover, the angel is clearly a *medium.*

Several years later, an angel makes a celebrated visit in the *New Poems* (1907) as "L'Ange du Méridien":

> O smiling angel, sympathetic stone,
> with mouth as from a hundred mouths distilled:
> do you not mark how, from your ever-filled
> sundial, our hours are gliding one by one.[26]

In this passage, the angel addressed is a figure carved in stone (though "sympathetic"), thereby emphasizing, as in the earlier poem, the angel's eidetic nature ("mouth as from a hundred mouths distilled"). More remarkable, from the present standpoint, is the sundial that the angel is holding; for the iconography of "L'Ange du Méridien" (a sculpture on Chartres cathedral) almost certainly invokes the themes (if not the actual devices) of the Heronic tradition. More specifically, the angel in this poem calls forth in poetic terms the correlation of the clock and the angel of method in mechanical philosophy. We can therefore regard the "impartial sundial, upon which / the day's whole sum is balanced equally" as mirroring the figure of the angel, as a materialization of the angel's "mechanical"—and clairvoyant—mind.

The angel that appears in the second Duino elegy retains a place in the discourse of souls, yet its character (as a bird) has become inscrutable, a sign of danger eliciting the poet's song:

> Every angel is terrifying. Yet, knowing that danger,
> I still sing to you, you nearly killing birds of the soul. . . .
> Angels, who are you?[27]

It is precisely on this note of uncertainty that Rilke two years later ponders the placelessness of the doll: "Only you, doll's soul, one could never say exactly where you really were. Whether you were in oneself or in the sleepy creature over there. . . . When were you ever really present?"[28] As de Man's thesis about lyric suggests, this final question must be addressed to every object that appears—only to disappear—on the horizon of lyric modernity. In one of Rilke's most haunting reflections on the enigmatic character of the doll, he writes, "One was so busy keeping you alive that one had no time to determine what you were" (49). The irony of the doll's precarious vitality turns on its immortality (its kinship to the angel) and the immateriality of its provisions; for the doll is "fed like the 'Ka' on imaginary food . . . being impenetrable and incapable of absorbing, at any point, even a drop of water" (43).[29] Even more disturbing is the impression that the doll is at once sentient and inert, awake and asleep; for the doll is "awake only for an instant as the eyes flick open, then off to sleep again with its disproportionate and insensitive eyes wide open" (43).

The doll is a "stranger to us" (47); yet, more than merely inscrutable, it is genuinely malevolent, like "something that made a noise and could hardly wait to submerge us and the whole room by exerting its full powers" (46). The doll's menace appears to reside in the ambiguity of its material presence; for although Rilke, like Kleist, compares the doll to a god or spirit, he also describes it as being "less than a thing" (47). Hence in contrast to "the intimate, the touching, the deserted, the thoughtful aspect of many things," the doll is "the horrible foreign body on which we had wasted our purest ardor . . . the superficially painted watery corpse" (45). Indeed, the riddle of the doll's materiality can be resolved only by elaborating the trope of the cadaver. Recalling Baudelaire's insistence on children's desire "to get at and see the toy's soul," Rilke exclaims, "O, doll-soul, not made by God, you soul, begged on a whim from some impetuous elf, you thing-soul exhaled laboriously by an idol and kept alive by us all . . . in the end we have quite destroyed you, doll-soul, when we thought to care for you in our dolls; they were, after all, the larvae *[Larven]* which ate you away" (49). In this astonishing passage, Rilke asserts that we destroy the immaterial doll-soul by seeking to care for it, mistakenly, in the material doll. Thus the authentic doll-soul, which is invisible, succumbs to our delusions about the actual doll, thereby recapitulating the dialectic of the visible and the invisible that governs the figure of the angel. In Rilke's eyes, the invisible doll is the authentic one. Furthermore, in an extraordinary inversion of assumptions about the immateriality of the soul, the actual dolls become the maggots *(Larven)* that consume the cadaverous (and somehow vital) substance of the doll-soul. It is precisely at this moment that the ambiguity of the German word *Puppe* (and the English word "puppet") comes most powerfully into play. For *Puppe* means both "doll" and "pupa"; hence the doll, in Rilke's essay, must be understood as a *chrysalis* that undergoes a material transformation. Yet it is not the physical doll, but the doll-soul, that Rilke describes as suffering the transformation undergone by a cadaver, a paradox that recalls Epicurean notions of a flame-like material soul. Furthermore, the doll-larvae that consume the doll-soul are themselves "ghosts" or "masks": the German and English term "larva" derives from the Latin *larva,* meaning "ghost" or "mask." (This sense survives in obsolete usages of both terms.) Thus an immaterial corpse (the doll-soul) is consumed by material ghosts (the doll-larvae). Finally, it becomes evident that the doll's etymological correspondence to metamorphosis (as a pupa) only confirms its relevance to the inherent modernity of lyric, since, in de Man's view, poetry that is intrinsically "modern" allows for "the metamorphosis of one object into a number of other symbolic referents."[30] In Rilkean terms, since the doll is the very emblem of the lyric object and its ambiguous substance, *every* object can be said to undergo a transformation in which the object's soul—its invisible foundation—is rendered in terms of physical corruption.[31]

Within a year of the composition of the "Dolls" essay, Rilke had composed the fourth Duino elegy, in which the doll finally encounters its double, the angel. Echoing Kleist's distinction, the poet refuses the dancer's "disguise," preferring instead the puppet's primitive grace:

> and now comes the dancer.
> O not *him!* No matter how lightly he steps
> he's in disguise . . . I hate these half-filled masks,
> I'd rather a puppet—at least he's complete. I'll take
> its stuffed body and its wire and its
> bland face. Here. I'm waiting.[32]

By asserting the puppet's superiority over the dancer, the poet sets the stage for the meeting of doll and angel:

> aren't I right
> to feel like waiting in front of the puppet show,
> staring into it so intently
> that an angel must appear as one of the players
> to counter my gaze and jerk the dolls to life.
> Angel and doll: a real play at last.
> Then those things will be united which we continually
> scatter by merely being. *(23)*

In this passage, Rilke, elaborating Kleist's aesthetic ideology, suggests that the simplicity of the doll's barbaric form is commensurable only with the incorporeality of the angel. The anguished dialectic of doll and doll-soul is resolved in the figure of the angel, as Rilke explains in a letter of 1925:

The angel of the *Elegies* is that creature in whom the transforma-
tion of the visible into the invisible, which we are accomplishing,
appears already consummated. For the angel of the *Elegies*, all
past towers and palaces are existent, *because* long invisible, and the
still-standing towers and bridges of our existence *already* invisible,
although (for us) still persisting physically. The angel of the *Ele-
gies* is that being who vouches for the recognition in the invisible
of a higher order of reality.[33]

From this last statement in particular, it becomes apparent that the
intuitions of Rilke's angel, especially its recognition of an invisible re-
ality *within* the physical realm, are strongly reminiscent of the angelic
mind conjured by Leibniz as an emblem of mechanical philosophy
(which grasps the invisible causes of sensible bodies). Thus, if the angel
is "that creature in whom the transformation of the visible into the
invisible . . . appears already consummated," then the doll is that figure
in whom metamorphosis appears as a problem, in whom the dema-
terialization of objects is incomplete, ambiguous, or even inscrutable.

Although Rilke's anatomy of the doll draws on themes from the
essays of Baudelaire and Kleist, the Rilkean figures of doll and angel
tend to submerge questions of grace or beauty in a milieu of uncertain
trauma—the effect of suffering visited on them, or to be visited on
their human counterparts. Rilke observes, "The things which were
happening to us incomprehensibly we mixed in the doll, as in a test
tube, and saw them there change color and boil up" (45). With its
dreadful manifestation as a corpse, the doll becomes a physical exper-
iment, and its traumatic air identifies it as a provocative and even
transgressive object. The violence implicit in La Mettrie's yoking of
hedonism and mechanical philosophy anticipates the modern conver-
sion of the ostensible object of pleasure, the automaton, into an ex-
perimental figure of boundless suffering, ill-will, and provocation.

The transformation of the double—the doll—into a relic of in-
scrutable loss informs Walter Benjamin's understanding of toys as well,
though his reflections also reveal how the traumatic aspect of the doll

can be regarded as implicit in Baudelaire's conception of the "barbaric toy." Benjamin's taste in toys inclined towards the primitive, as he reveals in accounts of his efforts to acquire examples of Russian toys during his sojourn in Moscow in late 1926 and early 1927.[34] Shortly after his return from Moscow, Benjamin published a brief article in which he explains, "The stock of primitive forms in use by lower groups in society, the peasants and the artisans, provided the sure foundation for the development of children's toys up to the present. . . . The spirit from which these products emanate—the entire process of their production and not merely its result—is alive for the child in the toy."[35] A year or so later, in a review article titled "Toys and Games," Benjamin translated this sociological rendering of his taste for the barbaric into a psychological register that implicitly accommodates the hidden trauma evoked by the doll. For Benjamin rejects imitation as the primary motive for children's play and their toys; instead, he claims, "a single rule and rhythm reigns over the world of toys: the law of repetition" (which he calls "the soul of toys").[36] In a brief allusion to Freud's *Beyond the Pleasure Principle*, Benjamin implicates the toy not only in the compulsive and mechanistic framework of inaccessible trauma but also in a register of archaic experience that complements his taste for the archaic style in toys. At the close of the essay, alluding to Baudelaire, Benjamin asks, "If a modern poet maintains that for each individual there exists an image which engulfs the world, how often does that image not arise from an old toy chest?" (132). In this passage, Benjamin not only discovers in the toy a sense of irremediable loss, but he also manages to suggest its affinity with his monadological theory of allegory. For the toy, like the monadic image, harbors "an indistinct abbreviation of the rest of the world."[37] In addition, Benjamin's equation of the toy and the monad occurs implicitly within the framework of philosophical atomism, since Leibniz's monadology is essentially a doctrine of immaterial atoms.

Benjamin's siting of the toy along the axes of trauma, seriality, and determinism participates historically, as well as theoretically, in the surrealist elaboration of the figure of the automaton. Jacques Lacan, whose exposure to the group of surrealists associated with the journal *Minotaure* (especially Roger Caillois) looms ever larger in our understanding of his revisions of psychoanalysis, developed a dyadic conception of the repetition compulsion, based on two terms drawn from Aristotle's *Physics*: *tuché* and *automaton*. The former term, normally translated as "fate," Lacan defines as "the encounter with the real," which, by its inherently traumatic nature (according to Lacan), triggers the mechanism of repetition.[38] The second term, *automaton*, normally translated as "chance," Lacan defines as "the network of signifiers" beyond which lies the inscrutable and traumatic "nucleus" of the real.[39] In Lacan's formulation, then, we can refer, on one hand, to the automaton of *chance* and, on the other, to the automaton as a material substitute for a traumatic absence. Thus the determinism linking fate and chance (the polar terms of the repetition compulsion) appears in the figure of the automaton, which evokes, in turn, the ambiguous materiality of a "screen object." Rosalind Krauss has drawn attention to correspondences between the Lacanian automaton and Duchamp's "readymade," and to the role of these two figures in what she calls surrealist "antivision," a fundamental modernist practice founded on a dialectic of the visible and the invisible. She writes of the subject's relation to the ambiguous visuality—and, by implication, materiality—of the automaton: "I enter the picture as a cast shadow, cast because, dumbly, I get in the way of it, I cannot see it. The point where it would be, if I could see it, is held for me by a marker, a place-holder, a structural substitute. This is the automaton, the readymade, the thing the gap produces and hides behind. This is what marks the point in the optical system where what is thought to be visible will never appear.[40] Were we to translate these insights into the discourse of philosophical atomism, we could say that the automaton, the toy conceived as a screen object, is a spectacular device that discloses, in the name of science, the immaterial foundation of the object—the invisibility of the real.

Although Lacan turns to antiquity for his terms, the Aristotelian context functions as little more than a screen for the primary influence on Lacan's conception of the automaton: Roger Caillois's theory of mimicry. At the beginning of the session on "The Eye and the Gaze," where he discusses Caillois, Lacan observes, "it is by *automatism* that we sometimes translate into French the *Zwang* of the *Wiederholungszwang,* the compulsion to repeat."[41] Pursuing the correspondences embedded in this translation, Lacan assimilates the automaton into the repetition compulsion by means of what he calls "the determining mutation of mimicry," a phenomenon, he notes, analyzed by Caillois in *Medusa and Company* (73). According to Lacan, "the most radical problem of mimicry," which he characterizes as unrelated to the functional purposes of adaptation, is "to know whether we must attribute it to some formative power of the very organism that shows us its manifestations" (73). In other words, does the repetition compulsion derive from a capacity of the body to transform itself physically (over time) in response to certain extremely powerful images? Only by turning to the relevant texts of Caillois—to the discourse of surrealism— can we determine the implications of what Lacan sought to achieve by assimilating the figure of the automaton—already associated in his analysis with chance and the materiality of the signifier—to an understanding of the repetition compulsion based on a theory of physiological mimicry. In doing so, we approach the most significant manifestation of the automaton in the twentieth century: the dolls and mannequins of surrealism.

In 1933–1934, Roger Caillois, then barely twenty years of age, wrote a book called *La necessité d'esprit*, published posthumously in France in 1981. In this text, we find the nucleus—and the essential iconography—of ideas later elaborated by Caillois in articles in *Minotaure* and in his book *Medusa and Company*. In *The Necessity of the Mind* he elaborates, with great diffidence, a thesis concerning what he calls "lyrical thinking," or the "lyrical mechanisms" of "automatic thinking."[42] At the core of his doctrine of lyric fatality is the figure of the mantis—the seer, the diviner, and the automaton of Caillois's text. He compares "the articulated rigidity of the mantis" to "an automaton" and refers to "its astonishing capacity for automatism" (including the notorious feat of the female decapitating and devouring the male during copulation).[43] Yet the mantis in Caillois's text is not to be understood principally as yet another incarnation of the automaton itself, but as a catalyst, as the focal point of a process that Caillois, and Lacan after him, regarded as essential to automatism and the repetition compulsion: the mantis is one of many possible *objects* of "automatic thinking" by which the human observer imitates psychologically, and also physically, the habits or the "look" of some creature and therefore becomes an automaton in the act of physiological mimesis. Caillois makes his case for the mechanical (or purely reflexive) nature of human mimicry by linking it to the appearance of *ocelli* (little eyes) on the death's-head moth (an example cited by Lacan). The body thus becomes a kind of "medullar canvas" (to use La Mettrie's phrase), a magic lantern of corporeal effects. One could even argue that the body in this state achieves the godlike grace of Kleist's marionette, whose exquisite yet mechanical "tropes" depend on the complete extinction of consciousness. Thus the human becomes an automaton not so much by adopting the particular habits of the mantis (which nevertheless presents a dreadful image of the automaton) as by means of the body's capacity to incorporate—even to the point of self-destruction—the *image* of another creature. In short, what Caillois calls "lyrical fact" is "a material realization in the external world of the virtual, lyrical, passional elements of consciousness" (85).

The natural automaton is therefore characterized by the utter plasticity of its body and by the permeability of the ostensible boundary between mind and matter, between the lyrical and the mechanical. Hence the "process of lyrical materialization" (which constitutes the nucleus of automatism) presumes that "the mental and supposedly inner world of representation would be *objectively* confused with the physical and supposedly outer world of perception" (12). This vision of a body without any permanent physical disposition, yet ruled by the mechanism of lyrical thinking, a body that approaches the condition of the doll in its unconscious capacity for mimicry, recuperates to a remarkable degree the Baroque sense of the natural body being contingent on the metaphysics of the toy. Yet Caillois reveals, by recourse to natural history, that the key to the toylike properties of the natural body, and indeed of matter itself, is not that they are machines but that the body imitates, in the manner that a clock possesses time (without *telling* time), and indeed constitutes nothing other than the material "possession" of a *look,* a life, other than its own. This process of unconscious mimicry helps to explain why the themes of the discourse of automata since antiquity persist after the demechanization of the toy, why the classical automaton yields to the doll in the course of modernity without sacrificing the problem of animation. Caillois preserves the fatality of the doll (the mantis), so essential to the discourse of automata, by insisting on the deterministic and "irrational" framework of mimicry. Just as the automaton symbolized, for Descartes and other mechanical philosophers, the lawfulness of nature and method, so, for Caillois and the surrealists, the doll symbolizes the autonomy and "objectivity" of unconscious processes (including chance).

It is not altogether surprising, given Caillois's insistence on "the rigorous determinism of the associations and syntheses of lyrical thinking," that he should repeatedly invoke the authority of scientific and mathematical paradigms.[44] We have already encountered the figure of the automaton at the convergence of rhetoric and analytical geometry in Kleist's essay on the marionette. Caillois, with similar intent, maintains, "After I had adapted surrealist writing to the exigencies of scientific method, all I had to do was to let the experiment begin" (26). Yet, as this statement indicates, the "exigencies" of science derive, in Caillois's view, not from some abstract sense of authority but from scientific *method*. Indeed, the "experiment" of lyric automatism conforms, in principle, to the deductive method, based on the role of *analogy,* which Descartes compared to an automaton and Leibniz to an angel. Caillois explains, "This method of exploration appears as a humble and circumspect application of the principles of analogy and continuity, a method used constantly and exclusively by the most rigorous scientific minds and one that is all the more legitimate in that it is difficult to see how the least theoretical investigation could advance without it" (20). Though one might question the "humble and circumspect" nature of Caillois's "method," there can be no doubt that the "lyrical mechanism" of automatic thinking conforms to the methodological principles of the "mechanical hypothesis," to the regime of analogy on which philosophical atomism is founded.

In addition, Caillois makes it clear that the significance of the term *lyric* in his doctrine of automatism is precisely what we would expect: poetry becomes a form of science. He writes,

> Surrealism can thus take as the maxim of its experience Hegel's self-evident aphorism: "Nothing is more real than the appearance considered as appearance." This aphorism is also an epigraph of all poetry which refuses to take advantage of its artistic privileges in order to present itself as a science. Poetry, then, becomes violently unilateral on principle, siding with the marvelous and the unusual; and it strives, independently of any other consideration and by whatever means, to take into account the irrational element within the object (8).

Though poetry is on the side of angels (and the "irrational element" in things), it shares with science a "method"—and a philosophy—of unyielding fatality and automatism. More to the point, Caillois argues, "the evolution of poetry has brought it closer and closer to an automatic activity" (52). Lyric poetry, conceived as "automatic writing," therefore becomes emblematic of the physiological automatism that underlies all mimesis as well as the protean "substance" of lyrical bodies.[45] It is no longer a question of the mechanical doll functioning as a symbol of lyric but rather of lyric functioning as a symbol of the automaton.

Poetry, then, epitomizes the "process of lyrical materialization" (12).

The instrumental figure in this "method" of images traversing the boundaries of corporeal and incorporeal, body and idea, is what Caillois calls the "ideogram." The mantis, for example, is an "objective ideogram," and it is in a chapter titled "The Objectivity of Ideograms" that Caillois reviews the scientific and popular materials pertaining to the myth of the mantis (85). Yet Caillois associates the ideogram with "hallucinatory objectivization" and observes, "The image commonly acts through a sort of *lyrical authority,* which seems to be very easily assimilable to the phenomenon of hypnotic suggestion" (11). Thus, as the object and emblem of physiological mimicry, the figure of the ideogram represents the process of automatism as, on one hand, a model of *reading* and, on the other, as an instance of unconscious perception.[46] We are reminded of the hermeneutic implications of the clock metaphor in seventeenth-century probabilism. Yet Caillois's choice of the ideogram is more provocative (if no less arcane), since it seeks to grasp a process of physical automatism—the literal incorporation of an image—in terms of deciphering an alien script. Both the deductive method of theoretical physics and the surrealist "method" of automatic writing appear to involve the decrypting of incorporeal bodies.

During precisely the same period that Caillois wrote *The Necessity of the Mind*, Hans Bellmer, a German illustrator and graphic designer, constructed a life-size doll that was to become a prominent feature of the legacy of surrealism. He published ten photographs of it, along with a brief text, in *Minotaure* #6 in 1934, and constructed a second doll in 1935. Though any direct influence of these two individuals on one another is out of the question, Bellmer's doll displays remarkable affinities, both thematically and philosophically, with Caillois's formulation of lyrical automatism. Indeed, the perversity of Bellmer's doll fully incorporates—and of course transforms—the ideogram of the mantis as well as the process of lyric synthesis. Moreover, the immediate historical inspirations for Bellmer's doll betray the submerged correspondences between the surrealist automaton and the broader discourse of dolls and automata. Bellmer acknowledged two sources of inspiration for his dolls. First, he attended in 1932 a performance of Max Reinhardt's production of Hoffmann's "The Sandman."[47] The story of the female automaton, Olympia, the offspring of two men, would soon be realized in surprising detail in Bellmer's life, for Fritz Bellmer, Hans's younger brother, was closely involved in the design and construction of both Bellmer's dolls.[48] In addition, Bellmer came under the influence of Lotte Pritzel, whose wax dolls had served as the immediate inspiration for Rilke's essay on dolls. Bellmer's friendship with her was "to be of great importance to him when he decided to construct his own doll in 1933."[49]

Bellmer's references to the historical discourse of automata extend well beyond the coordinates of Hoffmann and Pritzel. In 1939 he collaborated on a book of photographs of his second doll, paired with prose poems by Paul Eluard, titled *Les jeux de la poupée* (The Games of the Doll). In a prose introduction to this book, Bellmer cites as precedents for his doll the writings of Philo of Byzantium and Jerome Cardano (a sixteenth-century natural philosopher), both important figures in the Heronic tradition of pneumatic automata.[50] Later in his career Bellmer worked on illustrations of texts that reveal the philosophical orientation of his lifelong fascination with the doll. He produced drawings for Georges Bataille's erotic tale "Madame Edwarda" and another series, based on the works of Sade, titled "Petit traité de morale." These collaborations place Bellmer's dolls in a genealogy of libertinism and radical materialism, a line of descent from La Mettrie to Sade to Bataille, which links mechanical philosophy and eroticism through the figure of the automaton. In addition to these projects, Bellmer produced a series of images titled "Les marionettes," based on Kleist's essay on the marionette theater.

The ties between automata and spectacular culture implicit in many of the texts referred to or illustrated by Bellmer help to explain his dolls' intrinsic orientation toward photography and other visual media. Bellmer's mannequins were made to be photographed. Indeed, neither of the dolls was exhibited as an artifact to be observed firsthand; each appeared originally only in photographs produced by Bellmer (those in *The Games of the Doll* were hand-colored). The first doll made its appearance in a tiny volume of ten photographs privately printed in 1934, titled *Die Puppe* and prefaced by Bellmer's lyrical essay "Memories of the Doll Theme." These and several other images of the doll appeared in *Minotaure* #6 in 1934, the event that launched Bellmer's career as a surrealist. Photographs of the second doll (in black and white) appeared for the first time in *Minotaure* numbers 8 and 10, in 1936 and 1937. Altogether, Bellmer produced thirty photographs of the first doll and over one hundred photographs of the second. The presentation of Bellmer's dolls, which were dismantled and rearranged to take part in the narrative fragments of individual photographs, therefore consists in nothing other than their repeated appearances in these photographs. Indeed, what Bellmer conceived as the genetic "multiplication" of his dolls in photographs calls to mind Caillois's insistence on the correlation of automatism, mimicry, and the repetition compulsion. Even more remarkable, the spectacle of unconscious mimicry is incorporated—literally internalized—in the construction of Bellmer's first doll. With the help of his brother Fritz, he installed in the abdomen of his first doll a circular panorama mechanism divided into six miniature scenes representing "the thoughts and dreams of a young girl."[51] Each panorama scene was lit internally by a small flashlight bulb: "the device was operated by a button on the left nipple, which turned the mirror one-sixth of the circumference of the disc. A viewer looking through the doll's navel could see each panorama in turn."[52] Not only does this somatic peep show manifest in a single device the correlation of optics and automation implicit in the Heronic tradition, but it also confounds the Baudelairean *species* of primitive and scientific toys. In Bellmer's doll, the "joujou barbarique" incorporates a prototype of the modern visual apparatus.

The reciprocity of Bellmer's dolls and Caillois's theory of lyric automatism goes well beyond the iterations (and revisions) of doll and

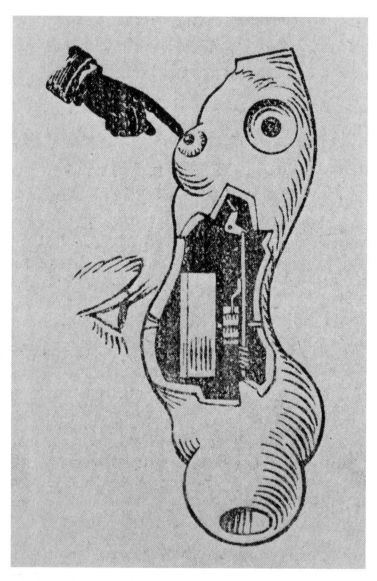

Figure 5.   Hans Bellmer, drawing of First Doll, panorama mechanism, from *Die Puppe* (1934). Courtesy Artists' Rights Society (ARS).

photograph. The preface to *The Games of the Doll* indicates that Bell-mer had integrated the concept of the game, or chance, into his con-struction of the doll and that he also associated the mechanism of chance with poetry: "The game belongs to the category of 'experi-mental poetry,' and bearing in mind such poetry's method of provo-cation, the toy will take the role of a provocative object."[53] In other works from the same period, Bellmer put into practice his views about the correlation of automatic writing (specifically poetry) and the doll. In 1939, for example, he collaborated with the poet Georges Hugnet on a tiny volume combining drawings by Bellmer and examples of automatic writing inspired by the doll.[54] In addition, seeking to explore the principle of the doll's articulation in writing, Bellmer himself com-posed poetic anagrams (words and sentences resulting from the re-arrangement of the letters in a given word or sentence) and frequently alluded to his dollmaking in terms of this literary device: "It is clear that we know very little of the birth and anatomy of the 'image.' Man seems to know his language even less well than he knows his own body: the sentence, too, resembles a body which seems to invite us to decompose it, so that an infinite chain of anagrams may re-compose the truth it contains."[55] In the composition of anagrams, he explains, "This sense of an alien responsibility and of one's own technical lim-itations—only the given letters may be used and no others can be called upon for help—leads toward a heightened flair, an unrestrained and feverish readiness for discoveries, resulting in a kind of automa-tism" (85). These passages reveal how closely Bellmer's notion of the doll as a corporeal *anagram* corresponds to Caillois's description of the trance of automatism induced by a "lyrical *ideogram*." In both cases, the iterations of the doll are compared to the practice of automatic writing.

Bellmer's theory of the anagrammatic doll leads him to reflect on corporeality in a manner that frequently recalls the themes we have encountered in the discourse of automata. Given his propensity for randomly and mechanically recomposing the elements of the doll, it is not surprising that Bellmer, like Kleist, invokes the relevance of mathematical formulas: "As in a dream, the body can change the center of gravity of its images. Inspired by a curious spirit of contradiction, it can add to one what it has taken from another; for example, it can place the leg on top of the arm or the vulvus in the armpit in order to make 'compressions,' 'proofs of analogies,' 'ambiguities,' 'puns,' strange anatomical 'probability calculations.' "[56] The metamorphosis of the doll, conceived as an anagram, implies a conception of lyric (comparable to that of Paul de Man, though inverting its allegorical structure) in which realism depends on the imperfect "irrealization" of the object. In a text published in 1957 (relating to *The Games of the Doll*), Bellmer states, "Concerning the monstrous dictionary of analogies and antagonisms which constitute the dictionary of the image, one must bear in mind that a particular detail, a leg perhaps, is perceptible, accessible to memory, and therefore available—in short, it is real— only if one's desire does not grasp it inevitably as a leg. An object that is identical only to itself is without reality."[57] From this perspective, the anamorphosis of the doll, conceived as the very foundation of realism, becomes an emblem of lyric modernity.

The perversity of Bellmer's recomposition of the doll implies an assault on literary and visual form, and on the very substance of the body: "I was aware of what I called the physical unconscious, the body's underlying awareness of itself. I tried to rearrange the sexual elements of a girl's body like a sort of plastic anagram. . . . I wanted to reveal what is kept hidden—it was no game—I tried to open people's eyes to new realities."[58] The doll, by its very nature a "provocative object," engenders "confusion between the animate and the inanimate; it must be a question of the thing personified, mobile, passive, adaptable, and incomplete."[59] More fundamentally, the doll, as an agent of "lyrical materialization," calls into question the distinction between corporeal and incorporeal: "An amalgam of objective reality, which is the doll, comes into existence as an amalgam of reality that is clearly superior, since it is at once subjective and objective."[60] The anagrammatic doll

Figure 6. Hans Bellmer, photograph of Second Doll (1935), from *Les jeux de la poupée* (1949). Courtesy Artists' Rights Society (ARS).

of surrealism, like the automaton of mechanical philosophy, consists of a genuine—and genuinely puzzling—amalgam of the "subjective and objective," of the material and immaterial; it is an object, like the "ideogram" of unconscious mimicry, traversing the borders of representation and corporeality.

Although Bellmer's doll theory recuperates to a remarkable degree—in the sense of memorializing something lost—the perverse body of mechanical philosophy, we should regard this theoretical consistency not as evidence of historical authenticity but rather as a telltale sign of philosophical *automatism* and the trauma that underlies it. Indeed, the ostensibly transcendent features of the lyric automaton, the most enduring ornament of philosophical materialism, can signify only the contours of a problem that is at once unavoidable and ungraspable. Vattimo declares, "Above all, matter seems a utopian notion because it literally has no place in our philosophical discourse."[61] He then adds, "There exists however a considerable exception to this absence . . . matter is present as a moment of dissolution, as a term which only functions insofar as it dissolves" (50). We must therefore take heed of the instructions whispered to us by our doubles, the toy and the doll: the radiant body of the gods can have no foundation other than the ephemeral substance of man.

CHAPTER 4

Meteoric Bodies

Just then by a happy chance, water-vapor was condensed by the
cold into snow, and specks of down fell here and there on my coat,
all with six corners and feathered radii . . . here was the ideal New
Year's gift for the devotee of Nothing, the very thing for a mathe-
matician to give, who has Nothing and receives Nothing, since it
comes down from heaven and looks like a star.

Johannes Kepler, The Six-Cornered Snowflake:
A New Year's Gift *(1611)*

What one believes is what matters. Ecstatic identities
Between one's self and the weather and the things
Of the weather are the belief in one's element.

*Wallace Stevens, "Extracts from Addresses
to the Academy of Fine Ideas"*

KEPLER'S STARLET

Prior to the eighteenth century, I have argued, mechanized toys and
automata were regarded—in the context of physics and the natural
philosophy of atomism—not only as emblems of corporeality but also
as practical demonstrations of the principles of pneumatics, the branch
of physics dealing with the mechanical properties of air and other
gases. The idea that mechanized dolls or toys (understood as *pneu-*

matica) might serve as emblems of atomism may seem less arbitrary (though no less problematic) if we recall, with Stephen Toulmin and June Goodfield, that "atomism has always appeared most plausible when applied to the physics of gases."[1] Indeed, they argue, "Outside the physics of gases, 'corpuscular philosophy' provided material more for manifestos than for solid explanations" (178). Thus Robert Boyle, the most prominent exponent of corpuscular philosophy in Britain in the seventeenth century, had his greatest success in a series of experiments carried out with his celebrated "air-pump," in order to provide a mechanical explanation for "the spring of air."[2] In its ancient and early modern formulations, therefore, atomism proved most effective at explaining the *body of air.* If atomism, the basis of scientific materialism, therefore remains philosophically and experimentally contingent on a discourse of "incorporeals," we have also seen how the most prominent symbol of corpuscular philosophy, the automaton, consistently evokes a paradoxical sense of bodies suspended between matter and immateriality. This doctrine of "subtle" bodies persists, I have argued, in the poetics of modern lyric in a manner that reveals the submerged relation between lyric substance and the discourses associated with philosophical atomism (particle physics, hedonism, automatism). The substance of song—the lyric "air"—encounters its scientific shadow in the body of air described and harnessed by pneumatic philosophy.

Atoms, I must reiterate, are not empirical objects among the world of things we experience. It has been necessary, since the dawn of materialism, to find plausible analogies to represent the atomic "reality" of bodies. One such analogy is pneumatics, the science of air, and its wondrous retinue of animated dolls. Corpuscular philosophy also turned, however, to certain categories of *natural* bodies as effective representations of atomic reality. Descartes, for instance, in addition to elaborating the metaphysical correlation of the automaton to the body and to matter itself, took a strong interest in the philosophy of "meteors"—a term whose meaning survives in our word for the science of weather, *meteorology*. At least until the eighteenth century, the term *meteor* referred to *any* atmospheric phenomenon (clouds, dew, winds, lightning, rainbows, comets, and so on); it was not until the twentieth century that the term was reduced to its modern astronomical sense, thereby severing our usage of the word *meteor* from the significance of *meteorology*. A member of the French Académie in the seventeenth century defined meteorology as "that part of natural philosophie which entreateth of the aire, and of the things engendered therein."[3] Descartes, like other natural philosophers engaged in the new physics, wrote on the subject of "meteors" as a means of demonstrating the method of mechanical philosophy, and also to disclose, by analogy to the science of atmospheric phenomena, the nebulous world of atoms. Meteorology, then, like pneumatics, pertained to mechanical bodies "engendered in the air," and both disciplines, for reasons concerning the stochastic nature of meteors, occupied privileged positions in the articulation of the corpuscularian hypothesis. In many respects, though the analogy may not be obvious at first glance, the dialectical substance of dolls finds its counterpart in the meteoric bodies of air.

In 1611, Johannes Kepler (1571–1630), the German mathematician and astronomer, published a treatise on the snowflake during his residence at the court of Emperor Rudolf II in Prague, a renowned patron and collector of scientific curiosities who possessed a famous collection of automata. Kepler's brief *tractatus* on the "six-cornered snowflake," subtitled *A New Year's Gift*, is remarkable not only for the manner in which it situates the snowflake in the science of "meteors," but also for its lyricism and self-conscious wit (though, unlike other early treatises on snowflakes, it was published without illustrations). Kepler clearly intends the reader to regard his corpuscularian anatomy of the snowflake as inseparable from the rhetorical and literary sophistication of his text. In this sense, Kepler's mechanical philosophy and, more precisely, his search for the principle of inorganic form embodied in the snowflake, deploy exquisitely the device of the Metaphysical

Figure 7.   Illustration of snowflakes, Olaus Magnus, *Historia de Gentibus Septentrionalibus* (1555). Besides the sketch of a six-pointed snowflake in the right-hand panel (said to be the first record of a microscopic object), all of the forms depicted in this image are fanciful—including what looks like a bell, a hand, and an eye. Courtesy Clark Library, Los Angeles.

conceit, which T. S. Eliot regarded as the supreme ornament of a unified sensibility. The opening sentences of Kepler's treatise are addressed to his benefactor, Johannes Wacker:

> I am well aware how fond you are of Nothing, not so much for its low price as for the sport, as delightful as it is witty, that it affords your pert sparrow; and so I can readily guess that the closer a gift comes to Nothing the more welcome and acceptable it will be to you.
>
> Whatever it is that attracts you by some suggestion of Nothing, must be both exiguous and diminutive, very inexpensive and ephemeral, in fact almost nothing. Although there are many such things in the world of Nature, the choice between them is open to

us. You will perhaps think of one of Epicurus's atoms: but that is simply Nothing. You have had Nothing from us, however, before now. So let us review the Elements.[4]

The gift Kepler seeks to bestow is "almost nothing," a trifle, at once a "diminutive" object and the text that attempts to explain it. Further, he seeks this "exiguous" body, which finds its absolute, though illegitimate, reference in the Epicurean atom, among the "Elements"—a reference to the famous analogy of Lucretius, who claims in *De rerum natura* that atoms are to bodies as letters are to words.[5] The analogy plays on the Latin term *elementum,* which means at once a constituent part of a complex whole (hence the four elements of meteorology) and a letter of the alphabet. Thus physics, as Kepler practices it, and more specifically the "philosophy of meteors" that frames his treatise, are inherently textual in nature. Michel Serres, in his study of the origins of physics, writes, "The idea that atoms are letters is a thesis which inaugurates the great classical philosophies—the idea of encrypting or encoding the global functioning of physical science. . . . Physics is really an activity of decipherment or decoding."[6] Further, he explains, "Physics is faithful to the world, since the formation of its text is isomorphic to the constitution of natural tissue" (196). Thus although the Epicurean atoms, or "elements," of Kepler's text are "simply nothing," they somehow constitute an "ephemeral" body that is not simply nothing but "almost nothing." Evidently, in the philosophy of meteors, nothing is always something. The Lucretian analogy of atoms and letters provides, moreover, the foundation for the model of reading implicit in the clock metaphor of seventeenth-century probabilism and in the angel of method conjured by Leibniz. Indeed, the etymology of the term *meteor* (μετεωρον, "something raised up," from μετα-αείρειν) suggests that the body "engendered in the air" may be the subtle body of an angel, caught up in the dialectic of rising and falling elaborated by Rilke in the angel of the Duino elegies. Meteoric and angelic bodies occupy a space between heaven and earth.

After briefly searching the "elements" for a gift suitable both to his benefactor's taste for elegant trifles—for *toys,* perhaps—and to the inclinations of a mathematician, Kepler notices the patterns of snow-flakes falling on his coat that day in Prague. And so, he decides, it is the meteoric body of the "six-cornered starlet," or the text of the snow-flake, that most nearly resembles a gift that is "almost nothing." He takes delight in an interlingual pun between the Latin word for snow-flake, *nix,* and the German *nichts* (nothing), calling it "an omen in the name" (7). Indeed, Kepler returns repeatedly in his treatise to the conceit of a body that is next to nothing. He playfully embarks on his analysis with a plea to his patron: "So accept with unclouded brow this enrichment by Nothing, and (if you have the sense) hold your breath for fear of once again receiving nothing" (7). By calling the mind "unclouded," Kepler alludes for the first time to a possible cor-respondence between the "six-cornered starlet" (which becomes more and more animated in the course of the text) and other kinds of bodies, as well as the correlation of external and internal "climates."

Kepler acknowledges the danger of elaborating the conceit of "Nothing" in order to ascertain the principle of the snowflake's form. Indeed, the lyric device of the conceit resembles in many respects the scientific method of hypothesis, and the meteoric body of the snowflake therefore depicts not only the subliminal atom but also the method by which one visualizes and objectifies the atom. Kepler asserts, "I shall push this notion as far as it will take me, and only afterwards shall I test its truth, for fear that the ill-timed detection of a groundless as-sumption may perhaps prevent me from fulfilling my engagement to discourse about a thing of Naught" (25). Eventually, he confronts the "folly" of his method, without however renouncing the need to adduce further "trivia" to correct the excesses of his "trivial arguments":

But this is folly, to be so carried away. Why, my endeavor to give almost Nothing almost comes to nothing! From this almost Noth-ing I have almost formed the all-embracing Universe itself! . . . So

I shall beat a retreat and take pains to see that what I have given and said should be Nothing. This will come about if, as quickly as my snowflake melts, I rebut these trivial arguments with as trivial counter-arguments and reduce them to—nothing (39).

Kepler proposes to correct and straiten his inquiry not by abandoning the method of the lyrical conceit, but by equating it with a principle of negativity that reduces its object and its discursive medium to nothing—or "almost Nothing." It becomes clear that the six-cornered starlet must be reduced, in the spirit of science and wit, to a trifle—to a Metaphysical toy conjured by the "gift" of a toy medium. Yet Kepler's treatise is not merely a work of "folly"; for, as one historian of science notes, "it defined a new realm of inquiry for exact science: the mathematics of the genesis of form."[7] Indeed, prior to the convergence of microscopy and mechanical philosophy in the mid-seventeenth century, "such scientific clarity on an issue bordering on the micro-realm was without precedent" (57). In his anatomy of the snowflake, Kepler thus established a threshold for "the mathematical physics of small systems" (57). All the same, the rigor of his method cannot be isolated from its lyricism. He closes his treatise by returning once more to its central conceit, and alerts the reader: "Nothing to follow" (45). With these words, Kepler not only confounds the "Nothing" that constitutes his text and the "Nothing" that follows it, but he also blurs the distinction between *textual* meteors and the "vapours" composing the prehistory and the afterlife of the snowflake.

The lyrical dimension of the meteoric body is not, in Kepler's view, solely methodological or representational, nor is it external to the material formation of the snowflake. He states, "There is then a formative faculty in the body of the Earth, and its carrier is vapour as the human soul is the carrier of spirit; so much so that no vapour ever exists without being found by a formative principle . . . formative reason does not act only for a purpose, but also to adorn" (33). Thus he aims to transpose nature's "playfulness" to "serious intention" (33), to the ends of physics, and he finds, concerning the snowflake's hexagonal form, that "aptness and beauty of shape, not material necessity, is in view" (41). In addition, the lyrical form (and substance) of the snowflake is not to be isolated, in Kepler's view, from the formation of *terrestrial* bodies: "Jewellers say that natural octahedra of the most perfect and exquisite form are found in diamonds ... the same faculty of soul which clothed the diamond within the Earth in a form furnished from the innermost treasury of its nature, that of the octahedron, when it emerged from the Earth in vapour, clothed with the same shape the snowflake arising from that vapour" (37). Kepler, moreover, takes a decisive step in his corpuscular anatomy of the snowflake when he asks, "What has an animal in common with a snowflake?" and finds "a resemblance to an animal in a starlet of snow" (31). In the context of mechanical philosophy, of course, the animal body is the organic image of the automaton, and it may well be that in Kepler's meteorology the "starlet of snow" functions as a counterpart to the automaton in mechanical philosophy.

The ephemerality of the snowflake, evoked—and objectified—so elegantly by Kepler, faithfully mirrors the position of meteorology in the classical organization of knowledge. For, as S. K. Heninger explains, "Meteors were imperfect mixtures of the four Elements. They were confined to the region of Air in the sublunary universe, since changing weather conditions could not conceivably transpire in the immutable region beyond the moon. ... Meteors, then, could occur only in the corruptible portion of the universe enclosed by the sphere of the moon."[8] The region of mutability and corruptibility coincides, of course, with that of mortality—hence Kepler's recognition of animal bodies on the horizon of meteorology. Yet the meteoric body is distinguished by its composite nature, by the fact that it falls (or rises) *between* heaven and earth, between astronomy and geology. The meteor, in this sense, is a medium, or an angel, as the angel's insignia, a halo woven of air and light, suggests. Michel Serres characterizes the domain of meteors as "a sort of habitat, visible though immense . . . and filled up entirely by the movement of bodies."[9] Further, he states, "Meteors are accidents, events: a hazardous milieu, the factual environment of essences, the *topos*" (85). The inherent instability and ephemerality of meteors stem, according to Serres, from "turbulence" (from Latin, *turba,* "crowd") that is "transelementary": "As for form, that which appears to be an accident—the whirlwind, the eruption, thunder, lightning—becomes law" (102). Further, he claims, in the realm of meteors, "Everything borders on the crowd, disorder, . . . tumult, chaos, and agitation. Everything borders on disturbance, destruction, explosion" (103).

Arden Reed, in his book *Romantic Weather*, formulates a similar thesis about meteors: "Historically speaking, it has more often been typical to associate meteorological phenomena with a certain drift or tropism away from the clear and distinct, the orderly, the formal, the necessary, and toward the uncertain, the disordered, the shifting, and the contingent."[10] Further, he states, " 'meteors' cannot achieve the ontological stability of a form—although if they never participate fully in presence, neither are they ever entirely absent. . . . The weather is not so much beyond formalism as before formalism" (11). Reed goes on to make a strong argument for the essential correspondence between meteorology and the aesthetic ideology of Romantic poetry, extending to the cusp of modernism (in Baudelaire's writing). Emphasizing the correlation between weather as a linguistic phenomenon (composed of elements) and weather as the sphere of natural turbulence, Reed contends, "Weather and writing may thus be different names for the same production" (247). More specifically, "Coleridge and Baudelaire articulate some of their most intense intellectual efforts and questionings around the weather . . . the dramaturgy of the weather enacts basic arguments about poetics and language. . . . For both writers language has a 'meteoric' composition (and decomposition), and to take a reading of their climates therefore is a way to study the particular character of their textuality" (61, 62). These statements leave no doubt as to Reed's equation of the lyric "air" and the meteoric body of air. If we add to this equation Baudelaire's interest in toys, we can see that the poetic meteorology analyzed by Reed is part of a larger meditation on the nature of lyric substance.

In their discussions of atmospheric phenomena, both Serres and Reed give prominent attention to the sixth book of *De rerum natura*, which treats the subject of meteorology (including pestilence, or plague, which is regarded by Lucretius as a meteoric phenomenon).[11] Serres states, "Atomic physics fully realizes itself in the book of Meteors."[12] Reed, on a similar note, ends his lengthy introduction to a philosophy (and poetics) of meteors by declaring, "Meteorology will remain at best a stochastic science" (77). By "stochastic," Reed means "random," "conjectural," or "probabilistic," yet he also cites Serres on the turbulence and rarefaction of stochastic systems: "The perception of randomness *[le stochastique]* replaces the outline of form"; and further, "Matter is no longer imprisoned within schema. Fire dissolves matter, causing it to vibrate, tremble, oscillate, and finally to explode into *clouds*."[13] Although Reed's elaboration of the turbulence of meteoric phenomena is rooted in the Lucretian philosophy of materiality, he never mentions the doctrine of atomism, nor does he consider the *corporeality* of meteors. One is reminded of Vattimo's point about the peculiar absence of materiality as a topic in contemporary theory. Serres, on the other hand, does address the question of form—that is, the formation of bodies—though he tends, like Reed, to distinguish between the essential turbulence of meteors and the world of objects precipitated from the stochastic "cloud of atoms." He speaks, for example, of "the unfathomable depth of things in which the elements of divisibility sleep" (196). More precisely, he contends, "Turbulence is the functional figure of composition and formation. . . . It thus becomes the global figure of transformation. . . . Things, and therefore nature itself, are formed, as a conjunction of atoms, in and by this vortex" (115). Reed (once again citing Serres), makes a similar observation, emphasizing the fortuitous (and anomalous) character of objects: "Order is an aberration that sooner or later must occur. In this way, the stable, comprehensible world we ordinarily presuppose is reduced to 'the exception of meteors' " (10).

This tension between the stochastic "cloud of atoms" and the stable form of objects is precisely what Kepler ponders in the meteoric body of the snowflake. He undermines the distinction between form and vapor maintained by Serres and Reed, however, by elaborating the conceit of "nothing": the exquisite yet mechanical form of the six-cornered starlet is made of nothing (it is elemental), while the boundless and invisible body of "vapour" harbors the principle of form ("no vapour ever exists without being bound by a formative principle"). Kepler aims precisely to ascertain the mechanical properties of a body of air. By contrast, the absolute discrimination between object and meteor advanced by Serres and Reed is founded on a schism between meteorology and mechanical philosophy.[14] Serres repeatedly characterizes the meteor as a philosophical, historical, and topological anomaly: "Meteorology is a backwater of history.... The time *[temps]* of meteors does not encounter the time *[temps]* of history; their type of order and disorder has only recently come to the attention of scientific rationality."[15] Thus, he contends, "Our science, our mechanics, takes place generally, from Newton to August Comte, on Earth and in the sky—the descent of bodies and the path of the stars. Almost never in between the two" (107). Further, he explains,

> No one therefore reads the *Meteorology* of Lucretius or Descartes. ... Why this repression? Because philosophers, historians, the masters of science, care only for the ancient idea of law: exact determination, or rigorous over-determination. Power and order. What the weather is, or what the weather will be, infinitely exceeds their calculation, of which it takes no account. Because it [meteorology] is the occasion of disorder and the unpredictable, of the hazardous locale, of the unformed *[informe]*. Because it is the time *[temps]* of another time *[temps]* (86).

Serres's fundamental equation of *turba* and meteor therefore depends on his claim that meteors are inherently unlawful and incommensurable with mechanical bodies.

The discourse of the unforeseeable and the *informe,* as Serres and Reed present it, is extremely seductive and, indeed, useful in overcoming certain aspects of the conventional alienation of physics and poetics. It neglects, however, to take into account certain essential facts about the history of atomist discourse. Most important, in the seventeenth century, *corpuscular* and *mechanical* are equivalent terms; the revival of atomist doctrine coincides with the elaboration of mechanistic analogies (such as the automaton). Thus *all* atomistic phenomena, including the weather, are susceptible, in theory, to mechanical explanation—and, by analogy, to the principle of the toy. Further, to claim with Serres and Reed that meteors are anomalous and unintelligible phenomena (from the perspective of mechanical philosophy) simply ignores the close historical relation between atomism and pneumatics: atomism proved most successful at explaining the nature of bodies "engendered in the air"—bodies made of "nothing." Only by starting from this principle—*the mechanization of Nothing*—is it possible to account for the persistent immateriality of the automaton and the corresponding mechanicity of incorporeal phenomena, such as meteors. To ignore these fundamental incongruities obliges one to overlook, or misunderstand, the correlation between automatism and nebulosity in Romantic or modern lyric. Further, if one discriminates absolutely between meteors and mechanical bodies, the equation of antigravitational tropes and mechanical laws in Kleist's marionette remains simply unintelligible. In essence, to refuse the mechanization of "nothing" obscures the dialectical character of materiality in atomist doctrine.

We need only examine one of the unread meteorologies of the seventeenth century to discover how closely the philosophy of meteors conforms to the method of mechanical philosophy, and how this compatibility finds expression in the essential reciprocity of terrestrial and meteoric bodies. Descartes read Kepler's treatise on the snowflake before publishing his own (illustrated) meteorology, *Les météores*, in 1637 as one of three appendixes to the epochal *Discourse on Method*.[16] That Descartes regarded meteorology as a fundamental demonstration of the hypothetical method of mechanical philosophy is evident from the first paragraph of his analysis of the rainbow: "The rainbow is such a remarkable phenomenon of nature, and its cause has been so meticulously sought after by inquiring minds throughout the ages, that I could not choose a more appropriate subject for demonstrating how, with the method I am using, we can arrive at knowledge not possessed at all by those whose writings are available to us."[17] In addition, at the beginning of the *Meteorology*, Descartes indicates that to produce a mechanical explanation of meteoric phenomena, one must first consider the nature of *terrestrial* bodies: "I here explain the nature of clouds in such a way that we will no longer have occasion to wonder at anything that can be seen of them. . . . I shall speak, in this first discourse, of the nature of terrestrial bodies in general, so that, in the next one, I may better explain the nature of vapors and evaporations" (263). Leibniz, too, stressed the mechanical correlation between bodies and meteors. In fact, he liked to compare the body and its substance to a *rainbow*.[18] Descartes, for his part, couldn't resist comparing clocks and snowflakes: "I noticed some which had six tiny teeth around them, similar to those in the wheels of a clock" (312). Like Kepler's six-cornered starlet, the Cartesian snowflake begins to resemble a machine.

At the core of Descartes's conception of meteoric bodies is a doctrine of rarefaction (sublimation) and condensation: "Any agitation of the air that can be felt is called *wind,* and any invisible and impalpable body is called *air.* Thus, when water is greatly rarefied and changed into very fine vapor, we say that it has been converted into air" (287). The "impalpable and invisible body" of air thus converts to vapor and cloud, to rain or snow, and so on. Indeed, the process of precipitating palpable bodies from subtler bodies extends to "miraculous" conversions that disclose the common substance of meteors and animals:

And to the extent that there are exhalations of many diverse natures, I do not even judge it to be impossible that the clouds, by pressing them, sometimes form from them a material which seems, according to its color and consistency, like milk, or blood, or flesh; or else in being burned, becomes such that we take it for iron, or for rocks; or finally, in becoming corrupted, engenders certain small animals in very little time; thus we often read, among the miracles, that it rained iron, or blood, or locusts, or similar things (329).

Here meteoric precipitation is conceived in terms of both genetics and phenomenalism (suggesting, perhaps, a genealogy of illusion), such that the animal body is regarded as a "corruption" of the "transparent body" of air.

The body of the rainbow in particular engages the question of phenomenalism in the philosophy of meteors. For the rainbow, as Descartes explains, is one of those "things that we may see in the air without their actually being there" (331). The appearance of such things is identical to their substance or essence, since they are nothing more than appearances. Thus, to account for the meteoric body of the rainbow, one must provide a mechanical explanation of an optical illusion by establishing precisely the role of optical refraction, as Descartes does in his essay. The rainbow therefore marks the point where optics (which Descartes called the "science of miracles") and the philosophy of meteors intersect.[19] Descartes's reflections at the conclusion of his anatomy of the rainbow reveal his awareness of meteorology's relation to spectacular culture and the body politic. The final paragraph discusses the production of artificial rainbows: "And this makes me remember an invention for making signs appear in the sky, which would cause great wonder in those who were ignorant of their causes. I suppose that you already know the method of making a rainbow visible by the use of a fountain" (344). He goes on to explain—with the help of a technical diagram—how "we would see through their means a great part of the sky full of the colors of the rainbow" (345).

Figure 8. Painted-glass portable fireworks theater (unknown manufacturer, eighteenth century). This artifact combines the two dominant tropes of the rhetoric of materialism: toys and meteors. Courtesy Theater Instituut Nederland.

His final remarks reveal not only the difficulty of producing a "meteor" of this kind, but the ideological character (and scale) of the illusion he is contemplating: "I admit that skill and much work would be necessary in order to proportion these fountains, and to cause the liquids there to leap so high that these figures could be seen from afar by a whole nation, without the trick being discovered" (345). Thus the "natural magic" of the rainbow lends itself to the production of an image (a "sign") of nationhood, an illusory body that defines, quite literally, the horizon of the political imaginary.

When Descartes pondered the creation of a false rainbow in daylight, the production of artificial "meteors" to mark important occasions of state had already become a historical reality in the development of elaborate fireworks displays.[20] Indeed, the public fascination with these nocturnal spectacles, and the technical capacity to produce them, coincides with the Baroque enthusiasm for mechanical toys and for life-size automata in more exclusive settings (such as the mechanical Orpheus in the gardens of Saint-Germain-en-Laye). In terms of seventeenth-century natural philosophy, fireworks *(feux d'artifice)* belong to the discourse of incorporeals but also, by implication, to meteorology (which explains Descartes's interest in a false rainbow). More precisely, from the perspective of materialism, fireworks are to be regarded as a kind of artificial weather, or atmospheric toy. The incorporeal body of this nocturnal spectacle is distinguished on one hand by its ephemerality (like the weather) and on the other by its artificiality (like the toy). The corporeality of fireworks thus serves as a dazzling medium between the automaton and the meteoric body. The spectator witnesses in fireworks a body ruled by violent expenditure—a reminder of the court or state that sponsors it.

MISTER THUNDER

> A poem is a meteor.
> *Wallace Stevens, "Adagia"*

> The whole of appearance is a toy.
> *Wallace Stevens, "The Dove in the Belly"*

The correlation between toys and meteors in corpuscularian philosophy of the seventeenth century (and in the use of fireworks as an element of public diversion) survives for modern poetics (and, I might add, for modern materialism) in the poetry of Wallace Stevens. More explicitly, Stevens's work offers a complex and sustained meditation on the weather as "a sense of nature" equivalent to the "sense" of poetry—a cryptic formulation that points to the influence of Vico on

Stevens's poetics.[21] Further, his correlation of poetry and weather (of lyric and meteoric bodies) implies a more general equivalence between matter and *materia poetica*. Critics frequently allude to Stevens's interest in the idea of the weather, yet they rarely consider his attention to weather as a material phenomenon, or the materialist implications of his poetic meteorology.[22] Too often, references to weather and climate in Stevens's poems are viewed only as figures of speech and, thus, as one more symptom of his purported idealism and insistence on "abstraction." If, however, we take into account the role of meteorology in the history of materialism, Stevens's references to the weather must be treated in a more complex fashion. Just as the mechanical bird in Yeats's Byzantium poems no longer appears, once we grasp its relation to the iconography of materialism, to be simply an emblem of poetic idealism, so, too, must Stevens's meteorology, read from the perspective of materialism, raise important questions about the presumed idealism of Stevens's poetry (if idealism implies a disregard for the problem of materiality). The same thing could be said about the materialist inference of the dolls and automata of surrealism. In Stevens's case, we can hardly avoid the implications of materialism if we take seriously his comment that "poetry and materia poetica are interchangeable terms."[23] Indeed, the materialist orientation evident in this statement establishes its basic terms through his correlation of poetry and the weather.

The many references to weather and meteoric bodies in Stevens's poetry must be taken on their own terms; yet it is also clear, from the nature of his observations, that he means to recall the Baroque "philosophy of meteors" and to revise it as a vehicle for modern poetics. While Stevens's elaboration of the weather is of interest to students of lyric poetry and modern poetics, it is also of value, because of its subtlety and ingenuity, to the history of materialism. Like Baroque meteorology, Stevens's sense of the weather as a topos (quite literally) is based on a theory of "elements": between heaven (referred to by Stevens as the "lunar" element) and earth lies the realm of "things of medium nature," the realm of meteors.[24] The weather occupies the middle, and so do men: not, he says,

> Under the mat of frost and over the mat of clouds.
> But in between lies the sphere of my fortune
> And the fortunes of frost and of clouds.
> *("Like Decorations in a Nigger Cemetery," 151)*

Of this sublunar region, he declares,

> To believe in the weather and in the things and men
> Of the weather and in one's self, as part of that
> And nothing more. So that if one went to the moon
> Or anywhere beyond, to a different element,
> One would be drowned in the air of difference,
> Incapable of belief, in the difference.
> *("Extracts from Addresses to the*
> *Academy of Fine Ideas," 258)*

Further, when Stevens refers to the weather, as "the mobile and immobile flickering / In the area between is and was" ("An Ordinary Evening in New Haven," 474), we can already begin to discern the qualities attributed to meteoric bodies by natural philosophy.

Before proceeding, however, I want to emphasize certain figures and observations in the passages I have just cited. Most important, when Stevens speaks of the weather, we must bear in mind that the "fortunes of frost and of clouds" are identical to those of humanity and, more specifically, to the "fortune" of the poet, whom Stevens elsewhere calls a "pundit of the weather" ("Like Decorations in a Nigger Cemetery," 156). Nor is this comparison solely metaphysical, since, when he refers to "the things and men of the weather," he is claiming that bodies of air and the bodies of men, both occupying "the area between is and was," share certain phenomenological properties. This domain is distinguished, as the phrase indicates, by its peculiar temporality. In addition, the airy substance of this realm—indeed the very existence of meteoric bodies (including the poet's)—is a function of "belief." "What / One believes is what matters," Stevens says in another poem ("Extracts from Addresses to the Academy of Fine Ideas," 258)—a position that raises issues already familiar to us from the doctrine of analogy in scientific materialism.

I want to call attention to the phrase "the air of difference," which denotes the element of fatality, yet signals the correlation between meteoric bodies and the lyric "air." For Stevens elsewhere states,

> Poetry is a finikin thing of air
> That lives uncertainly and not for long
> Yet radiantly beyond much lustier blurs.
> *("Like Decorations*
> *in a Nigger Cemetery," 155)*

Lyric poetry appears in these lines as a radiant body of air, but it is also a made thing, dainty, delicate—almost nothing, we could say, in Kepler's phrase. The poet, then, is not only a "pundit of the weather" but also a maker of meteors and trifles, of toys ingeniously wrought.

The correspondence between toys and meteors in Stevens's poetry rests, however, on more than the connotations of the term "finikin." For the "pundit of the weather" is also "a man gone mad, after all, for time, in spite / Of the cuckoos, a man with a mania for clocks" ("Like Decorations in a Nigger Cemetery," 156, 157). In his world, "Everything ticks like a clock" (157), and he goes mad "in spite of the cuckoos"—modern relics of an ancient discourse of mechanical birds. Indeed, the weather man, who is one of "an ocean of virtuosi" (156), and whose madness the birds cannot prevent, lives in a world described as a "mechanism / Of machine within machine within machine" (157). Thus the weather, and also the mind and the body of the weather man, are each a kind of machine—a proposition with remarkable similarities to the general thesis of the Baroque philosophy of meteors.

The question remains: in what way is the weather like a machine, a mechanical singing bird? Another poem tells us that the "virtuoso" of the weather shares in

> common fortune, induced by nothing,
> Unwished for, chance, the merest riding
> Of the wind, rain in a dry September,
> The improvisations of the cuckoos
> in a clock-shop.
>
> > *("Examination of the Hero*
> > *in a Time of War," 275)*

Here the "common fortune" of the virtuoso, the automaton, and the "meteors" of a dry September hinges on the principle of "improvisation"—the idea that machines engage in improvisation. The weather, too, we might say, exists by improvisation, with the result that meteors might be construed as machines, and vice versa. The virtuoso therefore calls for "the phenomenon" to be

> painted by mad-men, seen as magic . . .
> Even enthroned on rainbows in sight of the fishes of the sea, the colored
> Birds and people of this too voluminous
> Air-earth.   *(277–78)*

As an effect of improvisation, then, any phenomenon—rainbow, machine, or human—can be "seen as magic." A vision of "common fortune"—a synthesis of humans and toys and meteors—occurs, remarkably enough, in a description of fireworks:

> Do you remember how the rocket went on
> And on, at night, exploding finally
> In an ovation of resplendent forms—
>
> Ovation on ovation of large blue men
> In pantaloons of fire and of women hatched,
> Like molten citizens of the vacuum?

Do you remember the children there like wicks
That constantly sparkled their small gold?
                    ("Two Tales of Liadoff," 346)

The rockets explode to become bodies, imitating the weather and hatching figures of fiery flesh. These "molten citizens of the vacuum" are human meteors, but also a means of diversion—atmospheric toys.

The principle of meteoric improvisation informs the clocks and automata of Stevens's poems even when the poem makes no explicit mention of clouds or rainbows or snowflakes. The weather, it seems, goes without saying. In "Notes toward a Supreme Fiction," for example, there is a music box:

> Perhaps there are times of inherent excellence,
>
> As when the cock crows on the left and all
> Is well, incalculable balances,
> At which a kind of Swiss perfection comes
>
> And a familiar music of the machine
> Sets up its Schwärmerei, not balances
> That we achieve but balances that happen.   *(386)*

In this surprising passage, the clock-like mechanism ("a familiar music of the machine") summons "its Schwärmerei"—swarms of revelers that call to mind the "metaphysical changes" swarming in the air of "Esthétique du Mal" (326). The principle of *enthusiasmos* embodied in the Schwärmerei therefore suggests that meteoric events overtake the automaton, or the music box, at certain "times of inherent excellence." These moments of dissolution also constitute, however, "a kind of Swiss perfection," an equinox of "incalculable balances," suggesting that the integration of machine and meteor pertains to the mechanical (or magnetized) thinking of the angel that appears in Leibniz and Rilke. Stevens does indeed envision the "virtuoso" to be an angelic figure (related to the "pundit of the weather"):

the virtuoso never leaves his shape,
Still on the horizon he elongates his cuts,
And still angelic and still plenteous,
Imposes powers by the power of his form.
("A Primitive like an Orb," 443)

The angel's "virtue" (and his power) thus relies—and works—on the material of the weather on the "horizon." Indeed, Stevens links the angel explicitly to the weather:

Our divinations,
Mechanisms of angelic thought,
The means of prophecy,

Alert us most
At evening's one star
And its pastoral text,

When the establishments
Of wind and light and cloud
Await an arrival
*("One of the Inhabitants
of the West," 503)*

In this passage, it seems, the automaton has become immaterial—a "means of prophecy"—suggesting that the substance of this angelic mechanism now resembles the weather that occasions its speech. The machine of "divination" in turn renders the "establishments of wind and light and cloud."

Beyond the correlation of toys and meteors, Stevens's poetic meteorology faithfully renders the dominant features of the Baroque philosophy of meteors. For example, the idea of a "thing of air that lives uncertainly and not for long" immediately calls to mind the instability and ephemerality of meteoric bodies described by seventeenth-century philosophers of the weather. The realm of meteors, according to Stevens, is "a permanence composed of impermanence" ("An Ordinary Evening in New Haven," 472), a "calculated chaos" ("Repetitions of a

Young Captain," 307): what he calls "my fluent mundo" ("Notes toward a Supreme Fiction," 407). Further, Stevens repeatedly stresses, as does natural philosophy, the mutability of air and the meteoric body:

> Cloud-casual, metaphysical metaphor,
> But resting on me, thinking in my snow,
> Physical if the eye is quick enough,
> So that, where he was, there is an enkindling, where
> He is, the air changes and grows fresh to breathe.
> The air changes, creates and re-creates . . .
> *("Chocorua to Its Neighbor," 301)*

The domain of weather—the "area between is and was"—thus figures repeatedly in Stevens's poems as the space of metamorphosis, a realm of transient visions and fiery changes:

> the air, the mid-day air, was swarming
> With the metaphysical changes that occur,
> Merely in living as and where we live.
> *("Esthétique du Mal," 326)*

In addition, one of the many correspondences between poetry and weather implicit in the term "air" turns on the principle of metamorphosis. The poet refers, for example, to

> The instance of change that was the poem,
> When the cloud pressed suddenly the whole return
>
> From thought, like a violent pulse in the cloud itself
> *("Two Tales from Liadoff," 347)*

From these passages we discover that the "violent pulse," the "instant of change," occurs "merely in living as"—that is, the swarm of "metaphysical changes" in the air (like the "Schwärmerei") mirrors a "sense" of life conditioned by imagination. All "things of medium nature" inhabit the weather of "as if."

The most famous meteoric body in Stevens's poetry is, of course, the "snow man"—a figure enmeshed in dozens of references to snow and winter throughout Stevens's poetry. In the poem titled "The Snow Man," we encounter for the first time the one who "regards" things with "a mind of winter":

> the listener who listens in the snow,
> And, nothing himself, beholds
> Nothing that is not there and the nothing that is.
> *("The Snow Man," 10)*

The correspondence between the substance of the listener and the substance of the "element" he beholds (snow) depends on the ambiguity of "nothing." Grammar, of course, obliges us to treat nothing as a substantive—a requirement the poem exploits to create a figure made of nothing: the snow man. What's more, "nothing," in this poem, is a substance capable of being both present and absent at the same time—a characteristic it shares with other meteoric bodies in Stevens's poetry. And because snow is almost nothing (like Kepler's starlet), it shares in the ambiguous materiality of language, so that the listener, and also his song, is made of snow (or nothing). Snow, Stevens says in another poem, is the favorite medium of the "wise man," who avenges the loss of things "by building his city in snow" ("Like Decorations in a Nigger Cemetery," 158). Indeed, the ephemeral (and ethereal) nature of snow is such that Stevens likes to confuse it with air or light, as he does in "The Poems of Our Climate":

> The light
> In the room more like a snowy air,
> Reflecting snow. A newly-fallen snow
> At the end of the winter when afternoons return.   *(193)*

Ultimately, we should understand the snow man, made of nothing, to be *no man*. Stevens confirms this equation when, echoing a famous line of "The Snow Man," he refers to "No man that heard a wind in an empty place" ("Extracts from Addresses to the Academy of Fine Ideas," 255).

Clearly, the figure of the snow man concerns an ethereal substance or medium that comprises the mind and the "elements" of nature, and thus implicates the mind in the foundation of matter. What is not evident from the passages I have cited, however, is the degree to which Stevens explicitly situates the snow man in the history of materialism. For Stevens is attentive, in other poems, to the relation between snow-flakes, and the forms produced by their accumulation, to

> parts not quite perceived
> Of the obvious whole, uncertain particles
> Of the certain solid
> > ("Man Carrying Thing," 350–51)

More precisely, the "uncertain particles" of snowflakes mark the limit of Stevens's anatomy of the snow man:

> Things floating like the first hundred flakes of snow
> Out of a storm we must endure all night,
>
> Out of a storm of secondary things,
> A horror of thoughts that are suddenly real.
>
> We must endure our thoughts all night, until
> The bright obvious stands motionless in the cold.   (351)

The shape composed of ethereal flakes—the snow man—turns out to be an emblem both of atomism and of the *enigma* of atomism, as when Stevens asks, in another poem, "When was it that the particles be-came / The whole man?" ("Things of August," 494). The "bright, ob-vious" thing consists of invisible "things"—snowflakes, or thoughts—"A horror of thoughts that are suddenly real." Hence the real is com-posed of the unreal, the material of the immaterial. In another poem, Stevens suggests more specifically that we might regard the elements or particles of things as *images,* or fragments of vision: "Snow sparkles like eyesight falling to earth, / Like seeing fallen brightly away" ("No Possum, No Sop, No Taters," 294). This beautiful passage calls to mind the illustration in the treatise by Olaus Magnus depicting snowflakes as eyes and other body parts. Correspondingly, the dazzling substance of snow in Stevens's poetry becomes an imageric substance, as if real things were made of pictures. At the same time, the body consisting of vision (or particles of vision) falls brightly away, returning to nothing, a radiant blur.

The "snow man" is only the most famous of the many types of "meteors" appearing in Stevens's poetry. Some are related directly to the weather: clouds, rain, mist, rainbows, thunder; others indirectly so. The first poem of *Harmonium*, for example, tells of the plight of young "bucks" in Oklahoma who find, with every step they take, "A firecat bristled in the way" ("Earthy Anecdote," 3). The poem remains puzzling, even inscrutable, until we see the stand-off between the "bucks" and the "firecat" as an encounter between the "earthy" body and the meteoric body of lyric. Generally, the weather functions for Stevens, as this poem indicates, as a kind of bestiary of elemental creatures, but also as a theater of metamorphosis:

> The rain is pouring down. It is July.
> There is lightning and the thickest thunder.
>
> It is a spectacle. Scene 10 becomes 11,
> In Series X, Act IV, et cetera.
>
> People fall out of windows, trees tumble down.
> Summer is changed to winter, the young grow old,
>
> The air is full of children, statues, roofs
> And snow.
> ("Chaos in Motion and Not in Motion," 357)

The sense of artifice and improvisation is heightened here by the reference to scene changes and the comical incongruity of things filling the air.

As in the natural world, the meteors in Stevens's poetry often occur in numbers. For example, the ensemble of meteors that makes up a thunderstorm (rain, lightning, thunder) appears to suggest, in Stevens's poetry, the rhetorical nature of meteoric bodies, as well as the manner in which individual meteors combine to produce larger meteoric bodies. For rain, to Stevens, is "minstrelsy" (or nakedness), thunder an "illusion," and lightning a "metaphor." As an ensemble, these meteors comprise the primary figures of a storm, itself a meteoric figure of transformation. Here is one of Stevens's renderings of the body of rain:

> There was such idiot minstrelsy in rain.
> So many clappers going without bells
> That these bethous compose a heavenly gong.
>
> Bethou him, you
> And you, bethou him and bethou. It is
> A sound like any other. It will end.
> *("Notes toward a Supreme Fiction,"* 394)

The final remark, recalling the finitude of the rain's "idiot minstrelsy," confirms its meteoric nature. In another poem, Stevens elaborates the rain's curious body:

> Item: The cataracts
> As facts fall like rejuvenating rain.
> Fall down through nakedness to nakedness
> To the auroral creature musing in the mind.
> *("Montrachet-le-Jardin,"* 263)

One meteoric body meets another in a cataract that is both deluge and refrain, a knowledge of nakedness. What's more, in the chaos of a storm, now and again, one body illuminates another:

> The bouquet stands in a jar, as metaphor,
> As lightning itself is, likewise, metaphor
> Crowded with apparitions suddenly gone

And no less suddenly here again, a growth
Of the reality of the eye, an artifice,
Nothing much, a flitter that reflects itself.
 ("The Bouquet," 448)

The body of lightning, like metaphor, illuminates other bodies in the
world of a storm and transforms them. Like the snowflake, it is "a
growth of the reality of the eye," but it is also, like all other meteoric
bodies, "nothing much": an "artifice." Thunder follows lightning, one
body echoing another:

the inevitable blue
Of secluded thunder, an illusion, as it was,
Oh as, always too heavy for the sense
To seize, the obscurest as, the distant was.
 ("A Primitive Like an Orb," 440–41)

Thunder follows lightning, yet it is only an illusion, or a body in seclu-
sion. And its relation to rain, to minstrelsy, or to lightning "crowded
with apparitions" is governed by "the obscurest as, the distant was."
The bodies composing the storm of transformation are themselves fig-
ures of metamorphosis: evanescent, artificial, obscure, yet utterly naked
in their substance, in the apparitional forms of the meteor.

In certain respects, the weather in Stevens's poetry is a theater of
the *unconscious,* as the following description of the "auroras of au-
tumn"—which are meteorological phenomena—suggests:

It is a theatre floating through the clouds,
Itself a cloud, although of misted rock

It is of cloud transformed
To cloud transformed again, idly, the way
A season changes color to no end

Except lavishing of itself in change. . . .
The cloud drifts idly through half-thought-of forms
 ("The Auroras of Autumn," 416)

If one stops to consider the *content* of these "pageants out of air" (415), these spectacles of "half-thought-of forms" and colors changing "to no end," one is likely to be surprised. For Stevens's most sustained and complex meditations on the weather often involve images of racial—and specifically African-American—identity. The changing forms and colors of "The Auroras of Autumn," for example, could hardly be called "idle":

> The father fetches negresses to dance
> Among the children, like curious ripenesses
> Of pattern in the dance's ripening.
>
> The father fetches pageants out of air . . .
>
> Among these the musicians strike the instinctive poem.
> The father fetches his unherded herds,
> Of barbarous tongue, slavered and panting halves
>
> Of breath, obedient to his trumpet's touch   *(415)*

In this extraordinary passage, we discover that for Stevens, in this case, meteoric bodies are black (and female) bodies, "of barbarous tongue," obedient to the "touch" of the father's instrument. There is, to be sure, some confusion between the "ripening" body and the half-body of breath (the poem), but there is no uncertainty as to the racial identity of the "forms" and "colors" making up the "festival" of air in this poem.

Stevens's correlation of race and meteoric bodies in "Auroras of Autumn" is not an isolated case. In my analysis of the weather in Stevens's poetry, I have cited a number of passages from a poem titled "Like Decorations in a Nigger Cemetery." Although, with the exception of its title, this early poem contains almost no overt reference to racial identity or color, the strange correlation in Stevens's mind between the weather and the idea of the "nigger" reveals itself more explicitly in a later poem titled "The News and The Weather," which makes allusion to the aesthetic model of the earlier poem. Here is the entire second section:

> Solange, the magnolia to whom I spoke
> A nigger tree and with a nigger name,
>
> To which I spoke, near which I stood and spoke,
> I am Solange, euphonious bane, she said.
>
> I am a poison at the winter's end,
> Taken with withered weather, crumpled clouds,
>
> To smother the wry spirit's misery.
> Inhale the purple fragrance. It becomes
>
> Almost a nigger fragment, a *mystique*
> For the spirit left helpless by the intelligence.
>
> There's a moment in the year, Solange,
> When the deep breath fetches another year of life.
>
>   (*"The News and The Weather,"* 265)

In this section, which pertains to "the weather" of the poem's title, a negress, Solange, appears (as in "The Auroras of Autumn") in relation to certain meteoric phenomena. She appears to supply the voice (and the "fragrance") of the meteoric body. Indeed, the identity of the "nigger" in nature is multiplied through the "nigger tree" and the "nigger name" (a double name: Solange and Magnolia). In the third stanza, we discover not only the correlation of the negress and the weather but also the nature of this *black weather:* it is a "poison," a lethal substance, yet also an intoxicating "fragrance."

This poem reveals that, for Stevens, the weather is a kind of *pharmakos,* a "euphonious bane," which, although it may be "poison," is also capable of smothering "the wry spirit's misery." The meteoric properties of the black woman's body are concentrated in the phenomenon of the breath ("Inhale the fragrance"), with its power to revive and restore: "The deep breath fetches another year of life." More precisely, the meteoric black body restores "the spirit left helpless by the intelligence"—a cure with distinctly racist overtones. In addition, following the implications of this cure for the poet, in particular, the "purple fragrance" becomes "almost a nigger fragment, a *mystique*." Here Stevens alludes to the fragmentary nature of a poem inspired formally by *decorations in a nigger cemetery*—a poem composed of rude emblems or fragments. Stevens thus equates the restorative effects of the meteoric body (the "purple fragrance" of Solange) with a primitivist aesthetic that saves the white poet from his own "intelligence." All of these observations suggest that the meteoric body is equivalent to the black female body: the "nigger" is a meteor. What's more, in this poem, Solange, the "nigger"/meteor, is a kind of muse to the white, male poet.

The "climate" of race is staged in the theater of clouds, one of the most important sites in Stevens's poetic meteorology. Yet clouds are also figures, or beings, of what Stevens calls "the giant sense" ("Repetitions of a Young Captain," 308). All meteors are "giants," but clouds especially capture the essence of "these archaic forms, giants / Of sense" ("Things of August," 494). "Sense" is a crucial term in Stevens's poetic materialism, one that pertains to poetry as well as the weather (both are "senses" of nature). The cryptic appearance of "giants" on the horizon of Stevens's poetics, and their manifestation of "sense" in a way that is equally obscure, can be explained by reference to Vico's theory of myth and "poetic wisdom." Stevens's use and elaboration of this Vichian framework combine with the more obvious reverberations of Baroque natural philosophy in his poetic meteorology.

Vico's genetic theory of poetry is consonant with his historical doctrine of the three ages of man. The first race of men, according to Vico, were "giants": creatures who were shaped (quite literally) by their "bestial education" and who were "entirely immersed in the senses, buffeted by the passions, buried in the body."[25] In Vico's account, the faculty of "poetic wisdom," which underlies all scientific knowledge, stems from this epoch of giants whose understanding of things was fully determined by "sense." Indeed, the "theological poets" of sense, expounding the wisdom of the age of giants, are the archaic prototypes for all poets to come.[26] For, as Vico observes, "The theological poets were the sense and the philosophers the intellect of human wisdom" (241).

"Sense," as Stevens understands it, must be distinguished from rhetoric or figurative speech. He states,

> Our sense of these things changes and they change,
> Not as in metaphor, but in our sense
> Of them. So sense exceeds all metaphor. . . .
>
> It is like a flow of meanings with no speech.
>   (*"Bouquet of Roses in Sunlight," 431*)

Thus our "sense" of things lies "far beyond the rhetorician's touch" (431). The distinction between figure and sense may lie in the evanescent and changing nature of sense, so that "A giant, on the horizon, glistening" is also a "giant of nothingness, each one / And the giant ever changing, living in change" ("A Primitive Like an Orb," 442, 443). These "giants of sense" convey the metamorphic character of the weather, which may account for their peculiar immateriality (a quality shared by all meteoric bodies). Hence,

> The giant of sense remains
>
> A giant without a body. If, as giant,
> He shares a gigantic life, it is because
> The gigantic has a reality of its own.
>   (*"Repetitions of a Young Captain," 308*)

The material "nothingness" of the giant has a reality of its own, yet it must not be confused with rhetoric.

The giants on the horizon are characterized, like all meteors, by distance (and perhaps by distance from the poet), yet Stevens also permits the "giant" to be confused with the poet. In a poem called "Jumbo," the giant appears in familiar guise, as "the transformer, himself transformed," and as

> The companion in nothingness,
> Loud, general, large, fat, soft
> And wild and free.   *(269)*

Yet the poet also refers to him as "Cloud-clown, blue painter . . . man that never is," as well as "Ancestor of Narcissus" and, most tellingly, an "imager" and a "musician" (269). These epithets indicate that the poet himself, like a cloud, is a "giant of nothingness"—a composite substance, at once subject and object, forming the meteoric element. Indeed, clouds in Stevens's poetry often appear to be associated with writing or lyric composition. In one instance, he states,

> this book
> Is a cloud in which a voice mumbles.
> It is a ghost that inhabits a cloud.
> *("The Lack of Repose," 303)*

In another poem, he refers to "a storm of torn-up testaments" ("Dutch Graves in Bucks County," 292), and elsewhere states, "The imaginative transcripts were like clouds, / . . . nameless, flitting characters" ("An Ordinary Evening in New Haven," 479). Stevens even goes so far as to equate "a voice in the clouds" with "Dichtung"—the German word for poetry ("The Man with the Blue Guitar," 177).

The correlation between nebulosity and inscription (or the poetic voice) is part of a much larger structure of association between the weather and poetic composition in Stevens's poetry. As I have already indicated, the connotations of the word *air* (as song and as meteoric element) often provide the foundation for this association; yet Stevens also likes to make broader comparisons between the weather and literary language. His theory of "elements" thus betrays the influence of Lucretius, who compares atoms (the elements of matter) to written characters. Stevens refers, for example, to "the weather in words and words in sounds of sound" ("The Pure Good of Theory," 332). Elsewhere, he declares simply, "Description is an element, like air or water."[27] In another poem, he makes reference to the "weather of night creatures, whistling all day, too, / And echoing rhetorics more than our own" ("Montrachet-le-Jardin," 261). The weather in this passage appears to be associated not only with dreams but also with the more specifically literary domain of rhetoric—including the figure of echo. Other references to clouds as "doubles" suggest that Stevens views the weather as imitative in some fashion (though transient, as always):

> The figures of the past go cloaked.
> They walk in mist and rain and snow
> And go, go slowly, but they go.
> *("Poésie Abrutie," 302)*

A more explicit passage in another poem, however, casts "the doubling second things" of the weather in a different light:

> Eve made air the mirror of herself, . . .
>
> But the first idea was not to shape the clouds
> In imitation. The clouds preceded us . . .
>
> We are the mimics. Clouds are pedagogues
> The air is not a mirror but bare board
> *("Notes toward a Supreme Fiction," 383, 384)*

Whatever the valence of the mimetic relation between humans and meteors, we can be sure it is an enchanted relation, characterized by the transference of material properties from one body to another. The material affinities of the weather therefore presume an *iconic* relation between different kinds of bodies.

One of the most interesting examples of this type of relation in Stevens's meteorology finds expression in the technology of sound reproduction:

> All afternoon the gramophone
> Parl-parled the West-Indian weather. . . .
>
> All afternoon the gramaphoon,
> All afternoon the gramaphoon,

The world as word,
Parl-parled the West-Indian hurricane.
                    (*"The Search for Sound
                    Free from Motion,"* 268)

When this poem was written (1942), the gramophone, or the word referring to that device, was already an anachronism; the poet can therefore focus on the artifactual quality of the sound it produces. I am referring not to the sound of a recording played on the device, but to the sounds produced by the machine itself: the hissing, droning, and crackling that "parl-parles" the sound of a storm. Thus the poem incorporates, through the device of repetition in its own structure, the echoing of the storm by the gramophone. Yet this correspondence is certainly not mimetic (since it is not a question of a *recording* of a storm), unless one views the alteration of the word "gramophone" to resemble the word "typhoon" ("gramaphoon") to be an instance of sensual mimesis. Certainly, the principle of "world as word," if one wishes to characterize it as mimetic, is an enchanted relation, always characterized by a degree of transformation. In the end, as the poem reveals at its conclusion, the "gramaphoon" is a figure for the poet:

a creature that
Repeats its vital words, yet balances
The syllable of a syllable.   *(268)*

The relation, then, between the lyric device and the storm involves, as it always does in Stevens, the sensual echoing—and alteration—of meteoric bodies.

Stevens helps to define the literary properties of the weather by extending his meditation on air to the figures of wind and the "breath." To the extent that Stevens's meteorology is a reflection on the elements of poetic voice, it has a direct bearing on prosody and metrics, a topic that raises fascinating questions about the materiality of literary form.[28]

It is useful to bear in mind the inference of the poetic voice when Stevens says,

> There is a storm much like the crying of the wind,
> Words that come out of us like words within,
> That have rankled for many lives and made no sound.
>   (*"Sketch of the Ultimate Politician,"* 336)

For the words of this "ruinous storm" issue from the body:

> Our breath is like a desperate element
> That we must calm, the origin of a mother tongue . . .
>
> The cry that contains its converse in itself . . .
>
> Not wholly spoken in a conversation between
> Two bodies disembodied in their talk,
> Too fragile, too immediate for any speech.
>   (*"An Ordinary Evening in New Haven,"* 470–471)

The breath possesses all the essential features of the meteoric body: a "desperate element" through which the palpable body is disembodied, yet also formalized; a missing mother tongue too "immediate" for speech. The breath intones the body's absence:

> It is in this solitude, a syllable,
> Out of these gawky flitterings,
>
> Intones its single emptiness,
> The savagest hollow of winter-sound.
>   (*"No Possum, No Sop, No Taters,"* 294)

Here the breath conveys the "mind of winter," the sound of nobody, the snow man's cry.

In many instances, Stevens's elaboration of wind and breath—of the elements of poetic voice—makes reference to, or evokes, a "sense" of matter appropriate to the forms of poetry and the weather. Yet this formulation of lyric substance is also congruent, in a broader sense, with the pictures of materiality (and the controversies surrounding them) supplied by modern physics. The wind, for example, is nothing, and nothing else:

> Item: The wind is never rounding O
> And, imageless, it is itself the most,
>
> Mouthing its constant smatter throughout space.
>   *("Montrachet-le-Jardin," 263)*

The reference here to "imageless" substance (which nevertheless approximates the letter "O") calls to mind one of the most prominent features of modern debates about material substance. The substance Stevens calls "smatter" he also, more frequently, calls "ether," a term with a distinct place in the history of natural philosophy. The "voice in the clouds," he informs us, is "a voice of ether" ("The Man with the Blue Guitar," 177). Elsewhere, he refers to "animals of ether" that drop, like images, "from heaven and float in the air" ("Study of Images II," 464). In another poem, he explains the element of belief:

> It is like a thing of ether that exists
> Almost as predicate. But it exists
> It exists, it is visible, it is, it is.
>   *("The Auroras of Autumn," 418)*

The ethereal body, like a snowflake, is almost nothing, but "it is visible, it is, it is." The need to insist on its presence, as well as the possibility of missing it, or not seeing it, stem from its ephemeral nature. Thus, the poet writes about "comets":

> The knowledge of bright-ethered things
> Bears us toward time, on its
> Perfective wings.
>   *("Analysis of a Theme," 349)*

And sometimes the poet's reference to the "voice of ether" is more technical, recalling the specter of atomism, as when he calls the poet "a part, but part, but tenacious particle, / Of the skeleton of the ether" ("A Primitive Like an Orb," 443).

Though Stevens's elaboration of a term such as "ether" is helpful in placing his meteorology in the history of materialism, we must ultimately turn to more descriptive passages in Stevens's poetry to determine the premises of his materialism and the theory of "matter" implicit in his meteorology. We must, first of all, emphasize the ambiguity of the poet's task:

> He wanted that,
> To face the weather and be unable to tell
> How much of it was light and how much thought
> ("*Extracts from Addresses to the Academy*
> *of Fine Ideas,*" 257)

Although the objective may be to arrive at uncertainty, it is clear that the substance of weather is an amalgam of "thought" and other materials, such as light. Indeed, the abstracting of tangible things, and the embodiment of "abstract" elements (such as air), are stable and fundamental principles of Stevens's materialism:

> The weather and the giant of the weather,
> Say the weather, the mere weather, the mere air:
> An abstraction blooded, as a man by thought.
> ("*Notes toward a Supreme Fiction,*" 385)

The forms of abstraction and corporeality, however, are inherently unstable; for, in this case, "a man" is an abstraction "blooded" by thought, and the weather is "mere" utterance. That is to say, Stevens treats as abstractions what we conventionally regard as material bodies, and he materializes the agencies of thought and speech. Thought is blood, climate a song, and so on. He also encourages the reader to find terms for the antinomy of mind and matter, thought and object, in visual experience, or in the eye itself. The possibility of "imageless" substance (air) implies that we must speak about "the giant of the weather" in terms of vision:

It must be visible or invisible,
Invisible or visible or both:
A seeing and unseeing in the eye   *(385)*

The kind of passage I cited above, about "the giant of the weather" (a man blooded by thought), occupies the middle ground of Stevens's materialism, since it achieves a kind of balance between "the make-matter, matter-nothing mind" ("Repetitions of a Young Captain," 306) and the more evanescent "sense" of an object. By contrast, Stevens's materialism—his vision of lyric substance—can veer at times towards greater abstraction, with the implication that matter is a kind of marvelous fiction:

A human thing. It is an eminence,
But of nothing, trash of sleep that will disappear
With the special things of night, little by little,
In day's constellation and yet remain, yet be.
("Chocorua to Its Neighbor," 300)

Here the body's substance—the "trash of sleep"—is at once immaterial and cadaverous, a "species" of the "special things of night"—a mere spectacle. Yet the same spectacular body—in the same poem—also displays the other face of Stevens's materialism: its sensuality and its compliance with the meteoric body. Thus the poet does not permit the "prodigious shadow" of the human to escape the phenomenology of the weather:

The substance of his body seemed
Both substance and non-substance, luminous flesh
Or shapely fire: fire from an underworld,
Of less degree than flame and lesser shine.   *(297)*

It is not impossible to discern a correlation between the "shapely fire" mentioned here and the "trash of sleep" in the earlier passage (both are transient phenomena, merely "seeming" to be), yet the latter passage is more faithful to the material "sense" of the body it depicts, even if flesh be flame.

We can therefore assume that a "knowledge of bright-ethered things"—even at its most abstract—harbors a theory of "matter." Indeed, one should be alert to intimations of "general theory" in Stevens's poetry whenever the principle of abstraction or thought is supplanted by song, and whenever song becomes the element of flesh:

> Thus theory of description matters most.
> It is the theory of the word for those
>
> For whom the word is the making of the world,
> The buzzing world and lisping firmament.
>
> It is a world of words to the end of it,
> In which nothing solid is its solid self.
> *("Description without Place," 345)*

The dispersion of solids in the theory of description alludes to the gravity of Stevens's poetic materialism, and to its theoretical specificity:

> It is not in the premise that reality
> Is a solid. It may be a shade that traverses
> A dust, a force that traverses a shade.
> *("An Ordinary Evening in*
> *New Haven," 489)*

Hence the "theory of description" makes of solid things precisely what atomism makes of our bodies: a world of words (and pictures), where bodies are made of dust and shadows, where language is a kind of force traversing the substance of things. In the natural philosophy of Stevens's poetry, the "flickings from finikin to fine finikin" cannot be distinguished from "The swarming activities of the formulae" (488): poetry completes the task of science. The medium becomes the object: "For the poem is the cry of its occasion, / Part of the res itself and not about it" (473). Yet the poet aims "to be unable to tell / How much of it was light and how much thought." That is to say, the world the weather man sees is haunted by his own body and "blooded" by abstraction: it remains duplicitous—at once intuitive and abstract—despite the mind's will to unify it. Thus the poet declares:

> The enigmatical
> Beauty of each beautiful enigma
> Becomes amassed in a total double-thing.   *(472)*

Indeed, the enigma of "mass" consists precisely in its doubleness, which confounds "beauty" and "mass," aesthetics and physics, image and body, in a discourse of lyric substance.

ANIMAL MAGNETISM

Natural philosophy explains the correspondence between meteoric and ponderable bodies, in part, by reference to the continuum of sublimation and precipitation. Thus the spectrum of materiality is anchored at one end by the figure of the animal-machine and at the other by the discourse of *subtilitas,* a Baroque hypothesis concerning the existence of a medium finer than air that permeates all bodies. This subtle medium (sometimes called "ether") is said to be the foundation, or frame, of the materials and forces constituting all bodies (from stone to flesh to light to gravity), and hence it also places bodies *in contact,* though they may be far removed from one another. Catherine Wilson describes the role of *subtilitas* in the formulation of modern materialism: "The corpuscularian philosophy established itself in the first half of the 1600s as the product of the progressive refinement of the Renaissance notion of 'subtlety,' and a materialization of hidden resident spirits."[29] The doctrine of "subtle" bodies therefore concerns what I have called the "mechanization of nothing" in philosophical materialism. Wilson explains that *subtilitas* pertains to "things that can only be known with difficulty because they are neither clearly perceivable by us nor clearly thinkable" (40). From the perspective of corpuscular philosophy, subtle bodies correspond to the bodies composed of air, or vapors, that form the province of pneumatics and meteorology. The discourse of subtle media, like the philosophy of meteors, functions to materialize, or at least to represent intuitively, the subliminal and virtually unintelligible "reality" of atoms.

Though the ether is subtler than air (seven hundred thousand times rarer, according to Isaac Newton), Descartes and other materialists characterize it as a meteoric phenomenon, as an *internal climate* of the body, and also by the term "animal spirits." Descartes's most extensive treatment of the ether occurs, not surprisingly, in the *Meteorology*, the *Optics*, and in the *Treatise on Man* (all written between 1629 and 1633). Though ether circulates in the "pores" or spaces between the corpuscles constituting a body (and between bodies), its physical character is essentially corpuscular. In the *Meteorology*, he refers to "that very fine *[subtil]* material by means of which the action of light is communicated," and he further describes the "nature of light" as "the action or movement of a certain very fine material whose particles must be pictured as small balls rolling in the pores of earthly bodies."[30] In the former passage, he refers the reader to the *Optics* and his treatment of "the air or other transparent bodies through the medium of which we see" (68–69). There he describes the ether as "some very subtle and very fluid material, extending without interruption from the stars and planets to us" (69).

The correlation between climate and the subtle fluid permeating all bodies appears in several of Descartes's essays, including the *Meteorology*, where he introduces the analogy of the wind: "Although this very fine material does not separate the parts of hard bodies, which are like intertwined branches . . . nevertheless it agitates and stirs them . . . just as the wind can shake all the branches of the bushes composing a hedge without removing them from their places in doing so" (266–67). Furthermore, the agitation of this subtle fluid precipitates the rarefaction, or sublimation, of bodies, thereby producing the "vapors" associated with meteoric phenomena (269). In the *Treatise on Man*, Descartes translates the subtle corpuscular medium into a doctrine of "animal spirits" and develops more fully the meteoric analogy: "The parts of the blood which penetrate as far as the brain serve not only to nourish and sustain its substance, but also and primarily to produce in it a certain very fine wind, or rather a very lively and pure flame, which is called the *animal spirits.*"[31] In this passage, a doctrine of the material soul (later to appear in La Mettrie) has been translated not only into the meteoric phenomena of wind and flame (one of "the various fires that are kindled in the air") but also, more specifically, into the physiology of the nervous system. Thus Descartes compares the body's "animal spirits" (which "cease to have the form of blood") to atmospheric phenomena, to a corporeal climate of nervous energies and transmissions, thereby establishing a more precise correlation between meteors and mechanical bodies. To illustrate how these subtle fluids (or forces) function in the body, Descartes returns to the scene where meteorology intersects with pneumatics and the discourse of automata: "The spirits have the power to change the shape of the muscles in which the nerves are embedded, and by this means to move all limbs. Similarly, you may have observed in the grottos and fountains in the royal gardens that the mere force with which the water is driven as it emerges from its source is sufficient to move various machines" (100). He elaborates the conceit in considerable detail, leaving no doubt that the "animal spirits" of the body's climate correspond to the vapors or fluids described—and harnessed—by pneumatic philosophy:

> One may compare the nerves of the machine I am describing [the human body] with the pipes in the works of these fountains, its muscles and tendons with the various devices and springs which serve to set them in motion, its animal spirits with the water which drives them. . . . Moreover, breathing and other such activities which are normal to this machine, and which depend on the flow of spirits, are like the movements of a clock or mill, which the normal flow of water can render continuous (100–101).

Thus the subtle body of animal spirits (the blueprint of the nervous system) belongs, with the rainbow, the mechanized toy, and fireworks, in the arena of spectacular culture. Yet Descartes returns to the subject of the weather and animal spirits in *The Passions of the Soul* to remind his reader that such phenomena can be conceived only in material terms (and, more specifically, in a form that recalls the body of fireworks): "For what I am calling 'spirits' here are merely bodies: they have no property other than that of being extremely small bodies which move very quickly, like the jets of flame that come from a torch."[32]

Isaac Newton alludes to the materialist doctrine of *subtilitas* in the final paragraph of his *Principia* (1713), describing a "most subtle spirit which pervades and lies hid in all gross bodies."[33] In the queries of the third edition of the *Opticks* (1717), he develops more fully the idea of an "Aethereal Medium" in relation to his doctrine of forces and attractions (gravity, magnetism, electricity), thereby laying the foundation of modern theoretical physics. In queries 18 and 24, he describes the aether as a material medium that establishes a continuum between "fits of light" and muscular contraction:

> And is not this Medium the same with that Medium by which light is refracted and reflected, and by whose Vibrations Light communicates Heat to Bodies, and is put into Fits of easy Reflexion and easy Transmission? . . . And is not this Medium exceedingly more rare and subtile than the Air, and exceedingly more elastic and active? And doth it not pervade all Bodies? And is it not (by its elastick Force) expanded through all the Heavens? . . . Is not Animal Motion perform'd by the Vibrations of this Medium, excited in the Brain by the power of the Will, and propagated from thence through the solid, pellucid and uniform Capillamenta of the Nerves into the Muscles, for contracting and dilating them?[34]

In the final query of the *Opticks*, moreover, Newton speculates on the role of this "medium" in remote (or subliminal) relations between corpuscular bodies: "Have not the small Particles of Bodies certain Powers, Virtues, or Forces, by which they act at a distance . . . ? For it's well known that bodies act upon one another by Attractions of Gravity, Magnetism, and Electricity" (375–76).

A scientific and popular discourse of mechanical bodies animated— and indeed constituted—by a "climate" of incorporeal substances and forces gradually emerged during the eighteenth century. The Austrian Franz Anton Mesmer (1734–1815) formulated his theory of "animal magnetism" from ideas current in this milieu. Robert Darnton de- scribes the place of Mesmer's theory in this context: "Science had cap- tivated Mesmer's contemporaries by revealing to them that they were surrounded by wondrous, invisible forces: Newton's gravity, made in- telligible by Voltaire; Franklin's electricity, popularized by a fad for lightning rods and by demonstrations in the fashionable lyceums and museums of Paris. . . . Mesmer's fluid seemed no more miraculous, and who could say that it was less real than the phlogiston that Lavoisier was attempting to banish from the universe, or the caloric he was apparently substituting for it."[35] Although Darnton refers to "the New- tonian pose of most mesmerist writing" (115), it is not difficult to discern that mesmerism, with its dependence on atmospheric analo- gies, corresponds as well to Cartesian meteorology and its residual thesis of "animal spirits."

Mesmer, a theoretician, healer, and magician, defended his M.D. thesis in medicine in 1766 in Vienna, where he first developed his theory of an "imponderable fluid" called, initially, "animal gravity." Before Mesmer settled on the notion of animal *magnetism,* he toyed with the idea that the corpuscular medium might be related to gravity or electricity. His most notorious public experiments in Vienna were conducted with a young female patient who, prior to his induction of a "magnetic trance," had already undergone long episodes of electrical shock treatment.[36] Based on the experiments of a colleague in Vienna, who applied magnets to patients' bodies to relieve pain by drawing off harmful "fluids," Mesmer developed a technique that dispensed with

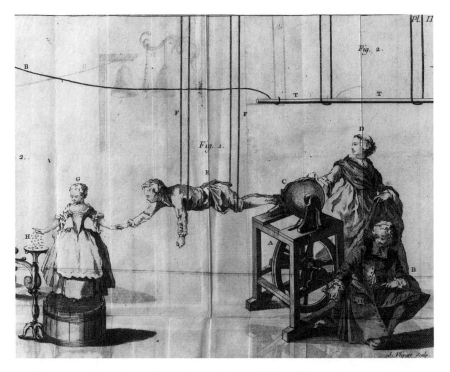

Figure 9.   Engraving of experiment by Sir William Watson (1715–1787),
published in Paris in 1748, showing the conveyance of animal electricity. The
electrical charge is generated at the point where the suspended male figure's
feet touch the revolving glass sphere, and is conveyed through his body to
the young girl on the left, whose hand attracts the flakes on the pedestal. An-
ton Mesmer's theory of animal magnetism evolved from related experiments
carried out in Vienna a decade or so later. Courtesy Burndy Library, MIT.

the magnets and allowed the physician to redistribute and harmonize
the flow of the "imponderable" magnetic fluid in the body merely by
touching the patient's body. As a result of this technique, patients ex-
perienced what Mesmer called "magnetic sleep," sometimes accom-
panied by "fits" or convulsions.

In 1778, Mesmer left Vienna to establish a clinic in Paris, which
flourished until the French Revolution. Drawing the majority of his

clientele from the aristocracy and fashionable society, Mesmer presided over the darkened rooms of his elegant clinic in "a violet robe of embroidered silk," as music of the pianoforte and a "glass harmonica" played in the background. Patients sought relief from their "magnetic crisis" around the *baquet* (a large basin of magnetized water from which iron rods protruded). Significantly, Maria Tatar explains, "Many of the patients who consulted Mesmer were society women suffering from a fashionable ailment of the time known as *vapeurs*. The disease, which today might be diagnosed as a mild form of hysteria, rendered its victims vulnerable to nervous fits and fainting spells."[37] Thus the etiology for "animal magnetism" points to the influence of "vapors," that is, to the conception of meteoric bodies formulated by mechanical philosophy. This view is corroborated by the report of the Royal Society of Medicine, called on in 1784 to investigate Mesmer's practices (with a commission led by Benjamin Franklin). One of its members, A. L. Jussieu, "attributed the effects of mesmerizing in part to the *'atmospheres'* surrounding bodies."[38] The fundamental link observed here between the "magnetic" cure and corporeal "vapors" or "atmospheric" properties leaves no doubt that the discourse of "animal magnetism," by seeking to moderate the hysterical climate of the female body, treats the body as a meteoric phenomenon.

Soon after his arrival in Paris, Mesmer published in 1779 a small treatise on animal magnetism titled *Mémoires sur la découverte du magnétisme animal*. From the statements in this document, it becomes clear how much the theory of animal magnetism owes to the doctrine of subtle bodies and to meteorology, both closely aligned, as I have indicated, with corpuscularian philosophy. It is also evident that animal magnetism depicts the subliminal world of atoms and should therefore be regarded as a fantastic, though not incredible, translation of scientific materialism into a social and political register. In his treatise—a form that anticipates the manifestos of the modern avant-garde—one discovers, among twenty-seven propositions, the following claims about animal magnetism:

1. A mutual influence exists between celestial bodies, the Earth, and animate bodies.

3. This reciprocal action is subject to mechanical laws unknown until the present time.

10. The property of the animal body which renders it susceptible to the influence of celestial bodies and to the reciprocal action of those bodies surrounding it, manifested by its analogy with the magnet, I have determined to call animal magnetism.

11. The action and force of animal magnetism, characterized in this way, can be communicated to other bodies, whether animate or inanimate.

14. The action takes place at a remote distance, without the aid of any intermediate body.

15. It is augmented and reflected by mirrors, like light.

21. This system will furnish new insights into the nature of fire and light, as well as the theory of attraction, of the ebb and flow of things *[du flux et du reflux]* of magnetism, and of electricity.[39]

Mesmer's theory of animal magnetism revised the discourse of incorporeals and effluvia (which included rainbows as well as magnetism) in a manner that requires comment. First, animal magnetism, though imperceptible and in some ways implausible, is subject to mechanical laws—a reminder of the intrinsic relation between mechanicism and bodies composed of "Nothing." Second, the "action" of animal magnetism can be conveyed between animate and inanimate bodies, and over long distances, thereby problematizing the practice of healing by touch, from which Mesmer's technique descended (and which it continued, in some fashion, to replicate). Third, by virtue of its correlation to the physics of light, animal magnetism displays an affinity with optics and the science of mirrors and hence with the nature of illusory phenomena (such as the rainbow). Last, by referring several times to the flux of animal magnetism, Mesmer emphasizes the *turbulence* of the mesmerized body and hence its relation to the stochastic realm of atoms. In a magnetic trance, the body assumes the properties of a cataract, a phenomenon that combines obstruction and transgression: it is at once a veil and a deluge.[40]

Despite its fantastic and fraudulent character, the medical concept of animal magnetism survives into modernity because of its representation of automatism and the corporeal unconscious. In the 1840s, at the beginning of a significant revival and revision of mesmerism in England, the Scottish surgeon James Braid (1795–1860) coined the term *hypnotism* to describe what he called the "nervous sleep" of animal magnetism.[41] What interested Braid, and other physicians who published on the subject during the period, was the use of mesmeric techniques to replace anesthesia in surgery. John Elliotson, who occupied the chair of medicine at University College, London, was an early advocate of medical mesmerism, and in 1843 he published a study titled *Cases of Surgical Operations without Pain in the Mesmeric State.* Another prominent figure in British mesmerism, William Carpenter, observed of the anesthetic properties of the magnetic trance, "This 'mesmeric sleep' corresponds precisely in character with what is known in medicine as 'hysteric coma'; the insensibility being as profound, while it lasts, as in the coma of narcotic poisoning or pressure on the brain."[42] The characterization of the mesmerized body as at once comatose and hysterical again evokes the meteorological phenomenon of the cataract. Carpenter, however, goes on to explain, "The first state thus induced is usually one of profound comatose sleep. . . . But after some little time, this state very commonly passes into one of somnambulism, which again corresponds closely on one hand with *natural,* and on the other with *mesmeric* somnambulism" (16–17). Thus the profound insensibility induced by "magnetization" yields to, or comprises, an ambiguous corporeal state of unconscious wakefulness: the spell of the sleepwalker.

Researchers of the period concluded, as Carpenter explains, that "not only may the general reality of the Mesmeric Somnambulism be fully admitted, but a scientific *rationale* may be found for its supposed distinctive peculiarities, without the assumption of any special 'magnetic' or 'mesmeric' agency" (22). Eminent physiologists of the period, such as Benjamin Carpenter and Thomas Laycock, quickly realized that Braid's research on animal magnetism pertained to the automatic reflex functions of the brain, and that mesmerism provided a significant historical representation of *automatism*. In 1872, Darwin published *The Expression of the Emotions in Man and Animals* (with photographs by Reijlander), a study of unconscious body movement, in which he adopts Herbert Spencer's thesis on the physiology of laughter (and other forms of spontaneous expression) as "an overflow of nervous force undirected by any motive."[43] Darwin cites Laycock, and Benjamin Carpenter's *Mind and Brain*, on the relevance of mesmeric phenomena (338), as well as Duchenne's *Mécanisme de la physionomie humaine*. From the conclusions of these eminent physiologists, it is clear that science regarded the magnetized or mesmeric body essentially as an automaton. This view, which corroborates the persistent historical equation of mechanical and meteoric bodies, calls to mind the Baroque figure of the mechanical doll animated by magnets or the human body moved by "animal spirits." The scientific rationalization of animal magnetism anticipates, moreover, developments such as Caillois's interest in automatism and unconscious mimicry and Bellmer's view that his doll articulates a corporeal unconscious. Marina Warner, in a recent essay on "ceroplasty" and Madame Tussaud's wax museum, remarks on the historical coincidence of the emergence of mesmerism and the fashioning of life-size wax dolls (often fitted with internal mechanisms to animate the figure). Reflecting on the figure of Sleeping Beauty (the oldest waxwork in the museum, dating from 1765), Warner remarks, in reference to mesmerism, "It would be interesting to explore the evolving ideas about sleep and dream states in the period when waxworks became popular."[44] While it would no doubt be interesting to consider the waxwork as an emblem of the *psychology* of mesmerism, the Sleeping Beauty in Madame Tussaud's museum, regarded as an automaton, might also be viewed as emblematic of the *physics* (and the physiology) of animal magnetism.

WEATHER UNDERGROUND

The spontaneity and automatism of the mesmerized body, as well as its pliability, historically have found expression in a variety of social movements, often those associated with political or cultural extremism. Robert Darnton begins his study of the decline of the Enlightenment by observing, "Mesmerism aroused enormous interest during the pre-revolutionary decade; and although it originally had no relevance whatsoever to politics, it became, in the hands of radical mesmerists like Nicholas Bergasse and Jacques-Pierre Brissot, a camouflaged political theory very much like Rousseau's."[45] Further, he contends, "One should not be surprised, therefore, to find radicals like Marat devoting themselves principally to fantastic treatises on light . . . nor to find that Mesmer's partisans included several important future leaders of the revolution" (44). Taking into account Darnton's survey of the writings of Bergasse and Jean-Louis Carra, it appears that the crucial link between mesmerism and revolutionary doctrine is articulated not so much by the physics of light as by *meteorology*. Carra, for example, elaborated a politics of "atmospheric fluids" in his *Examen physique du magnétisme animal* (1785); further, Darnton notes, "He detected an impending apocalypse in the extraordinary weather of the 1780s"—a "global convulsion" that had been precipitated, according to the prestigious *Journal de Physique*, by "the unequal distribution of electric and phlogistic fluids" (109–11).

An assessment of the political climate of the "mesmerist revolution" therefore presumes, as Darnton explains, that mesmerist doctrine described phenomena—especially automatism—that traversed (like Caillois's principle of lyrical thinking) the boundaries of matter and immateriality, physics and ethics: "Like Carra, Bergasse built his mesmerist system on the popular contemporary theory of reciprocal moral and physical causality, which formed a central theme in many mesmerist writings" (113). On this basis, one could discern an isomorphic relation between the "fits of light" posited by Newton, the convulsions of the mesmerized body, the turbulence of the weather, and political rupture. Bergasse, who regarded himself as a kind of "mesmerist Rousseau" (118), embraced at once the ideal of a primitive, harmonious society, the political ideology of revolution, and mesmerist physiology. Thus, he declares, medicine is "an institution that belongs just as much to politics as to nature" (124). According to this model, the "crisis" of the meteoric body could be relieved only by undergoing a convulsion (often conceived in pedagogical terms) that would redistribute the mesmeric fluids and restore the Epicurean state of repose *(ataraxy)*—a concept later realized in modern electroshock therapy. Combining the nature philosophy of Rousseau and the automatism associated with animal magnetism, the "mesmerized natural man" (123)—who resembles La Mettrie's man-machine—is revolutionary precisely insofar as he (or, more appropriately, she) is at once an automaton and a meteoric phenomenon, mechanistic yet volatile, wholly governed by necessity and instinct, yet spontaneous: an emblem of the vitality of the material unconscious. In the mesmerized, natural body of the revolutionary, a "philosophy of sleep" coincides with the doctrine of meteorological turbulence. The subtle body of the automaton is a cataract of imponderable "fluids."

Preserved and revised in the discourses of vitalism *(Lebensphilosophie),* nineteenth-century nature philosophy, and in the medical discourse of automatism, the cultural and political features of the "mesmerist revolution" reemerged in a highly problematic fashion in the context of modernism. For the topos of the mesmerized, natural body is essential to the origins of contemporary counterculture, to the genealogy of modern dance and its relation to feminism, and to the physical culture (including mass spectacle) of National Socialism in Germany (all sometimes combined in the career of a single figure). Thus the path of the mesmeric body through modern culture defies the political antinomies (progressive/reactionary; conservative/revolutionary) on which much contemporary criticism is based. Martin Green has written an important book on the artists' colony and health

Figure 10. Engraving of the electrocution of the Swedish physicist Georg
Richmann (and his assistant) in 1753, as he attempted to duplicate Benja-
min Franklin's lightning-rod experiment. The balletic suspension of their
bodies, induced by electric shock, evokes and anticipates not only the con-
vulsions of the body politic called for by radical mesmerists three decades
later in Paris, but also the mesmerized body of modern dance. Courtesy
Burndy Library, MIT.

resort at Monte Verita in the Swiss village of Ascona on Lago Maggiore.[46] Active from about 1900 to 1920, the community at Monte Verita served as the context for influential "experiments" in various activities, including anarchist politics, feminism, pacifism, vegetarianism, natural healing (sun baths, air baths, water cures), nudism, and sexual freedom.[47] Many of the *Naturmenschen* at Monte Verita grew their own food and constructed the "light and air huts" in which they lived. The antinomian thrust of the "Asconan idea" sought to recuperate, through various means, a knowledge of the body and to articulate an Epicurean vision of culture based on this knowledge. Among those who lived at Monte Verita, or visited and helped to disseminate its ideas, were D. H. Lawrence, Isadora Duncan, Max Weber, Carl Jung, the anarchist theorist Pyotr Kropotkin, Hermann Hesse, the dadaists Hugo Ball, Sophie Taeuber, and Tristan Tzara, the theologian Paul Tillich, the painters Emil Nolde and Alexei Jawlensky, and feminists such as Ida Hofmann (one of the founders of Monte Verita) and Suzanne Perrottet.

At the core of Asconan practice (though I do not wish to exaggerate the homogeneity of the community) was the "dance farm" collective under the guidance of Rudolf Laban (1879–1958) and his most brilliant student, Mary Wigman (1886–1973), a figure of towering importance in the history of modern dance.[48] Though it drew on varieties of movement in contemporary sport and physical culture, the dance developed by Laban and Wigman was never entirely distinct from the "nature cure" or "natural physical therapy" practiced by some of the dancers at Monte Verita as a source of income, or from the ambiguous healing powers attributed to Laban and Wigman by some of their followers. In addition, the dance ensemble was a central component of the Dada movement in Zurich, performing regularly at the Cabaret Voltaire in 1917 and 1918. This complex amalgam of physical culture and the avant-garde calls to mind the therapeutic convulsions and trances induced in the Epicurean environment of Mesmer's clinic in Paris. Influenced initially by eurythmics (the movement theory of *plastique animée* developed by Émile Jaques-Dalcroze) and by *Seelentänzer* (soul dancers) such as Isadora Duncan,[49] the *Ausdruckstanz* (expressive dance) of Laban and Wigman was distinguished from these earlier schools (and later from the modern formalism associated with Martha Graham) by its emphasis on energy, spontaneity, improvisation, and ecstatic gesture. Laban believed that whereas music expresses the emotions and literature reason, dance expresses the suprapersonal drives, the "drives that dominate living beings."[50] Wigman's impulsive and vehement style of dance was dominated by thrusting, swaying, or jerking movements, and by "vertiginous whirling." Critics reviewing her performances described "the dissolution of the dancer into swaying movement discharging tension" and referred to Wigman as "demonically possessed."[51] The titles of her early solo dances repeatedly evoke states of demonic or ecstatic possession: "Witches' Dance," "Idolatry," "Ecstatic Dances," "The Great Demon," "Dance of Fatality." A description by Wigman of her own performance style offers a more intimate portrait of her demon: "I looked into the mirror by chance. What it reflected was the image of one possessed, wild and dissolute, repelling and fascinating. The hair unkempt, the eyes deep in their sockets, the nightgown shifted about, which made the body appear almost shapeless."[52] Lincoln Kirstein, a champion of ballet and modern formalism, ridiculed "her half-controlled self-hypnotized projections of grief, passion, ecstasy."[53] These descriptions indicate the degree to which Wigman's early modern dance recuperates for the emerging avant-garde the hysterical body of the mesmerist trance.

The sources for Wigman's convulsive style are diverse, as I have indicated, yet we should note that the members of Laban's "dance farm" (nearly all female) were studying Darwin's book on unconscious body movement, *The Expression of the Emotions in Man and Animals*.[54] The correlation between nineteenth-century mesmerism and modern dance is reciprocal, however, since it was not uncommon for scientific research on hypnotism or automatism to invoke examples of related phenomena, such as "demoniacal possession" or a religious sect of Convulsionnaires.[55] The published version of William Carpenter's lectures on mesmerism includes an appendix describing an instance of "dance mania." Just as the mesmerized body came to be associated with automatism, so the "dance mania" of Laban and Wigman is shadowed by mechanistic analogies. Laban wrote, "In their group the dancers look like a machine which works methodically and vigorously at this rousing prayer."[56] Critics coined the phrase "absolute dance" to describe Wigman's innovations, and Susan Manning repeatedly characterizes her gestural style as an "autonomous language" isolated from any sort of musical or scenographic accompaniment—a modernist doctrine of reflexivity and impersonality that verges on the province of automatism.[57] Particularly revealing on this point is the teleology of Laban's dance theory and his system of notation, which he eventually applied to the study of labor and automation in industrial settings. In 1947 he coauthored a book with F. C. Lawrence on "industrial rhythm" and was featured, in 1954, as "Industrial Magazine's Man of the Month."[58]

If the sources and applications of the mesmerized body in modern dance are diverse, its ideological affinities in the broader context of modernism are equally heterogeneous. Critics and dance historians repeatedly emphasize the antipatriarchal character of early modern dance. Susan Manning begins her study of Wigman by stating, "Long before I had read feminist theory, it was clear to me that early modern dance comprised a feminist practice. Pioneered by women, early modern dance rejected the codified movement vocabulary of ballet"; and, more specifically, "Wigman's solos challenged the eroticization of the female performer and the voyeurism of the male spectator."[59] Her troupe of dancers at Ascona, and later at her studio in Dresden, usually consisted entirely of women. The antipatriarchal thrust of Wigman's work explains, at least in part, her participation in the dadaist Cabaret Voltaire in Zurich. Manning points to "parallels between Wigman's dancing and Dadaist dances—the use of the mask, the dissociation of music and movement, the primacy of the dance idea."[60] Another critic, Anabelle Melzer, declares "the meeting between the Laban-Wigman dancers and the dada performers . . . one of the most interesting liaisons in the history of avant-garde performance"; further, she explains, "By 1917, a stable working relationship is evident between the Laban-Wigman dancers and the Dada Gallery performers. All dance events at the Gallery were performed by dancers of the Laban-Wigman school and whether choreographed by one of the dancers or by [Hugo] Ball or another of the dadas, a semblance of stylistic unity, an agreement on medium and method seems apparent."[61] At the Cabaret Voltaire, Wigman performed to a recitation of Nietzsche's *Thus Spake Zarathustra*, a stark coupling of language and movement (or philosophy and movement) which suggests that Wigman must be regarded as one of the precursors of contemporary performance art.[62] Indeed, one of her solo concerts in 1917, "Ecstatic Dances," was subtitled "A first evening of ritual performance art."

The correlation of automatism and ecstatic release in the mesmeric dance practice of Laban and Wigman focused from the beginning on what Laban called the individual's "festive being" and the idea of *festival*.[63] In keeping with the collectivist ideal of Monte Verita, the ecstatic release of "festive being," which occurs in a trancelike state, was most appropriately experienced in a group: the mesmerized body of the automaton translated into hysterical body of the chorus.[64] The aesthetic ideology of Laban and Wigman took a profoundly disturbing turn in the late 1920s, however, in its relation to National Socialism. For Laban and Wigman transformed the radical mesmerist practice of dance into a highly effective tool of the fascist revolution. In a shift that Manning describes as "the passage from modernism to fascism" (166), Wigman developed a vision of "communal theater" based on "the transition from the dance group to the movement choir" (148), culminating in her production of *Totenmal* (Call of the Dead) in 1930.[65] Manning describes

the extent to which *Totenmal* modeled a prototype for Nazi theatre—in its theme, the cult of the fallen soldier; in its format, the

combination of a movement choir and a speaking choir; and,
above all, in its strategy of not appearing "political." . . . Revising
the tradition of festival, borrowing forms from the left and reo-
rienting them towards the right, *Totenmal* set a precedent for
Nazi dramaturgy (149).

Faced with such a dire contradiction in Wigman's work between ideo-
logically progressive avant-garde practice and fascist politics, Manning
has no choice but to situate Wigman's dance at "a convergence of
feminism and nationalism" (2). Thus she explains, "In works com-
missioned for National Socialist dance festivals in 1934 and 1935, she
[Wigman] consolidated a format for group choreography that substi-
tuted a representation of *Volksgemeinschaft* (folk—i.e., Aryan—com-
munity) for the earlier community of women dancers" (3).

Manning seeks to explain the collaboration of Wigman—and many
other German dancers—by means of the *Lebensphilosophie* and nature
philosophy shared by the two movements: "The same impulses that
occasioned the founding of Hellerau and Monte Verita—the desire to
escape urban industrialization and find a life more attuned to nature,
the valuing of emotion and intuition over intellect and rationality,
utopianism mixed with a sense of approaching apocalypse—also un-
derlay Nazi ideology. Many of the dancers heard in Nazi rhetoric an
echo of their own beliefs" (172–73). At the height of her success as a
dancer and choreographer, Wigman not only played a central role in
the Nazi dance festivals of 1934 and 1935 but also continued to run
her dance studio under the explicit sanction of the Ministry of Culture.
What's more, in 1936, Wigman published a book of essays, *German
Dance Art*, that offered, according to Manning, an "explicit statement
of support for fascist aesthetics" (191). Although she received no public
commissions from the Cultural Ministry after 1936, she never publicly
voiced disapproval of the regime, and she remained a "figurehead of
German dance" until she stopped performing altogether in 1942.

Wigman's career under National Socialism culminated in one of the most visible expressions of Nazi culture: her choreography of "Olympic Youth," the main component of the ceremonies staged for the 1936 Olympics in Berlin. Filmed by Leni Riefenstahl, a protégé of Wigman who trained at her Dresden studio, Wigman's nocturnal spectacle calls to mind, through its use of searchlights and fog machines, the artificial "weather" of pyrotechnic display. These effects are not surprising, given the occasion, but they acquire a special resonance if one regards them as translating Wigman's preoccupation with the meteoric body into the artificial weather of mass spectacle. We can then see the eerie texture of fog and light enveloping the stadium (captured in the final image of Riefenstahl's *Olympia*) as a vision of the mesmeric body—that is, as an episode in the history of materialism.

To gain some perspective on the ideology of Wigman's aesthetic formalization of the weather, it may be useful to glance briefly at a different formulation of artificial meteors in an entirely different context. Coinciding roughly with the span of Wigman's career (1910–1940) and her exploration of the meteoric body in modern dance, a new device—the cloud chamber—emerged from the science of meteorology to influence profoundly our "picture" of material substance and the methods of experimental physics. The cloud chamber, invented by C. T. R. Wilson in 1895, was originally built to reproduce the atmospheric and optical effects of clouds in a pressurized glass chamber. From its origins as a machine designed to produce artificial weather, the cloud chamber evolved into a device capable of "making visible the paths of ionized particles" through pressurized gas—the most important means of registering new particles in the history of modern physics. Peter Galison explains the relevance of Wilson's fascination with meteoric bodies to his invention of the cloud chamber: "Though the eventual use of the cloud chamber has led atomic, nuclear, and particle physicists to appropriate Wilson as one of their own, his life's work is incomprehensible outside the context of weather. One must come to terms with the dust, air, fogs, cloud, rain, thunder, lightning, and optical effects that held the rapt attention of Wilson . . . in order

Figure 11.   Finale of the 1936 Olympic ceremonies in Berlin. Still photograph from Leni Riefenstahl's film *Olympia*. Courtesy Leni Riefenstahl Produktion.

for the invention of the cloud chamber to make historical sense."[66] Although Wilson's fabrication of meteoric bodies appears to be free of ideological intent (unlike Wigman's meteorology), it quite obviously shares the mimetic assumptions underlying the Victorian portrayal and classification of atmospheric phenomena, ranging from Luke Howard's cloud nomenclature (which we use today) to meteorologic imagery by John Constable, J. E. Millais, and other Victorian painters.[67] Thus we can see that the intent of Wilson's recreation of meteoric bodies differs sharply from Wigman's expressionist meteorology—as do the ideological affinities of these divergent pictures of meteoric substance.

In contrast to the ideological purity of Wilson's materialism, relations between avant-garde practice, mass culture, and reactionary pol-

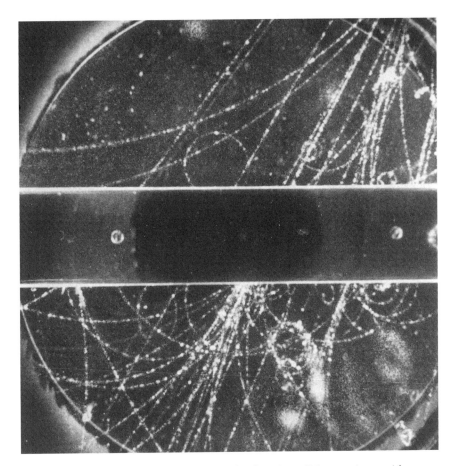

Figure 12. Cloud-chamber photograph of nuclear disintegrations, with electronic elements. Plate 88 from Rochester and Wilson, *Cloud Chamber Photographs* (New York: Academic Press, 1952).

itics leave one not only perplexed but, in the case of Mary Wigman and other modernists like her, genuinely disheartened. For there is something shocking about the juxtaposition of fascism and feminism (which remained a vital element of her work) in the dances Wigman produced for the Nazis. Manning and Green are surely correct in stressing the elaboration of physical culture and *Lebensphilosophie* as a

Figure 13. John Millais, *The Blind Girl* (1856). Like Constable's cloud paintings, this image evokes the correspondence between ponderable and imponderable bodies, between the two figures in the foreground (note the lyric connotation of the accordion) and the double rainbow. Courtesy Birmingham Museum of Art, England.

way of explaining the convergence of counterculture and National Socialism. Yet, even from this perspective, the essential relation between politics and Wigman's vision of corporeality remains inscrutable. One cannot begin to understand the evolution of the mesmerized, organic body in Wigman's dance practice without some sense of the "scientific" correlation of mechanical and meteoric bodies, without considering the subtle body of the automaton.

The interlocutors of Kleist's essay on the marionette theater align the puppet's mechanical "grace" (which is possible only because of the doll's complete lack of consciousness) with "the path of the dancer's soul."[68] In addition, the mechanics of the line, or trope, described by the marionette coincides, according to Paul de Man, with the *anamorphosis* of the line—with a distortion of representational reality, which therefore places the automaton and the dancer in a complex relation to mimesis.[69] Hence, if the political features of Wigman's "dance idea" tell us anything about the fate of the mesmerized subject in modern culture, it is that the regime of the antigravitational body of the puppet tends to treat imitation (in the case of fascist spectacle) as a practice that serves the ends of allegory and thus to swerve away from the goals of political realism.

CHAPTER 5

The Material Abyss

L'atomisme, c'est le matérialisme précis.
> *Gaston Bachelard,* Les intuitions atomistiques

The atom does not enter into the daylight of appearance, or it
sinks down to the world's material foundation when it does enter
it. The atom as such only exists in the void. The death of nature
has thus become its immortal substance.
> *Karl Marx,* On the Difference between the Democri-
> tean and Epicurean Philosophy of Nature *(1841)*

Whoever seizes the greatest unreality will shape the greatest reality.
> *Rainer Maria Rilke,* Correspondence

DUST TO DUST

The iconography of materialism (including the materialism of modern
lyric poetry) revolves, I have argued, on two axes: the concepts of the
machine and the meteor. Before I consider more carefully the figu-
rative economy of the atom itself—what Gaston Bachelard calls "the
metaphysics of dust"—let me briefly review the twin axes of materi-
alist rhetoric.[1] Just as the mechanized toy gives palpable expression to
the lawful character of atoms, that is, to the ideas of substance and
method associated with corpuscularian philosophy, so, too, Michel Ser-

res argues, does the meteoric phenomenon depict the subliminal and stochastic world of atoms: "From clouds to wells, from lightning to fountains, meteors, along with the geography of oceans, waves, and springs, naturalize physics, like experimental proofs of abstraction. . . . The abstract model is faithfully reflected in the concrete model, by analogy: it is a spectacle, a speculation."[2] The same could be said about the reliance of atomism on pneumatics and the discourse of "effluvia" (rainbows and magnetism) to demonstrate the viability of its physical doctrine and to represent intuitively the insensible foundation of matter. All of these phenomena persuade us to grant to the invisible "cloud" of atoms a kind of veracity—if not that of a chair, then of something imponderable, like magnetism or an electrical storm. Physics, nevertheless, insists—or it once did—that chairs are made of atoms. Catherine Wilson explains,

> The idea that science destroys the image of the familiar world and substitutes for it the image of a strange one, wonderful to the imagination and at the same time resistant to the projection of human values, is essentially right. The paradox that understanding seems to imply alienation from what is understood is one presented in the intellectualist version of the scientific revolution, according to which a colorless world of particles was given to us in place of the world of experience.[3]

The essential problem of materialism thus concerns its reliance on analogy and also the strangeness of the tropes, images, and devices (such as meteors and clocks) it employs to depict the invisible foundation of material substance.

My aim in the present chapter, however, is to delve below the iconography of dolls and meteors to the figurative ground on which these popular (and more palpable) analogies rest—to the abstract realm of atoms. In this regard, meteorology and mechanics, insofar as they comprise the iconography of modern materialism, each constitute what Giorgio Agamben calls "a science without object"—a concept rooted in Vico's "new science" of myth and history.[4] (The problem of a science without object also pertains to the disappearance of the object—and the concept of mind—into the process of scientific mediation.) In the strictest sense, therefore, philosophical materialism, insofar as it is tethered to atomism, is a science without object, or without an empirical object—a paradox confirmed by the essential insights of quantum theory in the twentieth century. Even at the level of more intuitive analogies, the scientific discourse of meteoric and mesmerized bodies, as well as the uncanny properties of the automaton, make it clear that *materialism need not be associated with realism*. Indeed, although materialism and realism were yoked together in a peculiar manner in mechanical philosophy (through the figure of the automaton) and thereafter frequently confused in the humanities, the material object formulated by atomism defies intuition and experience. There is nothing realistic about the object of scientific materialism, and hence any foundational claim to authority or authenticity on the basis of materialism in the humanities is simply without foundation—unless, of course, the authenticity of literary or cultural "materials" derives from a theoretical framework divorced from scientific materialism. In the recent wave of historicism in literary studies, for example, any claim to realism or historical authenticity would have to derive from a materialist orientation that is rigorously *un*scientific—a program not likely to be articulated any time soon.

Given the overwhelming influence of science in shaping the principles of Western materialism, in terms of both substance and method, to imagine a materialist discourse that is not somehow a "science without object" is unthinkable. Moreover, as Agamben indicates, the dematerialization of bodies calculated and argued so persuasively by scientific materialism is not yet complete, nor does the completion of this task necessarily rest with science per se: "the idea of a science without object is not a playful paradox, but perhaps the most serious task that remains entrusted to thought in our time" (xvi). Since "the object to have been grasped has finally evaded knowledge," Agamben contends, "the quest of criticism consists not in discovering its object but in assuring the conditions of its inaccessibility" (xvi). That "criticism" (and not science) should be the instrument of a task inaugurated by science follows necessarily from the conditions of the object's inaccessibility: "The problem of possession is a problem of enjoyment, that is, of language" (xvii). Hence, criticism (in contrast to science) "neither represents nor knows, but knows the representation" (xvii). Agamben's thesis recalls Bertrand Russell's dictum that "science is what you more or less know, and philosophy is what you do not know."[5] "Criticism" must complete the task inaugurated by physics (a doctrine of materialism predicated on the dematerialization of bodies) because the intuitive properties of atomic substance remain entirely contingent on language and representation.

Yet Agamben, by placing the term *stanza* at the core of his thesis, indicates that it is lyric poetry (in conjunction with "criticism") that inaugurates and is destined to complete the task of scientific materialism: "What is secluded in the *stanza* of criticism is nothing, but this nothing safeguards unappropriability as its most precious possession" (xvii). Thus the lyric stanza (a term indistinguishable, in Agamben's text, from the topos of memory) reconciles poetry and criticism in its elaboration and defense of "nothing"—a task that calls to mind Kepler's mechanization of "nothing" in his treatise on the meteoric body. For the stanza, like Kepler's lyrical text, holds nothing: "Only if one is capable of entering into relation with unreality and with the unappropriable as such is it possible to appropriate the real and the positive" (xix). In other words, the theory of bodies associated with atomism is the unreality the critic (or the poet) must confront in its social and historical forms, in order to safeguard the reality of "nothing" and to ensure the inaccessibility of the object. I want to consider more carefully how the reliance on analogy—or, if you like, the priority of representation—undermines the equation of materialism and realism, as well as to examine how the microscope anticipates the role of modern visual culture in this equation.

To return for a moment to the question of discursive models, even Agamben's term *criticism* is too narrow to grasp the lyricism (and trauma) of encrypted bodies, since it represents a reduction of the scope of "natural philosophy," the discursive framework in which the corpuscularian hypothesis flourished in the seventeenth century. In Kepler's hands, for example, natural philosophy was characterized by its heterogeneity and its resistance to disciplinary boundaries. Many of the founders of the Royal Society in Britain, who were adherents of the "corpuscular philosophy," viewed themselves as successors to Democritus or Lucretius, in the sense that their atomism was a general philosophy of matter and not a narrowly defined science. As an adherent of corpuscular philosophy, one was at once an atomist, a materialist, a mechanist, and, conceivably (though not publicly), an atheist and a hedonist.

In the Aristotelian-Scholastic scheme of knowledge, natural philosophy, along with mathematics and metaphysics, constitute the speculative sciences. Natural philosophy functioned in the seventeenth century as the matrix of deductive reasoning (the method of hypothesis), shaping and testing the early phases of a new "science" such as atomism. From the perspective of its chief adversary, modern positivism, natural philosophy is therefore associated with "ontological luxuriance," "speculative hypothesis," and "qualitative, physicalistic reasoning."[6] Catherine Wilson explains the role of natural philosophy in the development of modern materialism: "The programmatic statements of the seventeenth-century atomists and corpuscularians are, then, not the meaningful figure against the background of a proliferating but inchoate empiricism; they are philosophy, which is to say they are not only, and perhaps not primarily, a support for science, but also a reaction to it and a substitute for it."[7] From this perspective, the programmatic aspect of corpuscularian philosophy, in its resistance to disciplinary models, appears to anticipate not only the pamphlets of radical mesmerism, but also the manifestos of the twentieth-century avant-garde.

With the proliferation of theoretical models in modern physics (which permits us to explain natural phenomena in divergent ways), the correlation of natural philosophy and metaphysics (under the old Scholastic rubric) becomes especially significant, as Ian Hacking explains: "As soon as what we would now call speculative physics had given us alternative pictures of reality, metaphysics was in place. Metaphysics is about criteria of reality. Metaphysics is intended to sort good systems of representations from bad ones. Metaphysics is put in place to sort representations when the only criteria for representations are supposed to be internal to representations."[8] If natural philosophy fashions hypothetical models of reality, metaphysics furnishes the regulatory and evaluative tools to assess and elaborate the theoretical pictures of unobservable bodies devised by natural philosophy (or its modern heir, theoretical physics). Metaphysics, which asks a few extra questions about physics, is therefore an inevitable consequence of relativism and the surfeit of competing representations of reality. In this sense, metaphysics is a necessary complement to scientific materialism, since atomism offers an explanation of material substance that requires us to choose between intuition and speculation, between two "pictures" of reality.

Though I won't pretend that the eclecticism of Baroque natural philosophy might serve now as a framework for understanding materiality, I do suggest that we can grasp the nature of the corpuscular, or subliminal, body (which forms the basis of any general knowledge of bodies) only by attending to the many ways that atomism has acquired, through representation, a kind of reality that claims the substance of our bodies. Most important, since World War II, atomism and the meteoric body have been represented to us through the discourse of the atomic bomb and nuclear war, ranging from the first images of Hiroshima to science fiction to U.S. government films on "safety procedures" for avoiding exposure to radiation in the event of an atomic blast.

Even prior to the public obsession with atomic warfare, however, the concept of the atom exerted a powerful influence on modern thought and the popular imagination. About the time when the conceptual riddles of quantum theory were first beginning to reach the public, a reviewer in *Nature* wrote in 1926,

> Whatever properties may ultimately be assigned to the atom, there is one which cannot be omitted—its power to seize and captivate the human mind. In fact, if we judged by the output of the printing press in the last few years, we might not unfairly assume that no sooner does any one fall within the influence of this radiating personality than he is seized with an irresistible determination to go home and write a book about it. Nor is the proselytising zeal confined to the pure physicist, whose protégé the atom may be presumed to be. We have books on the atom, some of them quite well done, by chemists, by mathematicians, by technicians, and by journalists, and addressed to all sorts and conditions of readers. Thus we have "Atoms for Amateurs," "Atoms for Adepts," "Atoms for Adolescents," "Atoms for Archdeacons," "All about Atoms for Anybody"—these are not the exact titles, but they indicate the scope of the volumes well enough—in fact, there seems to be a determination that no class of reader shall be left without an exposition of the subject suited to his condition and attainments. . . . If we add to these the enormous output of serious scientific contributions from the many laboratories engaged in investigating the structure and properties of the atom, it is clear that this infinitesimal particle exerts an attraction unique in the history of science over the minds and imaginations of many types of men.[9]

This survey of scientific and popular responses to atomism begins by converting the radiant "personality" of the atom (a trope informed, prior to the atomic bomb, by radiography and the discovery of radioactive substances) into a *magnetic* phenomenon (which exerts an "irresistible" attraction). That radioactive bodies are so easily transformed into magnetic ones in the mind of an educated reviewer only confirms the persistent instability of the discourse of incorporeals. Indeed, the power "to seize and captivate" is the defining feature of the invisible atom.

The priority of representation in atomism cannot be isolated from the formal and epistemological premise of discontinuity, which determines, as Gaston Bachelard explains, the two basic modalities of atomic bodies: "In effect, two systems of thought which involve the same elements, in the same relation, in the same general order, but simply in inverse relation are reducible, essentially, to a single form. The two systems basically follow the parallel, but inverse movements of analysis and synthesis."[10] The "analytic" system corresponds to the search for elementary particles of matter, thought, perception, discourse, and so on, whereas the "synthetic" system pertains to the notion of building up complex structures from simple elements. The modality of combination, composition, and synthesis reflects, inversely, the analytical and reductive drive toward elementary particles: "Synthesis is never more than a replication of an analysis; it repairs what analysis has dismantled" (153). Whether conceived destructively, as a search for radical and foundational elements, or constructively, through architectural metaphors of building and assembling, the complementary atomist "systems" of analysis and synthesis underlie the kinds of bodies fabricated in the image of atoms.

The formal and epistemological aspects of atomism continue, indeed, to inform our most basic approaches to the constitution of knowledge and perception—even when they go unrecognized as such. For example, a complex and charged demonstration of epistemological atomism emerged in the 1990s from the Rodney King trial in Los Angeles and, more specifically, from the defense counsel's analysis of the infamous video of King's beating by a group of police officers. Many believe that the jurors' not-guilty verdict (which ignited the Los Angeles riots) stemmed directly from an argument contingent on the defense counsel's frame-by-frame anatomy of the video evidence. Stanley Fish, who spells out the implications of this analysis in an editorial in the *New York Times*, complains, "How could a jury ignore the evidence of its own eyes? . . . First, the film was slowed down so that each frame was isolated and stood by itself. Second, the defense asked questions that treated each frozen frame as if everything in the case hung on it and it alone. . . . the event as a whole disappeared from view and was replaced by a series of discontinuous moments."[11] In his attack on the jury's naïveté, Fish unwittingly reproduces the classic opposition between associationism in psychology (the atomist doctrine that whole perceptions are mosaics assembled by habit from disparate sensations) and Gestalt theory. Fish clearly puts his money on Gestalt, a movement that began as a scientific explanation of optical illusion.

Fish continues his complaint with the air of someone who would not have been so easily fooled, had he been on the jury: "Why do arguments like these often have so much force? At first glance, it seems odd, even bizarre, to discount the cumulative effect of so many blows. . . . How is the trick done? Well, first of all by a sleight of hand. The eye is deflected away from the whole. . . . the parts, now freed from any stabilizing context, can be described in any way one likes." In this remarkable "critique," Fish spells out the implications of his earlier description: the defense counsel's strategy is a "trick," a means of undermining the spectator's confidence in his own perception, or, more dramatically, an illusionistic process leading the juror/viewer to believe that he has seen something that contradicts the manifest appearance of things. As a result of the counsel's decomposition of the video, the jury could not be certain of what it had seen, could not be certain that the video depicted a man being beaten without provocation and with excessive force. Understandably, Fish calls the jury's conclusion "bizarre." Yet the analytic method of epistemological atomism aims precisely to eliminate the "stabilizing context" in any structure (which it regards as phenomenological and hence illusory), in order to discern what it is precisely that we can know with certainty. Often a critique of this kind ends by asserting that truth, or certain knowledge, always lies beneath the threshold of intelligibility: we can know with certainty only the discrete elements of the perceptual whole, which remains hypothetical and, in the most uncompromising terms, unreal. Fish concludes by broadening his attack: "This strategy—of first segmenting reality and then placing all the weight on individual bits of it—is useful whenever you want to deflect attention from the big picture." By means of this "strategy," and in defiance of intuitive evidence, the defense manages to extract from the video not only an unblemished black body but, paradoxically, a culpable black body (the cause of an event that may never have occurred). The jury is blind to the body and the event that it sees.

The correspondences between Fish's commentary and the basic premises of atomist doctrine are instructive and far-reaching. Many of the charges made by Fish, concerning the method of disarticulation and speculation—a method of *reading*—practiced by the defense, also hold true for the basic premises of philosophical atomism. Indeed, Fish's analysis demonstrates how quickly an argument based on the formal principles of atomism (analysis and synthesis) can produce a metaphysical body that compels us to abandon perception. More fundamentally, the defense counsel's strategy and what Ian Hacking calls the "Democritean dream of knowledge" (as well as Fish's own method of analyzing the mysterious verdict) proceed from a profound mistrust of the appearance of things. The material body evoked by atomist doctrine is no less estranged from empirical reality than the unblemished and culpable black body produced by the defense counsel's analysis. Indeed, the hermeneutic of the defense strategy leads us back to the very foundation of ancient materialism: Democritus is said to have declared, "We are severed from reality"—by our senses. Thus, as Ian Hacking explains, atomism and the origins of materialism are founded on skepticism, on a moment of radical doubt that dissolves apparent surfaces: "The hand represented as flesh and bone is false, while the hand represented as atoms and the void is more correct."[12] Atomism therefore produces, as a consequence of skepticism, "the philosophical split between appearance and reality" (141), between existence and essence, between secondary and primary qualities. Furthermore, the "dream" of atomism inevitably breeds skepticism concerning the imperceptible reality of material bodies: how can we verify any particular version of the dream; and is the dream no more than a dream?

Heinrich Hertz, the great nineteenth-century physicist whose philosophical revisions of atomism influenced the logical systems of Bertrand Russell and Ludwig Wittgenstein, counters the skepticism haunting ontological atomism by converting "free and Democritean speculation" into an edifice of logical "pictures": "The totality of things visible and tangible do not form a universe conformable to law, in which the same results always follow from the same conditions.... If we wish to obtain an image of the universe which shall be well-rounded, complete, and conformable to law, we have to presuppose, behind the things we see, other, invisible things—to imagine confederates concealed beyond the limits of our senses."[13] In this profound and influential statement, Hertz reveals that the skepticism (and speculation) intrinsic to Democritean physics stems from the will to impose on sensuous experience what Bertrand Russell, following Hertz, calls "the reign of law."[14] The "dream" of atomism, which purports to explain the nature of bodies, therefore coincides with a principle of law that is effective only "beyond the limits of our senses," and which stands in opposition to the *lawlessness of visible reality.* Just as material atoms occur at the very limits of sensation, so too, according to Russell, are logical atoms the final *remnant* of analysis: "The atoms I wish to arrive at as the sort of last residue of analysis are logical atoms, and not physical atoms."[15]

Both the ontological and epistemological modes of atomism are motivated by "the reign of law." Thus the inherent lawfulness of materialism stands behind the implacable determinism of mechanical philosophy (represented by the cult of the machine) and the modern fatalities of logical atomism (which amounts to a new organum of immaterial automatism). The flight from the lawlessness of visible reality moreover coincides, as Hertz explains, with a regime of logical "pictures," which occur, like atoms, at the very limits of sensation and analysis. Indeed, as insensible bodies, atoms are constituted by such pictures, which arise only with the necessity of picturing the invisible. Atoms, and the pictures that determine their intuitive qualities, are therefore not merely residual but *excessive,* ontologically speaking. Or, conversely, the question of existence may be excessive with respect to atomic realism.

As a physical doctrine, then, atomism constitutes a philosophy of materialism founded on a discourse of invisible bodies—indeed, it equates the two. Matter is a kind of phantasm. Atomism, in Catherine Wilson's phrase, is "a vision of things *sub specie aeternitatis,*" demonstrating Fontenelle's observation that "true philosophers spend a lifetime not believing what they do see, and theorizing on what they don't see."[16] The formulations of quantum mechanics and the programmatic writings of Boyle and Descartes are no less remote and hypothetical than the great poem on nature by Lucretius. Atomism nevertheless remains, however abstruse its formulations of physical reality, the only authoritative ground on which to build a doctrine of materialism. Ian Hacking remarks, "Today the scientific realist attends chiefly to what was once called the inner constitution of things."[17] The mechanization of the world picture initiated by corpuscularian philosophy dismantled (and disenchanted) the Scholastic worldview, yet atomism posited an occult and imaginary world of its own. Indeed, as Wilson observes, "The scientific revolution involved a reframing of the problem of occult qualities" (56).

In an admirable discussion of the transition from Renaissance nature philosophy to the mechanical hypothesis of modern physics, Wilson points out that both schools were motivated by "the positive drive to uncover what is hidden" (46); "The advantage of the corpuscularian hypothesis was that its reconception of the scholastic distinction between occult and manifest qualities permitted occult qualities to be rationalized and, in principle, controlled" (54). Thus corpuscularian philosophy provided "a demonstration of the intelligibility of occult properties, their accessibility in principle through hypothesized schemes involving invisible effluvia composed of subvisible particles" (56). As a result, "The conviction that there are subvisible material causes for the most obscure phenomena drove out explanations that involved spiritual entities or correspondences" (61). In a similar fashion, some three centuries later, psychoanalysis gradually established a modern lexicon for the psychological occult, just as atomism had triumphed in the seventeenth century (in a much more decisive fashion than psychoanalysis) in a discursive struggle for possession of the material occult. From this perspective, the subliminal world of atoms constitutes a rationalized or scientific occult of natural phenomena— indeed, one could argue that atomism rationalizes and objectifies the *unreal* and hence emerges authentically as a "science without object." After science, Wilson explains, "The word 'occult' ceased to refer to qualities that were known to exist but could not be explained, and came to be a term for the scientifically unintelligible, for what cannot be explained by recourse to invisible particles. It remains in philosophical discourse as a pejorative term" (55). In physics, then, the occult continues to function only in practice, not in principle; for nothing is intrinsically obscure (immune to mechanical explanation) unless it is unreal, though atoms—the authentic elements of the material occult— remain permanently beyond the grasp of our senses. From a more critical perspective, therefore, one could argue that atomism regards all true qualities as occult, since only atoms exist.

Considered solely in terms of Democritean physics, atomism presents formidable problems: if bodies are actually composed of unobservable particles, how can we verify any of the properties that we attribute to them? How can we be certain that atoms are not hypothetical entities—mere "beings of reason"? These difficulties become genuinely paradoxical with the integration into atomist doctrine of the empiricism of Epicurus and Lucretius: matter is the *sole* reality, and all knowledge derives from the senses. The introduction of Epicurean empiricism establishes the framework for an irresolvable conflict between ontology and epistemology within atomist doctrine: only atoms truly exist, yet, according to the premises of empiricism, they are unknowable and indeed inconceivable. From the standpoint of radical materialism, imperceptible entities can play no part in our knowledge of the world—in fact, things without bodies do not exist.[18] Thus after Epicurus, atomism comprises an incoherent amalgam of empiricism and immaterialism, which, taken in its entirety, implies that the elementary particles of material bodies (the sole reality) are not merely unverifiable (in light of Democritean physics), but also inconceivable (if one admits the premises of empiricism).

EPICUREAN MARX

Although the eclecticism and intractable contradictions of atomism may appear to have little bearing on the broader implications of modern materialism, it was precisely these problematic aspects of the doctrine that led Karl Marx, in his Ph.D. dissertation on ancient materialism, to reconcile the basic tenets of his early Hegelianism with a critique of Democritus and Epicurus. No doctrine of materialism could escape the specter of atomism—a fact Marx well understood. Describing Epicurean philosophy as a typical expression of the Hellenistic period and the decadence of "Alexandrian philosophy," he defines it more precisely as "a syncretic combination of Democritean physics and Cyrenaic morality" (i.e., hedonism), and associates it with "exaltation and derangement."[19] Nevertheless, it is precisely the heterogeneity and antithetical nature of atomism that compel Marx to regard it as specifically modern, and as the most appropriate basis for a doctrine of modern materialism. He characterizes Epicureanism as one of "the prototypes of the Roman mind" and asks, concerning these "eclectic systems": "Is not their essence so full of character, so intense and eternal that the modern world itself has to admit them to full spiritual citizenship?" (35).

He discerns, moreover, that the modernity of Epicurean philosophy (and the other "eclectic systems" of Alexandria) derives not merely from its syncretism, but also from its appropriation of archaic doctrines, and from the historical "self-consciousness" that accompanies anachronism of this kind. Thus he asks, "What is the reason why the systems that follow after Aristotle find their foundations as it were readymade in the past, why Democritus is linked to the Cyrenaics? . . . Is it an accident that these systems in their totality form the complete structure of self-consciousness?" (35). In historical and philosophical appropriations of this kind, Marx contends that the earlier systems, such as Democritean physics, are "more interesting and significant for their content" (36), whereas the later, eclectic systems, such as Epicureanism, command attention for their "subjective form" (which he calls "the spiritual carrier of the philosophical systems"). It is precisely the "subjective form" of Epicurean materialism, comprising the paradoxes of atomist doctrine, that Marx selects as the model for his own theory of dialectical materialism.

Marx launches his critique of ancient materialism by arguing, in contrast to earlier commentators, that between Democritean and Epicurean physics there exists "an essential difference extending to the smallest details" (36). He immediately focuses on the "self-contradictory view" of Democritus concerning "the relationship between the atom and the world which is apparent to the senses"; he writes,

> Sensuous appearance, on the one hand, does not belong to the atoms themselves. . . . The principles [atoms] can therefore be perceived only through reason, since they are inaccessible to the sensuous eye if only because of their smallness. For this reason, they are even called *ideas*. The sensuous appearance is, on the other hand, the only true object. . . . this true thing however is the changing, the unstable, the phenomenon. But to say that the phenomenon is the true thing is contradictory. Thus now the one,

now the other side, is made the subjective and the objective. The contradiction therefore seems to be held apart, being divided between two worlds (39).

Emphasizing, therefore, what he calls the "antinomy" of idealism and empiricism intrinsic to atomism, Marx contends that for Democritus, "the antinomy, banned from the world of objects, now exists in his own self-consciousness, where the concept of the atom and sensuous perception face each other as enemies" (39). As a result, Marx observes, "Democritus, for whom the principle [the atom] does not enter into appearance, remains without reality and existence, and is faced on the other hand with the *world of sensation* as the real world" (40). Thus Democritean atomism produces a schism between pure (objective) matter and pure (subjective) consciousness.

Epicureanism is distinguished from Democritean physics, according to Marx, by its insistence that "the explanation should *not contradict* sensation" (45). More precisely, "sensation was in fact Epicurus' standard, since objective appearance corresponds to it" (40). Hence "the concept depends on the sensuous perceptions" (41). Epicurus does not seek to reconcile or, like Democritus, to discount the antinomy of idealism and empiricism; instead, Marx contends, "Epicurus *objectifies* the contradiction in the concept of the atom between essence and existence" (58). In other words, he withdraws the contradiction from the sphere of consciousness and regards it, instead, as intrinsic to the body of nature, so that "the whole Epicurean philosophy of nature is pervaded by the contradiction between essence and existence, between form and matter" (71). Thus matter itself, and not our consciousness of it, is fundamentally contradictory. The antithetical features of atomist doctrine are no longer seen as undetermining the principle of the atom, or negating sensuous appearance, but rather as intrinsic to both. Nature is full of contradictions, but there is no contradiction between the materiality of nature and the doctrine of materialism postulated by atomism: both are equally incoherent, as far as *objectivity* is concerned.

Crucially, for Marx, the dialectic of materiality issues directly from the necessity of picturing the invisible, of endowing the atom—a body said to be without qualities—with sensuous qualities. He writes, "The contradiction between existence and essence, between matter and form, which is inherent in the atom, emerges in the individual atom itself once it is endowed with qualities. Through the quality, the atom is alienated from its concept" (61). Thus by picturing the insensible atom and endowing it, paradoxically, with intuitive qualities, the method of hypothesis produces in nature a state of alienation that serves as the foundation of Epicurean phenomenology. Marx maintains, "Only the atom with qualities is the complete one. . . . the world of appearance can only emerge from the atom which is complete and alienated from its concept" (62). As Marx elaborates his sense of the alienation of matter caused by its pictorialization, it becomes evident how much not only his mature philosophy of dialectical materialism but also his theory of fetishism owes to his reflections on the dialectical character of the Epicurean atom. For commodity fetishes, like atoms, are "at once sensuous and suprasensible things." From this perspective, fetishism must be regarded not as an aberration of materialism, but as a *general theory* of materialism, based on the principles of atomism. Further, through his reflections on Epicurus, Marx intimates the greater design of his own emerging philosophy of materialism: "Epicurus confesses finally that his method of explaining aims only at *ataraxy* [wonder] of *self-consciousness,* not at knowledge of nature in and for itself" (45). Marx reveals the basic premises of his own philosophical orientation (as well as what he rejects) in a comparison of Democritus and Epicurus:

> The *sceptic* and *empiricist* [Democritus], who holds sensuous nature to be subjective semblance, considers it from the point of view of *necessity* and endeavors to explain and to understand the real existence of things. The *philosopher* and *dogmatist* [Epicurus],

on the other hand, who considers appearance to be real, sees every-
where only *chance,* and his method of explanation tends rather to
negate all objective reality of nature (45).

This portrait of Epicurus functions splendidly as a self-portrait of
Marx himself, the future historian and philosopher of the capitalist
phantasmagoria.

SNARE PICTURES

> A *picture* held us captive. And we could not get outside of
> it, for it lay in our language and language seemed to repeat
> itself to us inexorably.
>
> *Ludwig Wittgenstein,* Philosophical Investigations

The prominence given to the idea of the image in modern physics,
along with the consequent attacks on the iconology of materialism,
have made almost no impact on scholarship in the humanities seeking
to isolate the nature of corporeality and to characterize the material
substance of culture. Yet a reliance on analogy, stemming from the
need to picture the invisible, is evident in writings on atomism since
antiquity. Catherine Wilson explains, "In corpuscularian texts, mac-
roscopic experiences are invoked to give imagination a clear picture of
an imputed microprocess: the air was said to be composed of a mul-
titude of tiny springs; acid particles were said to be sharp, water par-
ticles flexible, and so on."[20] According to Wilson, the seventeenth-
century mind was attracted to the "literary dimension" of the doctrines
elaborated by ancient atomists, to "their intellectual economy, austerity,
and remoteness from experience" (29). Ostensibly in contrast to these
qualities (though in fact touching the core of the lyric dimension of
atomism), corpuscularian philosophy flourished in no small part be-
cause of its remarkable capacity for "rendering the causes of phenom-
ena perspicuous" (29). That is to say, mechanical philosophy was good

at creating vivid pictures of obscure and unlikely physical processes. Indeed, as Ian Hacking explains, such pictures and analogies are often so compelling that they outlive the theories they are meant to illustrate: "Models tend to be robust under theory change, that is, you keep the model and dump the theory. There is more local truth in the inconsistent models than in the more high-brow theories. . . . If there is any truth around, it lies in the approximations, not in the background theory."[21] Hacking draws a similar conclusion about the kinds of pictures produced by a microscope: "Visual displays are curiously robust under changes of theory. You produce a display, and have a theory about why a tiny specimen looks like that. Later you reverse the theory of your microscope, and you still believe the representation" (199). The foremost example of a picture surviving its theoretical foundation is, of course, the atom itself.

Modern descriptions of the atom as a vortex, or a system of particles orbiting about a nucleus, or a cloud, or even a wave, exhibit the same lyric propensity and proceed, as with the earlier models, by analogy "from observable phenomena to unobservable atoms."[22] Beginning in the late nineteenth century, the term *picture* became pervasive in the discourse of physics, as Edward MacKinnon explains: "Since at least the time of Hertz and Boltzmann, physicists had been accustomed to speak of scientific theories as giving 'pictures' of reality. The terminology had become familiar enough so that it could be used without analyzing what it means for a theory to provide a picture" (180).[23] This method of picturing the unknown inner constitution of things demolishes, however—at least in practice—the barrier between primary and secondary qualities, substance and appearance, on which atomism depends. As a result, MacKinnon observes, "One explains macroscopic properties of bodies in terms of properties attributed to the atoms constituting these bodies. Yet, one can only speak of the properties of atoms in terms derived from macroscopic bodies" (13). The unavoidable circularity of physical description in this context obliges us to speak of atoms in terms of sensuous properties that atomism considers, in principle, to be illusory or misleading. Hence intuitive knowledge of the authentic substance of material bodies is inherently unreliable—yet unavoidable if one wishes to discuss the atom as something other than a mathematical formulation.

The analogical, or figurative, character of atomism, coupled with its rejection of sensuous appearance, presents a treacherous foundation on which to build a doctrine of scientific materialism. Not surprisingly, given the tendency of visual models to persist after the demise of their theoretical foundations, critiques of atomism, from Aristotle to modern positivism, have focused on the problematic role of "pictures" in atomism, which are at once "irredeemably fictional" and subversive of the abstract character of atoms (since atoms are said to have no qualities other than extension and motion). In the early part of the eighteenth century, Bishop George Berkeley fashioned one of the most trenchant critiques of atomism, calling its conception of matter "an incomprehensible somewhat, which hath none of those particular qualities whereby the bodies falling under our senses are distinguished one from another."[24] According to Berkeley, corpuscularian philosophy, seeking the unknown inner constitution of things, deludes us by claiming that "the real essence—the internal qualities and constitution—of every the meanest object, is hid from our view: something there is in every drop of water, every grain of sand, which it is beyond the power of human understanding to fathom or comprehend" (section 101). Berkeley's attack on "infinitesimals" stems from his so-called common-sense empiricism (or phenomenalism), which holds that bodies are nothing more than the appearances they present to us. Hence his credo, *esse est percipi:* beings are percepts. The extreme antithesis of atomist hypothesis therefore tends, like atomism itself, toward a kind of immaterialism, since bodies, in Berkeley's view, are akin to ideas. (Berkeley's argument permitted him to claim that "matter" doesn't exist.) Modern positivism, inspired in certain respects by Berkeley's empiricism, challenges atomism on similar grounds, though it focuses more precisely on the assumptions inherent in the method of analogy. Moritz Schlick, for example, the leader of the Vienna Circle, disparages "this crude type of knowledge based on models" and contends, "Micro-laws and macro-laws could only be identical by a very improbable chance. There is no *a priori* justification for such an assumption, which is essential even for the most primitive type of knowledge based on models."[25] Atomism presumes an analogous, or isomorphic, relation between visible and invisible structures, an assumption that permits the use of pictorial models of explanation. Schlick and other members of the Vienna Circle, following the example of Ernst Mach's empirio-criticism, vigorously rejected the figurative method of atomism.

Fortified and revised according to Hertz's doctrine of mathematical, or logical, pictures, atomism—prior to the development of quantum mechanics—held that "pictures of physical reality are an essential part of the explanations physics supplies. On this point there was general agreement. There was much less agreement on, or even discussion about, such questions as whether these pictures should be interpreted as iconic models, functional models, phenomenal representations, conceptual representations, or something else."[26] Before we ask what *kind* of pictures are implicated in the method of hypothesis intrinsic to atomism, however, we must emphasize again the ineluctable role of representation in the atomist explanation of bodies. Even if it is possible today to visualize clusters of individual atoms, the philosophical assumptions of materialism have historically been shaped by the invisibility of atoms. Physicists acknowledge that the intuitive features of atomic substance—that is, its intelligible reality—depend entirely on pictures and tropes. Atomism, as a result, has as much to teach us about the nature of pictures as it does about the materiality of bodies. Indeed, whether they are conceived as intuitive copies, maps, or mathematical models, pictures function in atomism in a manner that places in question the referentiality of pictures, as well as the assumption that pictures represent things we can see. For images, in atomism, always occur at the very limits of sensation or analysis; they depict what cannot be seen. Thus the need for pictures arises only with the postulation of invisible bodies; indeed, one produces a picture—a body—precisely because the entity represented has none. Hence, as far as atomism is concerned, pictures do not depict visible reality; rather, they grant visibility to things that are invisible.

Positivism, however, maintains that pictures of unobservable bodies are unverifiable, hypothetical, and hence nonreferential. The kind of picture associated with atomism refers to nothing actually present in the world. This is not to say that such entities are without influence, but only that they are unreal in empirical terms. Surely it is not very fruitful to regard the pictures of bodies derived from atomism as imitations, since verification of any intuitive property of atoms is next to impossible. Nevertheless, through representation, unobservable bodies may acquire a profound sense of reality. If we accept the premises of the positivist critique, pictures of invisible things are to be understood primarily not as referential but as instrumental; that is to say, pictures of unreal things are *tools* that help *produce* a sense of reality contingent on the properties attributed to the invisible body. Ancient atomism, for example, functioned poorly (except in the case of pneumatics) as an explanation of natural phenomena. Yet it was extremely effective as a tool of metaphysics, which distinguished in the strongest possible manner between being (atoms and the void) and nonbeing (sensuous appearance). As atomism has become more convincing as an explanation of physical phenomena, its efficacy as a metaphysical tool has diminished, such that modern distinctions between being and nonbeing, real and unreal, have grown progressively weaker. Nevertheless, atomism raises the question of whether all pictures, including those representing visible phenomena, might be viewed as tools in some primary sense. Perhaps we should regard the aesthetic ideology of atomism—that pictures depict only invisible entities—to be the measure of all pictures.

Apart from the iconography of toys and meteors, the atom derives much of its authority as an image from its abstraction, from its capacity to provide a hypothetical and quantitative picture of a material universe, ostensibly heterogeneous, yet extended without limit in space and time.[27] The abstract character of the "picture" of corporeality furnished by atomism coincides with the *lawfulness* of materialism. In conjunction, however, with the iconology of atomism, the "reign of law" becomes susceptible to a kind of theoretical license. For the unverifiable nature of atoms allows for the possibility of ascribing impossible qualities (such as a space of indeterminate dimensions) to imperceptible entities. Hence a doctrine of abstract pictures offers little resistance to the encroachment of the unreal and the paradoxical on the domain of material bodies. In addition, the will to construct impossible bodies or environments—from the standpoint of intuition—is congruent with the capacity of logical pictures to predict reality—a power intrinsic to the method of hypothesis elaborated by Descartes, Leibniz, and other "mechanical" philosophers in the seventeenth century. The capacity to predict reality derives, as La Mettrie well understood, from the nature of automatism, from the lawfulness of the human machine.[28] In the famous introduction to *Principles of Mechanics*, Hertz explains the basis of the divinatory power of logical pictures: "We form for ourselves images or symbols of external objects; and the form which we give them is such that the necessary consequents of the images in thought are always the images of the necessary consequents in the nature of things pictured. In order that this requirement may be satisfied, there must be a certain conformity between nature and our thought."[29] As a result of this conformity between nature and the images we form of it (in conjunction with the logical purity of these images), Hertz concludes, "We are thus enabled to be in advance of the facts" (1). Hence it is the logical character of the world picture furnished by atomism that enables it to *produce* the fact of nature, conceivably in defiance of intuition, before we have experienced it.

I use the term "world picture" deliberately because Heidegger's conception of the law of representation governing the "Age of the World Picture" explicitly targets the discourse of atomism. In his essay on the *Weltbild*, he writes, "If physics takes shape explicitly, then, as something mathematical, this means that, in an especially pronounced way, through it and for it something is stipulated in advance of what is already known."[30] According to Heidegger, the constitutive (and exclusive) foreknowledge associated with atomic physics is the very essence of the mentality of the *Weltbild:* "Nature and history became the objects of a representing that explains. . . . Only that which becomes object in this way *is*—is considered to be in being" (127). Remarking on the modern correlation of "the gigantic" and "the increasingly small" (which first finds expression in "atomic physics"), he contends, "The gigantic presses forward in a form that actually seems to make it disappear" (135). Hence the gigantism of the *Weltbild* displays an affinity for the subliminal world of quantum mechanics. (We are reminded here of Wallace Stevens's sense of the gigantic—and, more specifically, the "giant of nothingness"—in poetic materialism.) More precisely, the divinatory pictures of atomic physics, which constitute the true substance of material bodies, prefigure a *world conceived as picture,* thereby inaugurating the regime of the *Weltbild.*

The iconography of atomism has migrated historically from imagery that is largely intuitive and often associated with spectacular culture to a gallery of forbidding and frequently paradoxical mathematical "pictures." Thus, on one hand, the toys and meteors of corpuscularian doctrine are unambiguously sensual and available to public consumption and revision; on the other, the icons of quantum theory ($e=mc^2$, for example) appear to signal the migration of scientific materialism beyond the limits of intuitive formulation—though not beyond the reach of popular culture. Although we can discern in the iconography of atomism a movement from sensuous pictures to abstract puzzles, from exuberance to a "crisis of visualization," we should not therefore assume that to conceive of the body as a rainbow or a clock is any less abstruse than to regard it as an equation that refuses to yield a coherent picture of intuitive experience. Nor should we assume—though this issue is more problematic—that the progressive abstraction of the pictures of atomism signals a decisive break with realism.[31] For the appeal of the atom was directly linked from the start to its abstraction. The same could be said of the "mechanical hypothesis." Indeed, the correspondence of toys and meteors raised questions about the integrity of matter long before the discourse of radioactivity transformed the premises of atomic physics.

To discern a philosophical and historical continuum in the lyric substance of the body is not to claim that there are no distinctions to be made, especially with regard to realism and our knowledge of something called reality. The fact that we *make* a doll or a machine, and that we are *visited* by "meteors," makes a great deal of difference to our conception of material reality and to the premises of realism. To view matter as a wave, or a vortex, in contrast to a field of discontinuous particles, is likely to have certain ideological, and even political, consequences. In this sense, the conceptual (and ideological) modulation of the terms *Vorstellung* and *Darstellung* has an important bearing on our estimation of the nature of atomist pictures. Conventionally, *Vorstellung* denotes a picture associated with perceptual or mental processes and hence lacking a distinct material dimension; *Darstellung*, by contrast, usually denotes an external picture, at once graphical and public, and often associated with the constitutive powers of language.[32] Insofar as conventional definitions of *Vorstellung* and *Darstellung* can be reduced to a contrast between immaterial and material images, the distinction is not especially useful in the context of atomism, since, as we have seen, the iconography of atomism tends to confuse these categories and to migrate historically from corporeal to incorporeal emblems (and vice-versa) without fundamentally altering the dialectical nature of materiality.

Yet if we take into account the functional or pragmatic implications of the terms, a contrast between *Vorstellung* and *Darstellung* becomes much more relevant to the issues at stake in the iconography of atomism. For the connotations of *Vorstellung* are decidedly passive, whether one regards it as corresponding to the "idea" of French and British empiricism (denoting a mental picture of an external sensation), or to the Kantian notion of sense impressions already informed by basic categories of thought and language. In either case, *Vorstellung*, according to Ian Hacking, is the key term in what John Dewey called "a spectator theory of knowledge."[33] *Darstellung*, by contrast, in its "public" and "graphic" connotations, implies from the start a degree of artifice, if not intentionality. The role of construction, as well as the public nature of the artifact, becomes more pronounced (though deprived of its sensual aspect) in Hertz's doctrine of logical pictures, which he characterized explicitly as *Darstellungen*. Hertz, as we have seen, was entirely frank about the manner in which we fashion models of corporeality, according to mathematical and logical premises that guarantee the integrity of such speculations. Following Hertz and the epistemological concerns of Ernst Mach, Wittgenstein developed his picture-theory of language by equating the system of logical pictures and the logical structure of language. Thus as the material instrument or expression of logic, language itself circumscribes—and embodies— our knowledge of the material substance of things. Hertz declares, "The consequents of the images must be the images of the consequents" (2). The system of logical pictures, as it is expressed through language, therefore constitutes a public "discourse," though it also retains a sense of objectivity, based on its logical formulation. Were we to evaluate the iconography of atomism in these terms, according to its pragmatic or functional qualities, we would say that the automaton, as an artifact, displays an important affinity with the constructivist ideology of logical pictures. By contrast, the philosophy of meteors, which pertains to phenomena that exceed any notion of subjective or public intervention, presents an entirely different framework for the elaboration of material bodies. In addition, any system of realism founded on the meteoric body would naturally reject a humanistic framework, as well as explanations of materiality based on convention, in favor of theological "pictures" of the body. A close look at the discourse of incorporeals, so essential to atomism, would reveal a secure foundation for theological materialism.

ANGELS AND ANIMALCULA

We might hope, ere long, to see the Magnetical Effluviums
of the loadstone, the Solary Atoms of Light, the springy
Particles of Air, the constant and tumultuary motions of the
Atoms of all fluid Bodies, and those infinite, insensible Cor-
puscles which daily produce those prodigious (though com-
mon) effects amongst us.

> *Henry Power,* Experimental Philosophy *(1664)*

Thou look'st through spectacles; small things seem great
Below; but up into the watch-tower get,
And see all things despoiled of fallacies.

> *John Donne, "The Second Anniversary"(1612)*

In truth, it was only a case of spinning out the old dreams
with the new images which the microscope delivered. That
people sustained such excitement over these images for so
long and in such literary form is the best proof that they
dreamed with them.

> *Gaston Bachelard,* The Formation
> of the Scientific Mind *(1947)*

Corpuscularian philosophy of the seventeenth century was closely as-
sociated with the development of not one but two devices of "subtle
manufacture," the automaton and the microscope. Enveloped by the
discourse of curiosity, these new machines veered in the public mind
between scientific inquiry and what Berkeley called the "empty amuse-
ment of seeing." In addition, both of these devices emerged from a
historical and geographical setting associated with the development of
fine instrumentation; hence practical advances in mechanization and
lens technology tended to exist in a reciprocal relation.[34] Conceptually,
this relation comprised inverted economies of scale: the microscope
brought infinitesimal objects into view, whereas the construction of
increasingly intricate automata depended on advances in miniaturi-
zation (often derived from the jeweler's art). The significance of mi-
croscopy in the development of modern optics (Descartes's "science of

miracles") reminds us that the mechanized doll, too, is a special and powerful kind of image. These ingenious toys (the automaton and the microscope), one associated with mechanical simulation and the other with lens-produced imagery, stand as direct antecedents to the modern discourses of automation and spectacular culture. And both devices were directly implicated in controversies over the corpuscularian hypothesis that a material world free from perceptual distortion exists beyond the limits of our senses. The microscope provided wondrous evidence, if not of atoms, at least of an invisible world teeming with imperceptible and hitherto unknown phenomena. Mechanical philosophy, in Catherine Wilson's view, conveyed "the promise of actually being able to see, with the help of the microscope, tiny machines and invisible processes."[35] Thus, she claims, "the micrographical picture is a picture on the way to the picture the corpuscularian would like to be able to draw" (247). Yet the images supplied by the microscope became the subject of a fierce (and enduring) philosophical debate: are the phenomena glimpsed through the lens merely *subvisible* (not visible to the naked eye), or should they be regarded as *invisible,* as entities whose visual character is an effect of the lens, or indeed as entities which have no verifiable material existence (except the evidence of the lens), and which we must therefore presume to be phantasms or "beings of imagination"? Thus, in conjunction with corpuscular philosophy, the microscope offered "the vision of a world in which angels and animalcula could occupy the same referential space, being merely invisible in different ways" (239).

In addition to furnishing substantive evidence of the imperceptible world postulated by atomism, the visual imagery produced by the microscope corroborated, mechanically, the pictorial method on which atomism depends. In his treatise *Experimental Philosophy*, published in 1664, Henry Power contends that the "modern engine," as he calls the microscope, promises to disclose "what the illustrious wits of the Atomical and Corpuscularian Philosophers durst but imagine."[36] More pointedly, he observes that "without some such Mechanical assistance, our best philosophers will prove but empty Conjecturalists, and their profoundest Speculations herein but gloss'd outside Fallacies; like our Stage-scenes or Perspectives that show things inwards when they are but superficial paintings" (65). In this telling analogy, Power confirms the integral role of technology in mechanical philosophy, yet he also compares the atomist construction of insensible bodies ("things inwards") to the creation of illusory space through the laws of perspective in painting. By miraculous effect, however, the micrographical image transforms the picture of atomism into something real—no longer simply a picture, but a plausible *vision* of the body.

After the microscope had revealed the existence of an invisible material world, it would never again be possible (quantum theory notwithstanding) to isolate notions of corporeal substance from visual technology and from the method of hypothesis confirmed, at least implicitly, by the microscope. Indeed, the microscope is the ancestor of the cloud chamber, along with a host of other mechanical, chemical, and electronic "detectors" that have shaped modern microphysics. As a figure of scientific method, the microscope quickly passed into a more general vocabulary of penetrating and perspicuous analysis. Marx, for example, explaining the method he was obliged to adopt in his analysis of Democritean and Epicurean physics, remarks, "The differences are so concealed that they can be discovered as it were only with a microscope," and hence he warns the reader, "I am forced to go into what seem to be microscopic examinations as far as details are concerned."[37] Since the "details" in this case are atoms, the analogy of the microscope is especially apt, though it is no less pertinent, in a broader sense, to the analytic model on which Marx based his method. David Hume, in a passage that could very well have inspired Marx's analogy of the microscope, claims that by rigorous analysis, "we may, perhaps, attain a new microscope or species of optics, by which, in the moral sciences, the most minute and the most simple ideas may be so enlarged as to fall readily under our apprehension."[38] Hume, by referring to "the most minute and the most simple ideas," also invokes the specter of atomism in his deployment of the microscope analogy. Yet there is an important lesson to be learned from Hume's analogy, for it represents a retreat from ontological to epistemological atomism, without however justifying his faith in the existence of elementary ideas. Hume, the founder of modern positivism, generally condemns models or "pictures" of unobservable entities as merely hypothetical. On this basis, we must therefore assume that the "atoms" of moral philosophy he seeks to isolate by his microscopic method may well turn out to be chimerical. Indeed, the history of microscopic analysis, whether literal or figurative, is fraught with ambiguities (as the legal anatomy of the Rodney King video demonstrates so provocatively).

Although the pictures supplied by the microscope may have confirmed the basic thesis of atomism (the existence of a material world beyond the senses), and even lent credibility to its analogical method, the status of the microscopic body was highly controversial and remains so today (especially in the most advanced techniques of micrographic technology). Faced with the visible evidence of the microscope (which exists at the very limit of sensation), philosophers concluded either that microscopes produce images of *invisible* things, in the sense of phenomena that exceed not merely the range of senses but the very principles of ocular vision; or that microscopes render images of *subvisible* things, which belong, in principle, to the spectrum of intuitive experience but lie beyond the threshold of our sensibility. The distinction between invisible and subvisible phenomena took time to develop and remained fundamentally ambiguous. On one hand, therefore, mechanical and corpuscularian philosophers regarded microscopic imagery as an unassailable argument for scientific realism (if not for atomic realism). On the other, empiricists such as Berkeley understood Robert Hooke's famous statement, that the microscope brings "new Worlds and *Terra Incognita's* to our view," to mean that the microscope reveals nothing commensurable with the objects of sensuous appearance.[39] From this perspective, the world of microscopic bodies is fundamentally alien to the world as we are equipped to perceive it, and hence the microscope must be regarded as an *impediment* to authentic knowledge.

When Hooke and others superimposed the rhetoric of colonialism on the distinction between visible and invisible worlds, they posed the question of materiality, sensible or insensible, after the analogy of cultural difference. We must therefore ask whether the invisible world of the microscope (equivalent to the *savage* New World) is commensurable with the visible world of the metropole. Whatever the response to such a question, Wilson establishes unequivocally the relevance of colonialism and travel narratives to the theoretic of microscopy: "Observers armed with microscopes are, however temporarily, like people with microscope eyes, residents of a world of their own, which has no common language with ours. . . . the discourse of the early microscope is the discourse of a traveler who reports on what others have not seen, who returns with unfamiliar descriptions of familiar objects" (241). Further, though we may wish to dispute her point about the "familiar objects" of microscopy, Wilson reminds us of Hooke's evocation of the voyeuristic pleasures of microscopy. In the *Micrographia* (1665), rejecting the Baconian method of divulging nature's "secrets" through experimental "violence," Hooke claims that the microscope, by contrast, allows us to "quietly peep in at the windows, without frightening her out of her usual bays."[40] Like the trope of colonial expansion, which casts the invisible world in the role of the racial other, Hooke's image of the microscopist (and philosopher) as a peeping tom portrays the invisible corpuscular body in terms of sexual otherness. Both analogies indicate that the discourse of microscopy provided a vivid, *mechanical* atlas of the material occult postulated by atomism.

Modern and contemporary assessments of the microscope continue to be dominated by the question of whether the microscopic body should be regarded as subvisible or invisible, as compatible or incommensurable with intuitive experience (and hence whether real or unreal). The standard American textbook on microscopy (Gage's *The Microscope*) argues, for example, that "microscopic vision is *sui generis*.

There is and there can be no comparison between microscopic and macroscopic vision." Ian Hacking cites Gage's statement and the views of Gustave Bergman as representing the anti-realist view of microscopy: "Microscopic objects are not physical things in a literal sense, but merely by courtesy of language and pictorial imagination."[41] By contrast, Hacking introduces his own argument for the realism of microscopic images with the following observation: "One fact about medium-size theoretical entities is so compelling an argument for medium-size scientific realism that philosophers blush to discuss it: Microscopes. First we guess there is such and such a gene, say, and then we develop instruments to let us see it" (186). Philosophers (i.e., positivists) blush to discuss the microscope because it establishes a sound argument for the realism of unobservable bodies. More important, for our purposes, Hacking aligns the mediated vision of microscopy with other visual technologies, and he concludes that the allowances we make for televisual "seeing," for example, are no more extreme or peculiar than the modifications imposed on natural vision by microscopic technologies (many of which now dispense altogether with the visible spectrum of light): "Looking through a lens was the first step in technology. Then came peering through the tube of a compound microscope, but looking 'through' the instrument is immaterial. . . . We see with an acoustic microscope. We see with television, of course" (206, 297–98). Hacking's argument reinforces (indirectly) the strain of materialism that holds that real bodies are made of pictures and obliges us (more directly) to regard the "special effects" of the modern technical media as pertaining (at least potentially) to unobservable bodies, which may nevertheless be as real as our own bodies. Citing an anonymous "technician" (whom he calls his "teacher"), Hacking reminds us that modern microscopy is once again knocking on the door of atomic reality: "X-ray diffraction microscopy is now the main interface between atomic structure and the human mind" (186).

A very different position on the nature of microscopic bodies is adopted, though never thoroughly articulated, by Lisa Cartwright in her recent book on the visual culture of modern medicine. Concerning the discursive territory of the microscope, she identifies bioengineering as the horizon of microscopic constructions of corporeal substance, and modern visual surveillance techniques as the ultimate descendant of the self-regulating mechanism of the compound microscope. Thus she contends, "The cinemicrosopic apparatus is implicated in the growth of fields like microbiology and bioengineering during this century— fields that engage in the technological analysis and manufacture of new kinds of bodies and new forms of life."[42] In a similar scenario, pertaining to the influence of the microscope on modern optical technology, she maintains, "Long before techniques such as remote sensing or video surveillance were introduced in Western warfare and industry, compound microscopy effectively embodied the optical paradigms that would come to be associated with these late-twentieth-century techniques of discipline and domination" (86). Clearly, in Cartwright's view, the highly mediated images produced by the microscope are now instruments of subjugation and no longer pictures we "dream with" (as Bachelard observes). All the same, without ever posing explicitly the distinction between invisible and subvisible bodies, Cartwright's study consistently evokes, and defines as its subject, the subliminal world of atoms. Hence she views microscopy as describing "a microphysics of the body" and cites one modern microscopist who contends, "He is the greatest discoverer who finds the pre-symptom, or the symptom of the symptom" (81). Microscopic images, she maintains, are instruments of "physiology's animated quest to chart the body's imperceptible nonsites" (82) and thus "arbiters of knowledge of inaccessible space" (85).

In the debate over the commensurability of microscopic images, Cartwright occupies a position of extreme antirealism, determined by her commitment to a Foucauldean paradigm of corporeal discipline and reformation. Microscopic imagery does not reproduce a dimension of the natural body; it *produces*, for ideological reasons, an imaginary body: "The microscopic motion picture is more than a representation of imperceptible living processes, and more than a scientific metaphor of life. It is a mechanism through which science reorganized its conception of the living body" (82). Further, she claims, microscopic images are "privileged modes for generating new configurations of life and subjectivity that conform to the instrument" (90). Even more boldly, commenting on the corporeal "disintegration" observed in a photomicrograph by one early twentieth-century researcher, Cartwright declares, "This disintegration was engendered by the microscope itself, through its techniques of bodily fragmentation and abstraction" (82). To combat this destructive process of pictorial surveillance and domination, Cartwright mounts an impressive critique of the phantasmic and coercive nature of microscopic imagery, and ultimately she declares herself to be an advocate of the "subjective" body, freed from the violence of the apparatus, which somehow also appears in the microscopic image: "I attempt to uncover the agency of the object—its partial autonomy from the cultural institution that studies it; its subjectivity. The unseen 'promicroscopic world' exists only in part as a phantasm of the Western viewing subject. It exists more significantly as a subjugated institutional history, a history of the agency of the object of the gaze, the subjective being represented in the bodily fragment posed on the micrographic stage" (88). Thus, in Cartwright's view, *two* bodies are present in the image: first, the imaginary, institutional, and utterly abstract body produced by the apparatus, which bears no relation whatsoever to the body as we perceive and experience it; and second, the subjective, material body that somehow persists in spite of the "agency of the gaze" embodied by the microscope.

There are two significant problems in Cartwright's reading of microscopy and its relation to the material substance of the body. First, because of the unqualified technological determinism of her approach, and because she chooses to ignore the philosophical orientation of early microscopy, Cartwright entirely misses the correspondence between the flagrantly hypothetical method of corpuscular philosophy and the mechanical speculation that she attributes to the microscopic image. That is to say, she charges microscopy with "disguising and systematizing" the body (105), yet she fails to recognize the corresponding effects of philosophical materialism or to grasp that the hypothetical body engendered by the microscope emerged historically in a context that viewed the apparatus as corroborating the imperceptible bodies conjured by the pictorial method of atomism. Far from producing such a body, the microscope from the seventeenth to the twentieth centuries has confirmed, at least in a general sense, the improbable body long theorized by the dominant school of philosophical materialism. The historical conflation of microscopic and corpuscularian bodies simply blocks any recourse, as far as knowledge is concerned, to a subjective, material body somehow preserved, like a ghost, in the microscopic image. And this, of course, is the other problem with Cartwright's analysis. *Any* conception of material substance is already thoroughly alienated—but also enchanted and made more compelling—by abstraction and pictorial strategies, apart from the effects of the microscopic image. By adhering so zealously to the ideological tenets of the Foucauldean model, Cartwright frequently overlooks the dialectical nature of microscopic images, not to mention the weird iconology of corpuscularian physics.

In addition, the operative notion of corporeality to which Cartwright appears to subscribe (it is never spelled out) obliges her to regard the body as it appears through the microscope as somehow insubstantial, as the product of a relentless winnowing away of material and historical qualities. She notes at the outset the "disintegration" suffered by the body in its microscopic identity and seeks in her study "to trace this dissolution of the corporeal body and its subject in the history of the microscopic image" (83). Why the manifest sensuality of the microscopic image, alternately wondrous and alarming to the observer, should be regarded as subversive of corporeality, as negating material substance, is never explained. In fact, Cartwright's analysis of the microscopic body evokes quite effectively the strange conception of material substance generated by the "pictures" of corpuscular philosophy. The material "disintegration" she identifies as aberrant, as an artifact of the microscope, corresponds eloquently to the fading, chaotic substance of the meteoric body, or to the magnetic effluvium of the mesmerized body. What she takes to be an absence of corporeality conforms in crucial ways to the corpuscularian iconography of material substance. The microscope, "by purging the familiar signifiers of corporeality from the body image" (91), depicts a body no less provocative in its defiance of intuitive experience than the phantasmic body envisioned by atomism—that is, by the discourse of materialism. There is no recourse, moreover, to a materialist account of the body that is not fundamentally anamorphic in its representational strategies. Material substance remains inaccessible and, thus, inherently lyrical.

The blind spot in Cartwright's analysis—the problem of materiality—can be explained in part by the fact that her conception of the microscope prevents it from functioning as a philosophical "engine." In Cartwright's view, the microscope is principally an instrument of *medicine,* which means it is an instrument of knowledge whose images are assumed to be generally stable and authoritative, and therefore capable of dominating the subjective body. As a philosophical device, however, the microscope is an "engine" of *unknowing,* and its vivid pictures are inherently unstable and ambiguous. It is not an instrument but a toy. Cartwright acknowledges that "the view of the invisible provided by the early single-lens microscope was a source of epistemological instability and anxiety" (84), yet she assumes that by the late nineteenth century any trace of uncertainty or obscurity in the image can be resolved and mastered technically. And she is right, to a degree: from the seventeenth to the nineteenth centuries the microscopic image was stabilized and formalized quite effectively, with the result that the chimerical features of the microscopic body were seen no longer as an impediment to knowledge but rather as a diagnostic field of inexhaustible significance and authority. Nevertheless, Cartwright emphasizes the persistent "unmanageability" of the microscopic body as well as the array of techniques, such as the use of aniline dyes, microsectioning, and sophisticated lighting strategies, that are necessary to render the object visible. She chooses, however, to regard these techniques as symptoms of a technological domination of the subject and not as "special effects" or evidence of the profound plasticity of the modern microscopic image. Reading over Cartwright's description of various microphotographs and films, one cannot help but be struck by the volatile nature of the images and by their capacity to thwart visual "penetration" or possession of the object. Indeed, Cartwright's primary analogy for the modernist aesthetic of microscopy is *cubism*—an image of multiple aspects usually associated with extreme relativism (hardly an effective tool of indoctrination). One film made from "two thousand successive cross-sections of a brain specimen" gave the impression of "a camera moving through a foggy indeterminate space in which atmospheric particles scatter light diffusely across the field" (97). Thus, she concludes, the microscopic image presents "the characteristics of a dense, 'foggy' field rather than that of a 'negative' space containing solid objects" (97). These descriptions suggest that the vision of material substance yielded by the microscopic image coincides with the "atmospheric" properties of the meteoric body. In this case, the hypothesis of meteoric substance cannot be isolated from the "foggy" character of the microscopic image. Certainly, given these qualities, it would be a mistake to exaggerate the stability and authority of the modern microscopic image.

The correlation between microscopy and meteoric bodies reminds us that Robert Hooke, who published his celebrated *Micrographia* in 1665, also published in 1667 a treatise titled *A Method for Making a History of the Weather*. Further, Kepler's microscopic anatomy of the snowflake was written about the time that the earliest societies devoted to microscopy were being formed in Italy and England. One need pursue the correspondence between microscopy and meteorology only far enough to confirm that Hooke and other prominent microscopists were corpuscularians and mechanical philosophers. Spinoza, who cites microscopic images as evidence of his theory of "imaginary entities," for a time made his living grinding lenses for microscopes. Marcello Malpighi, one of the five leading microscopists of the seventeenth century, conceded that "microanatomists are pursuing philosophy and not medicine."[43] Insofar as the microscope was an instrument of philosophy, the vividness, and also the instability, of its imagery was essential to its collaborative role in corpuscular philosophy and, more generally, in the visualization of subliminal bodies. For philosophy claimed that the invisible world revealed by the microscope was the true *material* world. Leeuwenhoek, the great Dutch microanatomist, mocked a fellow researcher who claimed to have an instrument so powerful that he could see "not only mites . . . but the atoms of Epicurus, the subtle matter of Descartes, the vapours of the Earth, those which our bodies transpire, and the influence of stars."[44] Yet Leeuwenhoek himself called the animalcula he spied through the lens "living Atoms," like the Italian, Divini, who described one minute creature as "the Atome of Animals."[45] When materiality is equated with invisibility, the invisible world becomes the province not only of atoms and animals but also, conceivably, of beings possessing the radiant body of an angel.

The phantasmagorical nature of the invisible material world coincides, moreover, with the discursive means by which the microscopic image was stabilized and formalized, by which it acquired a discipline. For the mechanical vision of microscopy, like the hypothetical vision of corpuscular philosophy, relied on analogy to make the invisible world intelligible. Thus Leeuwenhoek described animalcula as eels, and Hooke compared cell tissue to honeycomb and yeast to a forest. Wilson remarks that in the notebooks of early microanatomists, "Verbal description tends to be poeticized and the image deflected toward a known object of comparison" (222–23). Yet this process of elaborating or troping the visual artifact also contributes, as Wilson notes, to a

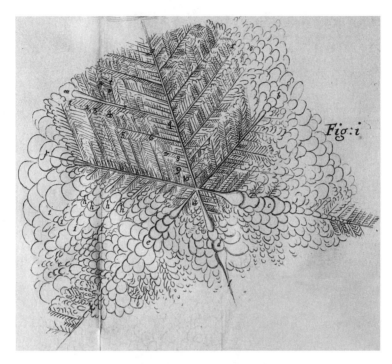

Figure 14.   Illustration of microscopic figures in the "prismatical body" of frozen urine. Robert Hooke, *Micrographia* (London, 1665). Courtesy Clark Library, Los Angeles.

process whereby the microscopic image becomes intelligible, realistic, and increasingly authoritative (or, as Cartwright would have it, authoritarian): "The unfamiliar and incomprehensible were tamed and made intelligible by being described and theorized in the language and concepts of the world of immediate lived experience and affect" (252). Hence the lyric dimension of material substance—its verbal dimension—is a dialectical process in that it simultaneously elaborates and impoverishes, amplifies and disciplines, the physical phenomena it represents.

    The philosophical aspect of the microscope, which pertains to unknowing and the inaccessibility of the object, coincides with its identity as a toy. The leading technicians and philosophers of microscopy, said to be "gripped by curiosity," were called "virtuosos," a community of researchers associated with libertinism, Epicurean philosophy, and the "experimental life." The exuberance and eccentricity of these "virtuosos" of the microscope risked producing a world of "scientific kitsch."[46] Hence the philosophical aspect of the microscope was perilously close to its role as a mechanism of spectacular culture. This conjunction of philosophy and spectacle contributed to the premature collapse of the microscopic revolution, and to the isolation of the microscope from scientific research for over a century. By 1692, Robert Hooke, the great English virtuoso, acknowledged, "I hear of none that make any other Use of that Instrument, but for Diversion and Pastime, and that by reason it is become a portable Instrument, and easy to be carried in one's pocket."[47] Within a century of its invention, the microscope, once hailed as a device that would reveal the unknown constitution of things, was estranged from science and became, quite literally, a toy of the upper classes. To this day, it is not unusual for a child to receive a microscope as a gift, complete with a box of prepared specimens. The microscope was the first example of what Baudelaire called the "scientific toy"—a device as important to the history of material substance as it is to the genealogy of the modern visual media.

The fact that Xavier Bichat, the founder of histology, refused to allow a microscope into his laboratory in 1800 can be explained only in part by the technical defects of the apparatus at that time. Equally important to the fate of the microscope in the newly evolving empirical disciplines was the enduring legacy of collaboration between microscopy and the speculative sciences. As Wilson notes, the microscope was, from its inception, "welcomed by those traditionally designated rationalist philosophers, and regarded with scepticism and mistrust by empiricists" (219). Hence the scientific rejection of the microscope and its mechanical vision coincided with a flight from theory and the speculative enterprise of corpuscularian physics. In this sense, the estrangement of science and the microscope preserved the apparatus as a philosophical toy, as well as its problematic equation of materiality and invisibility. This equation would be revisited only with the revival of theoretical physics and the proliferation of new optical media in the twentieth century—a conjunction signaling a renewed crisis of material substance.

CHAPTER 6

Radiant Species

THE PHYSICS OF APHRODITE

A faint erroneous Ray,
glanc'd from th'imperfect Surfaces of Things,
Flings half an Image on the straining Eye;
While wavering Woods, and Villages, and Streams,
And Rocks, and Mountain-tops, that long retain'd
Th'ascending Gleam, are all on swimming scene,
Uncertain if beheld.

James Thompson, "Summer,"
The Seasons *(1730)*

Are not gross Bodies and Light convertible into one another,
and may not Bodies receive much of their Activity from the
Particles of Light which enter into their Composition? . . .
The changing of Bodies into Light, and Light into Bodies, is
very conformable to the course of Nature, which seems de-
lighted with Transmutations.

Isaac Newton, Opticks *(1717)*

The spectacle of the invisible world revealed by the microscope offered
dramatic, mechanical evidence of the subliminal world postulated by
corpuscularian philosophy. Further, as Lisa Cartwright's study dem-

onstrates, modern microscopy continues to supply an authoritative material foundation for an invisible world that is apparently without limits, and to substantiate an ideology that depicts the subvisible body as the true measure (and arbiter) of the visible body. In addition, one could argue, as Ian Hacking suggests, that the microscope and its reception provide a crucial historical model for understanding the transformation of vision in modern spectacular culture, where distinctions between materiality and invisibility are continually eroded by new optical effects. Nevertheless, despite the evidence supplied by the microscope, the *poetics* of material substance, which calls for materialization of the invisible world, remains incomplete as long as the theory of vision on which it rests is not thoroughly and resolutely materialist in its orientation. Further, insofar as any notion of material substance is inherently lyrical, the theory of vision implied, or openly espoused, by a doctrine of materialism must likewise be treated as a poetic structure and its figures aligned with the poetic substance that it apprehends. Hence the Democritean physics of vision (and its modern legacy) can be expected to clarify significantly, and elaborate in unexpected ways, the atomist conception of material substance.

Analysis of the iconology of material substance shifts decisively when the basic questions reflect the metaphysical assumptions of materialism. For the idea of a picture without substance—a purely mental picture—is inconceivable according to the metaphysics of materialism, which holds that only material bodies exist. Hence, any picture—a statue, an optical reflection, or a thought—constitutes a body of some kind. In the context of atomism, the vexed relation between bodies and pictures is therefore, from a metaphysical perspective, a relation between bodies. The mechanical evidence of the invisible world provided by the microscope complements a theory of vision that regards the mental image as a material body. The convergence of bodies and pictures—of what are ostensibly primary and secondary qualities— occurs explicitly in the longstanding historical reciprocity of theories of light and matter, and in the contributions of optical theory to the development of natural philosophy and modern physics. In other words, our understanding of ponderable things—of bodies in a proper sense—often stems from insights concerning the subtle body of light, or from the riddles posed by imponderable bodies. The intransigent materialism of atomist doctrine therefore establishes the terms of a reciprocal relation between ponderable and imponderable phenomena, which converts impalpable images into bodies and vice versa. The incarnation of pictures authorized by atomism conforms to, but also inverts, the rarefaction of bodies so vividly conceived by meteorology and modern optical theory—the discipline Descartes called "the science of miracles."

The chiasmic relation between bodies and pictures, between corporeal and incorporeal phenomena, has its foundation in ancient and medieval conceptions of vision, derived principally from the doctrine of atomism. According to this model of vision (attributed to Democritus and called the theory of "intromission"), "Material replicas issue in all directions from visible bodies and enter the eye of an observer to produce visual sensation."[1] Thus, vision occurs when "tiny images flitting through the air" (as Descartes described the visual replicas) come *in contact* with the eye. Epicurus, who called the replicas *eidola,* maintained that "thin films, which we call idols, are constantly given off by objects, retaining the form and color of the object. . . . These are images of the same shape as solid bodies from which they come but in thinness far surpassing anything that the senses can perceive."[2] Further, according to Epicurus, mental images or dreams derive from the same physical process: "Both thought and sight are due to idols coming from objects to us" (15). Thus, concerning "a mental picture of the shape of an object or its concomitant qualities," Epicurus writes, "it is created by the continuous impact of the idols or by an impression left by them" (16). Thought is therefore a material residue of the atomic *eidola* that form the basis of visual experience.

Lucretius, who called the replicas of vision *simulacra,* offers a more elaborate description of the physics of visual experience in book IV of *De rerum natura*:

These images are like a skin, or film,
Peeled from the body's surface, and they fly
This way and that across the air . . .
Let me repeat: these images of things,
These almost airy semblances, are drawn
From surfaces; you might call them film, or rind,
Something like skin, that keeps the look, the shape
Of what it held before its wandering . . . the way
Cicadas cast their brittle summer jackets *[tunica],*
Or calves at birth throw off the caul, or snakes
Slide out and leave their vesture under the brambles. . . .
All things project such likenesses of themselves,
However insubstantial, from their surface.
So there are, all around us, shapes and forms
Of definite outline, always on the move,
Delicate, small, woven of thread so rare
Our sight cannot detect them.[3]

The atomic *simulacrum* is thus described by Lucretius as a "skin" or "tunic" that holds the shape and appearance of the body which sheds it. The simulacrum is thus a kind of effigy or doll, a subtle body that is at once the cause of visual sensation and *imperceptible* before it strikes the eye. Further, as a garment woven of invisible filaments, the simulacrum sustains the famous Lucretian analogy of atoms and letters, that is, the inherent *textuality* of atomic bodies (including, of course, the idols).

This theory of material effluence becomes, in the Middle Ages and thereafter, the doctrine of visual "species," a term of enormous complexity in which the orders of being and appearance converge.[4] In his treatise *The Multiplication of Species*, Roger Bacon describes the atomic idols as "radiant species," and Lindberg, summarizing Bacon's theory, explains, "Rays or species issue in all directions from every point on the visible object and reach all points of the surface of the eye."[5] Further, insofar as the simulacrum is a form of radiation, its multiplication pertains to its ambiguous corporeality and to the manner in which it is conveyed to the eye through the medium of air: "There is no change of place, but a generation multiplied through the different parts of the medium; nor is it body which is generated there, but a corporeal form that does not have dimensions of itself but is produced according to the dimensions of the air; and it is not produced by a flow from the luminous body, but by a drawing forth out of the potentiality of the matter of the air."[6] As this passage indicates, the material substance of the visual species is indistinguishable from the airy medium in which it multiplies. Hence Lindberg remarks, "Species are not bodies *per se,* because they do not have dimensions or corporeal natures distinct from those of the media in which they are situated. . . . Rather, the medium is the material cause, out of the potentiality of which species are generated."[7] As a consequence, Lindberg concludes, "The species of corporeal substance has exceedingly incomplete being, and therefore the medium prevails over it and endows it with dimensionality" (xvi). Despite the ephemerality of the species and its deviation from the criteria of the body, the species remains, in Bacon's view, corporeal in essence and in its mode of existence. Thus, as a medium and as an effigy of ambiguous material substance, the radiant species anticipates in remarkable ways not only the meteoric body but also the subtle body of the automaton and the doll of modern poetics.

Whether we choose to call the material cause of vision in this context an idol, a simulacrum, or a species, we must bear in mind that the visual image is *no different in substance and appearance from the radiant body projecting it.* Thus, from the standpoint of atomism, a visual image is not simply a body that borrows its substance from other bodies, or from its medium. Rather, it is a *part* of the body of which it is an image: the simulacrum is a skin, a radiant species, of the body from which it derives. The atomic effigy is therefore a *doll made of flesh and air,* an image that is fundamentally real. Thus the body and its image converge in the figure of the atomic idol. As the chief emblem of a materialist conception of vision, the radiant species calls to mind the dialectical atom and the phantasmagorical materialism that Marx conjured from the decadent corpus of Epicurean phenomenology. For the logic of fetish, in which the body coincides with its partial image (and is hence a thing at once "sensuous and suprasensible"), translates the physics of the visual simulacrum into a doctrine of political economy.

Because the body of the simulacrum is not entirely distinct from the medium through which it passes—or, more precisely, from *the body of air*—we should consider more carefully what bearing the philosophy of meteors may have on the subtle body of the image. For Lucretius calls the idols of vision "airy semblances," and the process of radiation precipitating the visual species indeed resembles the rarefaction of meteoric bodies. In fact, the great medieval theorists of vision (the founders of modern optics) were also meteorologists: Roger Bacon produced a commentary on Aristotle's *Meteorologica*, and Robert Grosseteste wrote extensively on the philosophy of meteors ("On Rainbows," "On Comets," "On Predicting Intemperate Weather"). Indeed, one modern commentator contends that the science of optics has its origin in the study of meteors.[8] We should also recall that Johannes Kepler, whose treatise on the snowflake thrives on the paradox (and ephemerality) of a body that is "almost nothing," translated the doctrine of species into the modern theory of the retinal image.[9]

One way of understanding the correspondence between meteors and radiant species is to emphasize, as Michel Serres does, the turbulence of atomic bodies, and to regard the process of rarefaction (by which bodies radiate simulacra) as occurring at the extreme limit or frontier of a body, in a region of phenomenological instability. Hence, as Serres claims, "Turbulence is productive. . . . it is the transmitter of simulacra."[10] The body and its radiant species are both volatile phenomena, and the processes of rarefaction and precipitation become entwined in the atomist conception of vision: "The form produces forms; the agent and the product are causes of one another" (133). Thus we could say that bodies radiate bodies in the turbulence of vision, or, with Yeats in mind, that images beget images. For the fate of the mechanical singing bird in "Byzantium" is to become a "shade" and finally an "image":

> Spirit after spirit! The smithies break the flood,
> The golden smithies of the Emperor! . . .
> Those images that yet
> Fresh images beget.[11]

Thus the fate of the automaton in the Epicurean milieu of the court resembles the turbulence of the meteoric body, or indeed the fluctuation of any body as it becomes visible, by transmitting veils of its own substance mingled with the air.

Although Yeats allows the lyric body of the automaton to escape, or suspend, its corporeal nature, and although the Epicurean term εἴδωλον is the same word Homer uses to denote a phantom, in the context of atomism the visual species is, by definition, a body. If it is possible to associate the Epicurean idol with death, then the ghosts of the underworld—material ghosts—must be associated not with dread or terror but with wonder and pleasure. Further, the Epicurean idol returns the Platonic *eidos,* associated with error and falsehood, to the body, to the object, and to the space of communication. And since the idol must make *contact* with the eye in order for vision (or thought) to occur, seeing and thinking should be regarded as variations of the sense of *touch.* In the world of corpuscular bodies, Serres observes, "Sensation is a generalized tact. The world is no longer at a distance; it is nearby, tangible. . . . Knowledge is no different from being" (134). Serres emphasizes the *erotic* character of corpuscular vision and knowledge: "Knowing is not seeing, it's making direct contact with things; and, what's more, they come to us. The physics of Aphrodite is a science of caresses" (134). From the perspective of the *tactics* of vision, the doll, regarded as a form of imagery and as the emblem of corpuscular philosophy, presents itself as the essential object of vision that is equated with touch or contact. Furthermore, the doll, conceived as a picture that must be touched to be fully apprehended, is the object not

merely of a "science of caresses," but of playful abuse and slow dis-
integration: a science of disappearance. For the substance of the doll,
through contact and use, becomes ever more tenuous and shows its
wear, its own history as a species of vision. The importance of begin-
ning to think about ordinary pictures as dolls cannot be overstated.
We must bear in mind, however, that the "physics of Aphrodite" and
the model of vision it implies are founded on the notion of a *radiant*
body, which borrows its substance from the subtle medium of its trans-
mission and reaches the eye without changing place. The body of the
atomic idol, and the body from which it radiates, are not all there.
The iconology of material substance therefore pertains to bodies made
visible by their own turbulence—by combustion, but also to a register
of subliminal perception crowded with fleeting material ghosts.

The chiasmic relation between bodies and pictures finds expression
not only in corpuscularian optics but also, more accessibly, in the phys-
ics of "incorporeal" or "imponderable" bodies—a category of bodies (or
agents) without mass or other palpable qualities. Indeed, the physics of
light is a critical component of any theory of vision. We have already ex-
amined the conjunction of atomism and the discourse of *subtilitas,* as it
occurs in pneumatic philosophy, meteorology, and animal magnetism.
The privileged relation of atomism to the subtle and spectacular bodies
of the atmosphere can be extended to a broader spectrum of incorporeal
phenomena. However, "imponderable" phenomena (such as cold, heat,
light, and electricity) often confounded the models and categories of cor-
puscularian theory, as did the so-called effluvia, which included gravity,
magnetism, and certain meteoric phenomena, such as rainbows. Any
theory of matter must distinguish between material substances and im-
material agents; yet by 1700, after a century of progress in physics, this
distinction was far from clear. Even the air could not be judged unam-
biguously to be either corporeal or incorporeal. Indeed, the eighteenth
century (the era of animal magnetism) saw the proliferation of "facti-
tious airs" and substances, often consisting only in the lyric and ephem-
eral nomenclature of experimental science: "pompholyx, colcothar,

and powder of algaroth; butter of arsenic, flowers of zinc, and martial ethops."[12] Depending on the criteria—and the appellation—the "lambent inflammable air" could be regarded as either a ponderable thing or a volatile "spirit." It was not until the establishment of the priority of mass in the late eighteenth century that the idea of "imponderable matter" became incoherent or paradoxical.

Scientific uncertainty about the intrinsic properties of material bodies prior to the nineteenth century resembles the wholesale revisions of corporeality currently under way in the humanities. Today's critique of socially and ideologically constructed bodies stops short, however, of the basic problem of materiality, and indeed it labors under a highly reductive notion of material substance. Rarely in literary or cultural studies is the substance of a body permitted to diverge from the palpable and massy qualities of the object, or to betray the effects of a revolution in modern physics, in which radiation becomes the matrix of corporeality.

Although coherent distinctions between corporeal and incorporeal phenomena were established by the exact sciences in the nineteenth century (accompanied by the objectification of incorporeal phenomena), it would be a mistake to exaggerate the historical stability of these categories. Despite the distinctions drawn between corporeal and incorporeal phenomena, scientific conceptions of palpable bodies consistently betray the influence of theoretical and experimental models associated with imponderable phenomena. In modern physics, for example, wave mechanics, which claims that "material points consist of, or are nothing but, wave-systems,"[13] was "born out of the generalization of the well-known analogy existing between the laws governing the propagation of light and those governing the motion of material bodies."[14] The "well-known analogy" between light and material bodies derives from Newton's speculations in the final queries of the *Opticks*. As a dogmatic atomist (like Galileo and Gassendi), Newton speaks of "Particles of Light," believing that vision consists of the transport of material bodies from the luminous object to the eye (a theory of intromission related to the doctrine of *species*). Thus, in query 29 of the *Opticks*, he asks, "Are not the Rays of Light very small Bodies emitted from shining Substances?"; and, in query 31, he contends, "Even the Rays of Light seem to be hard Bodies. . . . And therefore hardness may be reckoned the Property of all uncompounded Matter."[15] Newton's commitment to a particulate theory of light leads him to speculate (in book II, part III of the *Opticks*) that powerful microscopes might one day reveal the physical distinctions between the corpuscles of various colors: "Microscopes may at length be improved to the discovery of the Particles of Bodies in which their Colours depend."[16] More important, his corpuscular theory of light provided the basis for his belief in the transmutability of light and material bodies, a view that later served as the foundation for some of the most significant developments in modern theoretical physics. Einstein's hypothesis of light quanta, for example, which established the basic terms of the quantum theory of matter, drew inspiration, in part, from the Newtonian model. Thus spectroscopy, the physical analysis of light, has played an essential role in the modern formulation of corporeality. Indeed, radical and unexpected shifts in our understanding of material substance have often derived from the study of optical phenomena.

Given the essential duplicity of light and matter, it is not surprising, if we return to the optical theory of simulacra, to find the concept of "radiant species" entangled with the physics of light. Roger Bacon, adopting the Neoplatonic philosophy of Plotinus, believed that light, as a physical substance emanating from things, was itself a kind of image; more precisely, *lumen* (luminosity) is the corporeal form, or "species," of *lux*.[17] We have retained a sense of the correlation between light and likeness in the phenomenon of the illuminated manuscript, in which pictures are understood to be a source of illumination, to shed light on the text. The conflation of light and likeness, of radiation and body, can be explained in part by the fact that, as Lindberg explains, "the science of optics tended to coalesce around two interrelated, yet distinguishable problems—the nature and propagation of light, and the process of visual perception."[18] Indeed, historically, the *physics*

Figure 15.   Isaac Newton demonstrating the optical effects of a prism.
Advertisement for eyeglasses; courtesy Bausch and Lomb Optical Co.

of light takes precedence in the genealogy of optical theory; for medieval optics (associated with Grosseteste and Bacon) derived from the Neoplatonic "philosophy of light." The physical doctrine of the philosophy of light, resembling the basic premises of modern field theory, considered light to be the primordial "form of corporeity," as well as the origin of the propagation of the material world. In addition, according to Grosseteste, all causation in the material world operates on the analogy of the radiation of light.[19] As a result, Lindberg explains, "The study of physical light permits one to comprehend the origin and structure of the material universe. Optics has been given a place at the very heart of natural philosophy" (97). Further, "Because optics could reveal the essential nature of material reality . . . its pursuit became not only legitimate but obligatory" (99). Thus insofar as the atomic idol is a body made of light (and air), it provides insight into the nature of material substance, as well as the erotics of vision. On this basis, one could claim that to understand a body one must first understand the nature of its image. Pictures—those anomalous and imponderable things—therefore constitute the ground of corporeality.

The notion of corporeality implicit in the optical theory of radiant species is not far removed from the basic premises of modern wave mechanics and the quantum theory of matter. Thus the extension of electrodynamics to matter theory in the 1880s, and Max Planck's discovery of discontinuity in radiation in 1900 (as well as Einstein's 1905 hypothesis of light quanta), established the basic terms for the modern equation of materiality and radiation. The discovery in the 1890s of X rays, cathode rays, and other forms of radioactivity functioned as a prelude to the development of new conceptions of matter, especially the nuclear atom, outlined in Bohr's quantum model of 1913. Further, Louis de Broglie's development of the idea of "matter waves" in 1922 derived largely from his research on X-ray phenomena. Establishing the physical character of light and other forms of radiant energy was therefore a crucial step in the modern revision of matter. By the early decades of the twentieth century, it had become apparent that matter could be reduced to a complex structure of electrical charges—to a form of radiation—and that light consisted of particles (called photons). Thus at the very moment when particles of matter were dissolving into fields of radiation, the phenomenon of radiation was revealed to be discontinuous and, in some sense, corpuscular (though the idea of a discrete particle of matter was no longer tenable). In the sense that light can be regarded as the first "form of corporeity," the chiasmus of light and matter in modern science appears to have revived the physics of Aphrodite; or perhaps quantum mechanics has managed to objectify the radiant species of atomic vision and to calculate its inaccessibility. In any event, the body and its material substance are no longer conceived as a mechanical doll but as a mechanism of radiation.

HALF-LIVES AND ONE-AND-A-HALF LIVES

> When it comes to atoms, language can be used only as in poetry. The poet too is not nearly so concerned with describing facts as with creating images and establishing mental connections. . . . Quantum theory provides us with a striking illustration of the fact that we can fully understand a connection though we can speak of it only in images and parables.
>
> *Werner Heisenberg,* Physics and Beyond

In the world of Democritean physics, all that exist are atoms and the void. This hypothesis provides no basis for any type of *relation* between atoms, and without it atomist doctrine could not explain the cohesion of bodies. Modern atomism differs essentially from ancient atomism in its explanation of relations between atoms based on the notion of an "aethereal medium" or, more rigorously, on Newton's doctrine of "forces and attractions," which applies the concepts of gravitation and action-at-a-distance to the subliminal world of atoms. Since the development of Newtonian mechanics, some conception of radiant and incorporeal agency has been an integral—and increasingly dominant—component of atomist doctrine. Thus, since the beginning of the eighteenth century, material substance has been regarded as combining ponderable and imponderable phenomena—precisely the framework that enabled Mesmer to concoct his theory of animal magnetism.

Coincident with the development of Newtonian mechanics, Leibniz coined the term *dynamics* to characterize a theory of matter that emphasizes the force inherent in elements that are infinitely divisible; indeed, Leibniz equated material substance with force. In keeping with the phenomenal and contingent nature of mass in the science of dynamics, Leibniz also formulated a metaphysical doctrine of *immaterial* atoms—monads—that form the matrix of ordinary bodies but are not themselves bodies. Without entering the labyrinth of relations between Leibnizian physics and metaphysics, we should understand that the "Monadology" holds that material bodies are composed of immaterial elements—a paradoxical thesis that holds the key to modern conceptions of materiality. In 1755, under the influence of Leibniz, Kant published his own *Monadology*, a theory of infinitesimal point-atoms, which constitutes his most important work of physics. Several years after the publication of Kant's *Monadology*, Roger Boscovitch, a Jesuit mathematician from Croatia, published *A Theory of Natural Philosophy* (1758), in which, according to Edward MacKinnon, he developed "a theory of the atom as a point-center surrounded by alternating short-range repulsive and attractive force fields."[20] Boscovitch's point-atom anticipates in important respects the modern dispersion of the classical atom into fields of radiant energy, especially Kelvin's vortex model of the atom, formulated in 1867. Thus the historical sublimation of the atom, evolving from Lucretian and Newtonian particles to vortex rings (before it dissolved altogether in a sea of radiant energy), mirrors quite precisely the encroachment of incorporeal phenomena on the body of the Democritean atom.

Although it was still possible in 1890 to distinguish between matter and radiation, J. J. Thomson called the electron—essentially an electric charge—a "corpuscle." This designation revealed how the corpuscular model could be integrated into the investigation of the electrical properties of bodies, thereby superimposing the concepts of matter and radiant energy. In 1895, Wilhelm Ostwald (a Nobel Prize winner in 1908 and the first publisher of Wittgenstein's *Tractatus* on logical pictures in 1922) founded the energetics movement in physics, which sought to substitute energy for mass as the fundamental basis of physical theory. At the very moment when the existence of a subliminal entity resembling the atom was confirmed by Thomson's measurement of the unit electric charge, the corpuscular properties of the atom were submerged, or dispersed, in a field of incorporeal force. Thus, by the first decade of the twentieth century, the concept of radiation had supplanted mass as the essential ground of material substance.

This crucial development in scientific and philosophical materialism coincides historically with the emergence of modernism in literature and the arts. Only the corpuscularian hypothesis of phenomenal bodies composed of real, but imperceptible "elements" offers a vision of corporeality as utterly strange and counterintuitive as the modernist thesis that palpable bodies are composed of radiation. To make such a claim one must not only assume that the substance of corporeal bodies is explicable according to the discourse of incorporeals, but also be prepared to revive the paradoxical category of imponderable matter. Indeed, corporeality becomes equivalent to what was formerly regarded as an unstable and anomalous *medium* and, even more perversely, to phenomena entirely unknown and undetectable prior to 1890. The discourse of high Romanticism and Kant's "Copernican revolution" (our understanding of external reality is determined by inherent intellectual categories) come to mind as comparable moments of rupture in the humanities, yet perhaps only Berkeley's immaterialism (which holds that matter, as such, does not exist) matches, by its absolute rejection of modern physics, the perversity of the quantum hypothesis: bodies are composed of what history and intuitive experience regard as *nothing*.

The radioactive body—a revision of the doctrine of radiant species—and the concomitant medium of radiography signal fundamental changes in our notion of material substance. For the half-life of radioactive material often far exceeds the parameters of historical time, even as it infers, by its lethal effects, the principle of mortality. Further, since the half-life of a radioactive body may far exceed the duration of what we call "life"—like a god, it cannot be killed or eliminated— the radiant body functions at once as an emblem of immortality and, through the destructive effects on living flesh precipitated by its own decay, of ephemerality. Thus the half-life of radioactive bodies represents the animation of inert materials as well as the fatality of matter. Conceived in relation to visual culture, certain forms of radiation— the material medium of radiography, for example—extend the range of microscopic vision to the foundation of corporeal substance. Matter, already revealed by the microscope to be transparent,[21] becomes, under the gaze of radiography, as subtle and ethereal as the simulacra of atomist vision. More fundamentally, since radiation constitutes the only empirical evidence of the existence of atoms, it functions as a medium of perception or expression, coinciding with the residual *force* of the atom, which furnishes us with a "picture" of the interior of the atom. In this respect, radioactivity is the medium of objects (or substance) that we assume to be real but which remain, in the final analysis, hypothetical. In the world of intuitive bodies, however, the medium of perception (radiation) is also a destructive force that dematerializes the body as it brings to light, in an X-ray image, the hidden interior of the body.[22] According to the terms of radiant substance, therefore, the corporeal body coincides with the medium depicting its internal world and with a material force capable of decomposing the body. In this sense, the body is its own radiant image as well as the agency of its own disappearance.

If we regard the radiant body as the medium of perception-at-a-distance (the epistemological counterpart to the gravitational effects of action-at-a-distance), then the trope of radioactivity offers the most significant site of exchange between the discourse of materialism and the ideological construction of the modern technical media. Indeed, when we turn to the question of the how the modern physical doctrine of radiant bodies has been translated into social, historical, and imaginative reality, we find that the popular understanding of the physics of television, for example, conceives the transmission of subtle bodies in ways that are no less compelling than the models once furnished to corpuscularian philosophy by the discourses of pneumatic technology, meteorology, and animal magnetism. In the early part of the twentieth century, the discovery of radium (along with other radioactive substances) and the development of radiographic technology dominated the social and imaginative construction of radiant bodies. Later, the military applications of radar technology in World War I and, more important, the related development of the popular medium of radio in the 1920s significantly revised—and often politicized—the modern discourse of radiant bodies. Generally speaking, any development in media technology involving the irradiation and transmission of bodies adds a new chapter to the modern reformulation of the doctrine of radiant species.

FAIRYFLAKE

A small pre-Raphaelite with too much hair;
A Frankenstein of test tubes; a "refugee"—
A shaman full of secrets, who could touch
Physics with a wand and body forth
The universe's baby wrapped in stars.
From signs Phoenicians scratched upon the sand
With sticks he drew the contraries of space:
Whirlwind Nothing and Volume in its rage
Of matter racing to undermine itself,
And when the planets sang, why, he sang back
The lieder black holes secretly adore.

> *Howard Moss, "Einstein's Bathrobe"*

Poured on the stone block floor, these syllables
are barley groats I scatter on the reactor's core.

> *Allen Ginsberg, "Plutonian Ode"*

The social and imaginative construction of radiant bodies has been dominated since World War II by the threat of nuclear warfare and the iconography of the atomic bomb, beginning with the blast at Hiroshima and extending through the culture of the cold war period. No other vision of the radiant body so effectively discloses the inscrutable half-life of ordinary bodies, by evoking the traumatic and wondrous properties of radioactive substance. The discourse of the atomic bomb is especially germane to the imaginative and social materialization of radiant substance because it pertains directly to the enigmatic power of the atom and to the visualization of imperceptible phenomena, as well as to the simulation of events that strain comprehension. Indeed, at many levels of discourse, from *Look* magazine to civil defense films, from Hollywood science fiction movies to military strategy, one is confronted in the 1950s by an overriding need to *depict* the invisible medium of radiation, and to record its catastrophic effects on familiar objects (and animals), in order to simulate the possible fate of the human body in the event of a blast.

These manifestations of popular culture are only the most visible of various attempts to come to terms with the alterations of material substance implied by the development of the atomic bomb. American poetry of the postwar era has also produced its share of apocalyptic visions and poignant melodrama, but it offers in addition a more abstract—and ambivalent—response to the scientific and technological alienation of matter. Like journalism, government propaganda, and popular entertainment of the era, poetry bears witness to the mysterious and horrifying transformations of material substance staged in the prospect of a nuclear blast. In addition, like many of these sources, though more emphatically, poetry tends to place itself in ethical opposition to nuclear policy and, more directly, to the catastrophic effects of an atomic blast. In productions of this sort, the "gaze" of poetry, both imaginatively and ethically, does not differ significantly from other cultural sources of this era. A simple thematic reading of poems about atomic warfare or radioactive fallout therefore yields pictures of material substance that participate in a larger project of reimagining, and also preserving, the body. These pictures also yield evidence of a certain historical and imaginative continuity, extending from the meteoric body and the mesmerized body (the toy) to the radioactive body.

Postwar lyric departs, however, from the general tone of apprehension and horror in its willingness to identify with the imaginative power of science, which had formulated the conceptions of material substance rendered so thoroughly and vividly by the operation and aftereffects of the bomb. Lyric poetry of the 1950s covets the sublimity of radioactive substance precisely because it views radioactivity as an emblem of the lyrical body and as an inscription of its own imaginative powers. A number of extraordinary poems depict a struggle between physics and poetry for possession of the body—the radiant species— issuing from the apocalyptic climate of the bomb. By confounding lyric substance and radioactive substance, lyric poetry enters into a dangerously mimetic, yet historically authentic, rivalry with science over the disposition of materialism. In addition, however, there is a strain of "virtuosity" in modernist poetry that avoids entirely a confrontation over the radiant body of the atomic age and instead goes about its business of fashioning impossible creatures so finely observed, so lifelike, that one hesitates to call them unreal. The allegorical lyric of the modern "virtuoso" thereby discloses its affinity with scientific materialism—that is, with the lyricism of science. The poems I examine in the remainder of this study fall into three categories: poems addressing the theme of the atomic bomb; poems confounding lyric and radioactive substance, thereby disclosing the narcissism of the poet's relation to the physicist; and poems evoking by their "virtuosity" the method of natural philosophy (a talent for discerning and evoking invisible material worlds).

At all levels of the discourse on the atomic bomb, the compulsion to depict the invisible and destructive medium of radiation was coupled with a meditation on the nature of matter and ordinary bodies. The public obsession with radiation and its effects derived in part from the fact that this enigmatic power resides in the matter of everyday objects—indeed, in the ostensibly familiar substance of our own bodies. The discourse of the bomb and atomic power presents us with the idea of "an elemental but utterly alien force lurking in, and belonging to, the world's material foundations."[23] In the context of atomic power, therefore, ordinary material substance becomes fundamentally alienated from its intuitive existence, in a manner closely related to Marx's explanation of the dialectical materiality of Epicurean phenomenology. Conceived in nuclear terms, the substance of material bodies awakens to a monstrous, ulterior life utterly estranged from intuitive experience. In a poem called "New Dawn," for example, Robert Penn Warren writes,

> All harmless until, backed by vulgar explosive, the small will
> Crash through to
> The large mass
> To wake it from its timeless drowse. And that
> Will be that. Whatever
> *That* may be.[24]

In philosophical terms, the "That" awakened from "its timeless drowse" by a nuclear detonation is nothing other than the abstract life of the body posited by atomist doctrine and the premises of scientific materialism. What the discourse of the bomb reveals is the traumatic (and also wondrous) character of abstraction worked on the body by philosophical materialism—a metaphysical disturbance we have already observed in the increasingly traumatic representations of dolls and automata in modern culture. Indeed, taking into account certain definitions formulated by the emerging discourse of "trauma studies," one could regard the phantasmic body of scientific materialism and the iconography of the bomb during the cold war as textbook illustrations of mass trauma: "To be traumatized is precisely to be possessed by an image."[25]

In popular culture of the 1950s, the slumbering, alien life of material substance found expression in motion pictures as a retinue of radioactive creatures and dinosaurs—a monstrous birth first realized in *The Beast from 20,000 Fathoms,* a film released by Warner Brothers in 1953. It is significant, in this film, that the monster dislodged from the Arctic ice by an American atomic bomb test is not a new form of life but a creature released from a state of suspended animation. Thus, as Alexander Hammond explains, the movie depicts "the release of a primal force of nature long frozen in the unmelted structure of matter—a force that, once released, threatens mass destruction and radioactive poisoning."[26] This black and white, low-budget film established a distinct and enduring topos in science fiction film, extending from Warner Brothers' *Them!* of 1954 (depicting "giant ants springing out of the first atomic bomb test site to threaten Los Angeles") to the reconstituted dinosaurs of *Jurassic Park.*

In the shadow of the atomic blast, material substance assumes a metamorphic character not only in general terms but also in the brooding and meteoric life of mundane objects. In a world of "atomic hazards," objects and bodies tremble at the brink of annihilation; yet even survival in the aftermath of a blast implies alteration and improvisation. The government spokesman in a 1954 civil defense film, for example, schools the anxious (but resourceful!) viewer in the event of catastrophe: "Every milkman knows his truck can become an ambulance."[27] The prospect of an atomic blast causes every object to oscillate not only between divergent identities, or between presence and absence, but also, as W. H. Auden conceives it, between object and image, real and unreal:

> But this Horror starting already to scratch Its way in?
> Just how, just when It succeeded we shall never know . . .
> For nothing like It has happened before. It's as if
> We had left our house for five minutes to mail a letter,
> And during that time the living room had changed places

With the room behind the mirror over the fireplace;
It's as if, waking up with a start, we discovered
Ourselves stretched out flat on the floor, watching our shadow
Sleepily stretching itself at the window. I mean
That the world of space where events re-occur is still there
Only now, it's no longer real; the real one is nowhere . . .
I mean that although there's a person we all know about
Still bearing our name and loving himself as before,
That person has become a fiction.[28]

It is no accident that the lyric poet is drawn to the apocalyptic climate of atomic reality, in which ponderable bodies remain—and remain to be seen—yet are nothing more than anomalous or radiant species. For the inherent instability and ephemerality of the lyric object corresponds precisely to the catastrophic and labile body conjured in the shadow of the bomb and, more fundamentally, to the alien, pictorial body issuing from the lawful speculation of atomism and elaborated by scientific materialism. In a poem titled "The Fundamental Project of Technology," Galway Kinnell represents the body in the spellbinding "climate" of the bomb as a lyrical medium bridging the natural and the supernatural. At the site of the Hiroshima memorial in Japan, the poet writes,

Unlike the trees of home, which continually evaporate
along the skyline, the trees here have been enticed down
toward world-eternity. No one knows which gods they enshrine.
Does it matter?[29]

Kinnell plays on the materiality of objects in the theater of the bomb by contrasting the "trees of home," which merely "evaporate," with the trees at the site of the blast, which become like ghosts or shrines to unknown gods. Yet *evaporation* is precisely the fate of trees and bodies at ground zero; so perhaps the familiar trees of home are not so far removed from the trees "enticed down" to the nether world by memories, or perhaps by the lure of the bomb itself. In this memorialized place, wonder and trauma coincide in the lyric body of the atomic age. And although the discourse of the bomb seems far removed from the toys and emblems of mechanical philosophy, the intrinsic ambiguity of the nuclear body, suspended between the visible and the invisible, reiterates the uncanny effect of the automaton veering between nature and illusion, truth and fiction. The radioactive body is thus a crucial emblem not only of modern materialism but also of lyric poetry.

The impulse to depict the invisible medium of nuclear reality, to represent the radiant climate of the bomb, found expression in the United States in a massive project of simulation—manifest at all levels of discourse—that began less than three months after the bombing of Hiroshima on August 6, 1945. In Los Angeles, a nighttime "Tribute to Victory" took place in the Coliseum on October 26, 1945. Here is part of the *Los Angeles Times*'s account of "the gigantic show arranged by the motion picture industry":

> One of the most impressive effects of the program was a demonstration of the atomic bomb. . . . At a signal, a low-flying B-29 skimmed over the bowl, the multicolored searchlight beams tinting its gleaming silver with pastels. As the big bomber roared over the peristyle, a terrific detonation shook the ground, a burst of flame flashed on the field and great billows of smoke mushroomed upward in an almost too-real depiction of devastation. As the smoke snaked skyward, red and blue lights played over the white column with magic effectiveness.[30]

Although this early simulation of an atomic blast hinted at the "devastation" associated with Hiroshima—an image "almost too real" for the crowd—its primary task, accomplished with "magic effectiveness," was to superimpose the American colors on the fresh icon of the mushroom cloud. In addition, however, this nocturnal spectacle of a stadium shrouded in smoke and illumined by searchlights calls to mind the images produced by Wigman and Riefenstahl at the Berlin Olympics only nine years earlier—a pyrotechnic feat that evoked the radiant species of the atomic age.

By the early 1950s, however, the nation was hungry for images of devastation—not of Japan or the Soviet Union, but of the American landscape. Mass spectacle gave way to vividly illustrated articles in popular magazines depicting not only the blast but also its possible effects. The cover story for *Collier's* on 5 August 1950 evoked the prospect of "Hiroshima U.S.A." and calculated the effects of an atomic attack on New York City. An even more elaborate scenario appeared in *Collier's* on 27 October 1951, in a piece titled "Preview of the War We Do Not Want: Russia's Defeat and Occupation, 1952–1956." On 21 April 1953, several months prior to the release of *The Beast From 20,000 Fathoms, Look* published yet another preview of apocalypse, "How Hellish Is the H-Bomb?" Like many of these popular features, it portrays the possible effects of an attack on New York City. The illustrations for these articles (many produced by the same artist, Chesley Bonestell) call to mind the pyrotechnic events staged for the 1936 Olympics and for the postwar Victory Day celebration in Los Angeles. As icons of materiality, then, these illustrations record the permutations of the meteoric body in the atomic age.

The project of visualizing an unseen force and simulating its catastrophic effects emerged with greater realism and complexity in the propaganda and informational films produced in the 1950s by the federal government and the military for purposes of civil defense. (Many of these films appeared after, and perhaps in response to, the release of *The Beast from 20,000 Fathoms.*) These civil defense films addressed in detail a variety of survival tactics to be used in the event of "enemy attack." To make their point as graphically as possible, they also frequently included documentary coverage of atomic bomb tests and various "experiments" conducted in conjunction with the blasts. In addition, several of the films stressed the avid media coverage of the test blasts and the spectacular character of these events: "On the morning of shot day, observers gather at 'news knob' to await the momentous

Figure 16.   Illustration of New York City incinerated by a hydrogen bomb. From "How Hellish Is the H-Bomb?" *Look,* 21 April 1953.

event"; "To give us a ringside view of the event, high speed cameras stand like lonely sentinels, ready to photograph the hurricane of fury."[31] One commentator notes that the blast will be broadcast "coast to coast" from "media hill"—the observation area set aside for journalists.[32] The spokesman for *United States Civil Defense in Action* calls for the immediate formation of a volunteer "ground observer corps," meeting the need for "500,000 pair of trained eyes to continuously scan our skies" for signs of enemy attack.

All these films stress the need for citizens to view "the drama of people learning how to protect themselves in realistic exercises"; one commentator declares, "Survival is your business."[33] It gradually becomes evident, however, that the emphasis in these films on visualization, as well as the exhortations to witness and participate in simulations of disaster, is intended to overcome a powerful *resistance* to visualization in the viewer (the dialectical counterpart of a need to depict the invisible). At the conclusion of one film, a government spokesman exhorts, "Let us recognize the threat to our way of life, the threat to our survival: Let's face it!" The voiceover is accompanied by a special effects shot of a scattered crowd of silhouette figures witnessing a glowing mushroom cloud in the distance.[34] Thus, in all of these films, a tension develops between the compulsive visuality of the event and the sense that one is witnessing something unspeakable— that one should *not* be watching. In other words, knowledge of the invisible medium and its lethal effects is at once ethically contaminated—"evil" is not too strong a word for it—and necessary for "survival." At the same time, knowledge of the catastrophic medium and event can only be had through *pictures*—for, as one commentator puts it, "Should there be a real atomic attack, there will be no spectators."[35] Thus, like our knowledge of the subliminal world of atoms—though with greater personal, social, and political implication—our knowledge of the invisible world of nuclear disaster depends on pictures. Moreover, the conditions requiring these simulations and our close attention now constitute a permanent state of alert: "Civil defense is a

fact, not a plan—a permanent part of our daily life."[36] Another com-
mentator calls the simulations of civil defense "a forceful reality."[37]
Hence the invisible world of nuclear disaster, like the modern thesis
of radiant substance, becomes, through representational practice,
through pictures, a real part of psychological, social, and historical
existence. At the same time, natural intuition of palpable and objective
bodies persists, so that one's sense of corporeality veers between the
mundane presence of things and a vision of bodies consumed by ra-
diation, between fact and fiction.

The tension between simulation and reality (and we should note:
simulation, in the context of the bomb, pertains to the visible world
and reality to the invisible world) figures prominently in the films'
commentary on these "tests": "Only in practice now, a rehearsal, a
training exercise, but tomorrow this siren may mean the real thing—
what will you do? What will happen to *you?*"[38] As this warning in-
dicates, to witness or participate in simulations of nuclear "fury" im-
plies that we imagine our own possible extinction or survival, or that
we might somehow, by watching or performing, influence our own
fate and possibly the fate of others as well.

Postwar American poets who are attentive to the bomb often iso-
late—and demonstrate in their poetic practice—the logic of simula-
tion and spectacle intrinsic to nuclear reality. William Stafford, for
example, calls an atomic test blast in the desert

> something farther off
> than people could see, an important scene
> acted in stone for little selves
> at the flute end of consequences.[39]

The observer, "at the flute end of consequences," also knows that any
object placed in proximity to a test blast, appearing in the "scene" for
purposes of simulation, anticipates the fate of his or her own body in
the event of a real blast. What happens to the "test residence" built in
harm's way, and all of its pristine furnishings, illustrates or prefigures

the fate of one's own body, as well as the hypothesis of radiant sub-
stance.

Galway Kinnell, in his poem set in a memorial museum in Hiro-
shima, calls the simulacral strategies of the nuclear age "the mecha-
nisms of *pseudologica fantastica*." The poem begins by surveying the
relics of the blast on display:

> Under glass, glass dishes which changed
> in color; pieces of transformed beer bottles;
> a household iron; bundles of wire become solid
> lumps of iron; a pair of pliers; a ring of skull-
> bone fused to the inside of a helmet; a pair of eyeglasses
> taken off the eyes of an eyewitness, without glass,
> which vanished, when a white flash sparkled.[40]

Beyond the altered, yet still familiar objects, and beyond the vanished
eyes of the spectator (who saw nothing—only the spectacles survived),
looms the figure of the radiant body: the body whose radiant and
volatile substance is disclosed only by a nuclear event, the body dis-
appearing in the catastrophic medium of the atom.

The iconography of the fate of material bodies in the Hiroshima
blast is dominated by two figures: the "vaporized" human body and
the permanent, palpable shadows imprinted by the radiant force of
the blast. William Dickey, in a poem about the difficulty and necessity
of imagining atomic reality, distills the chiasmic relation of bodies and
shadows in the Hiroshima blast:

> The picture that is in my mind
> is of people, vaporized by an unexpected sun
> and only their shadows left burned into the wall behind them.[41]

Inevitably, this scene calls to mind the chiasmus of bodies and pictures
spelled out in advance for modernity by the doctrine of radiant species,
yet Dickey's "picture" rests on solid ground. Any compilation of pho-
tographs of the Hiroshima or Nagasaki disasters usually includes sev-

eral images of material shadows imprinted on stone bridges, metal storage tanks, and other structures, and occasionally the stone shadow of a vanished human body. In addition, Dickey's term "vaporize" is authentic, since Japanese eyewitnesses and later historians too adopted this verb to describe the fate of bodies close enough to ground zero to vanish with the blast—though of course it would be impossible for anyone to witness and survive such an event. Nuclear reality, like the subliminal world of atoms, has no spectators, though it is entirely constituted by pictures. We should also note that vaporization is a phenomenon associated with pneumatics and meteorology, and that by describing the disappearing substance of bodies in this manner, we link the radiant body of nuclear catastrophe to the philosophy of "meteors" and to the symptoms of "vapors" associated with animal magnetism. The idea of a material shadow would also, of course, find a place in the discourse of subtle bodies.

Several of the U.S. civil defense films devote considerable attention to the artificial environments and "test cities" constructed at the blast sites of the Eniwetok atoll in the South Pacific and in the Nevada desert. The civil defense spokesman in *Let's Face It* reveals that scientists and government officials had hopes for "construction of a complete city at our Nevada test site, but such a gigantic undertaking is not feasible." The viewer then sees, imposed on the film's photographic image of the desert landscape, a drawing of an imaginary city, which slowly vanishes as a real mushroom cloud from a blast rises in the background. Instead of the annihilation of a full-scale city, however, officials must settle for "representative units of a test city, built as though it were to last a thousand years"—meaning that the "test city" will be entirely authentic in every detail, though its generous thousand-year warranty inadvertently calls to mind the recently vanquished Third Reich. The announcer confides, "It's a weird, fantastic city, a creation right out of science fiction, a city like no other on the face of the Earth: homes, neat and clean, and completely furnished, that will never be occupied; railway tracks that lead to nowhere, for this is the

Figure 17.   Meteors in the atomic age: rainbow over Panmunjom, South Korea, November 1951. Courtesy United Press International.

end of the line." Among the "experimental elements being assembled" at the bomb site are a fleet of "test cars" (with numerals painted on them for identification), "samples of clothing," and a "synthetic forest" (real pine trees erected in the desert sand). In addition, the viewer glimpses female mannequins being loaded into the test cars.

Another film, *Operation Cue* (1954), focuses on the domestic side of radioactive fallout—"a test of the things we use and live with." The film's announcer, a female "reporter," guides us through the "test houses," stocked with brand new televisions and "household furnishings complete in every detail." She notes the "testing of textiles and synthetic fabrics" and "the food test program" (including a large box of brand-name foods, labeled "Grandma's Pantry: Food for a Family of Four"). She also confides, "As a mother and housewife, this appealed to me." In addition, our female guide takes a special interest in the "rows of mannequins lined up out in the open facing the blast, each item of clothing and each color carefully selected to give vital information." She explains that, inside the test houses, the "mannequin families represent Mr. and Mrs. America" (with large ID tags around their necks), though she also comments on the "mannequins sitting around so indifferently." And in the anxious moments leading up to the blast, she observes, "the test objects waited" in the silent desert.

After watching the elaborate preparations at the test site, the viewer of *Operation Cue* is treated to documentary film images of the dolls, houses, and synthetic forest weathering the actual blast and crumbling in its radiant climate, whose lethal effects are abetted by high winds and other atmospheric conditions. (In this respect, the bomb itself has a place in the philosophy of meteors.) Some twenty-four hours after the blast, our female "reporter" is permitted to return to ground zero. She inspects the surviving dolls and asks the viewer, "Do you remember this young lady? and this young man? See how the blast charred and faded his new blue suit." She also notices a "tattoo" left on the female doll's leg by her dress print.

The civil defense administrator of *Let's Face It* is more didactic— and abstract—in his commentary on the "debris and devastation." Prior to the blast, witnessing the army of tradesmen building the test city, he predicts, "Every brick, beam, and board will have its story to tell. When pieced together, these will give some of the answers, some of the information, we need to survive in the nuclear age." And, indeed, in the aftermath of the blast, he confirms and elaborates the textual analogy of the ruins: "Every bit of twisted steel makes its contribution; blackened ruins and ashes of a structure add another chapter; the shattered wreckage of a dwelling offers an eloquent testimonial. Piece by piece, like the parts of a jigsaw puzzle, our story is assembled, analyzed, and evaluated." Each dwelling, each and every object, each mannequin, contains a secret divulged only by the blast, by the object's partial or complete disintegration. These ruined elements, which stand for our bodies, are assembled as parts of a puzzle, and read like hieroglyphs, to tell the story of an invisible world accessible only through the models we build of it—a hermeneutical framework that reinscribes the Lucretian analogy of atomic bodies composed of textual elements.

Ostensibly, then, the purpose of witnessing the destruction of these artificial cities and their population of life-size dolls is to learn something about the material fate of things—and indeed the fate of materiality—in the nuclear age. A stentorian voice at the conclusion of *Let's Face It* observes, "The imprint left by the hurricane of fire and blast remains here for us to read and analyze. From studies of ruins and damage such as this, we get the hard-to-come-by knowledge that helps us form rules for survival in modern warfare." Inserted into an archaeological model of deciphering relics of ancient civilizations, these incinerated structures are in reality the ruins of the future. Hence there is a sense in which these toy cities are effigies, elaborately mounted and then sacrificed in order that we may avoid their fate. For it is quite obvious that these toy worlds were built as pictures of an invisible world, a world that is at once the prospect of nuclear disaster and an illustration of the atomist doctrine of radiant substance—both of which constitute a kind of metaphysical trauma. Just as our knowledge of the subliminal world of atoms is confined to pictures, so it must be possible to control the fate of bodies conceived in this manner by constructing other kinds of pictures, no less magical than the automata and meteoric bodies of corpuscularian philosophy. Indeed, the apocalyptic simulations of destruction in the 1950s, like all the other pictures associated with atomism, mediate between visible and invisible worlds, between intuitive and subliminal bodies.

Postwar lyric, as we have seen, illuminates but also implicates itself in the logic of simulation associated with the bomb. William Dickey's poem "Armageddon," for example, oscillates between "The possibility of absence / so complete we will hardly have known what absence was" and his need "to form images / to imagine the happening."[42] The poem begins with the assertion, "I see it in terms of images," yet soon declares, "It will not be like this." The alternation of vision and blindness shapes the poet's apprehension of the invisible world of "incident" and apocalypse.

The incommensurability of atomic events, and the relation of pictures to the looming absence of nuclear bodies, claim our attention more obliquely in a poem by Hans Magnus Enzenberger, who regards the dialectic of visible and invisible as a tension between "the category of totality" and the "important happenings" of intuition and mundane reality:

> Between the distant causes
> and the distant effects
> a hair
> glowing on the pillow.
>
> Some kind of imperialism
> dominates.
> The lichen at the doorpost
> survives.[43]

In his view, a form of "domination" distinct from that of the invisible, rooted in ephemerality, emerges through these details, which are radiant (and painful) in their own right:

> How invincible
> the toothache
> which abruptly at night
> illuminates me.

Yet the relation between lyric poetry and the radiant medium of apocalypse offers more than testimony to horrific events and an apology for intuition and the ephemeral body. The postwar American lyric poet is likely not only to contrast the physicist and the poet but also to find in the architect of modern physics a narcissistic image of his own lyric vocation. In addition, there is a distinct tendency in the poetry of this period to confound lyric substance (or some notion of the essence of poetry) with the phantasmagorical—and destructive—character of radioactive substance. The confrontation between lyric poetry and the fatalities of nuclear physics is imagined by Richard Wilbur, for example, in terms of the poet's resistance to the abstractions of an apocalyptic "prophet."[44] Gary Snyder, in two poems written about the same time as Wilbur's, depicts this polarity largely in terms of the territories occupied by two adversarial figures, the naturalist and the fighter pilot. In a poem called "Strategic Air Command," he divides the world into two realms, but he inverts the values assigned to these "elements" by Wallace Stevens:

> These cliffs and the stars
> Belong to the same universe.
> The little air in between
> Belongs to the twentieth century and its wars.[45]

Between the realms of heaven and earth is the realm of meteors, which Snyder in another poem ("Vapor Trails") calls the "field of all future war."[46] Evidently, Snyder equates the theater of atomic warfare with what he calls "the air world torn and staggered" by the "white blossoming smoke of bomb." The earthbound poet, by contrast, estranged from the realm of vapor trails and meteoric blossoms, directs his attention to patterns discernible in less volatile things:

> I stumbled on the cobble rock path
> Passing through temples,
> Watching for two-leaf pine
> —spotting that design.[47]

Yet the poet's delineation of two antithetical realms may not be as firm as it appears. For the poet's song—the lyric "air"—cannot be entirely dissociated from the realm of meteors, from what Snyder calls "the little air" between the cliffs and the stars.

The submerged relation between poet and physicist figures directly in a poem by Howard Moss, in which he stages an illicit embrace at dawn between Albert Einstein and the poet-ephebe:

> The Dawn took the horizon by surprise
> And from the marsh long, crayoned birds
> Rose up, ravens, maybe crows, or raw-voiced,
> Spiteful grackles with their clothespin legs,
> Black-winged gossips rising out of the mud
> And clattering into sleep. They woke my master
> While, in the dark, I waited, knowing
> Sooner or later he'd reach for me
> And, half asleep, wriggle into my arms.[48]

The poet calls Einstein "my master," perhaps in part because the physicist is awakened by birds "rising out of the mud / And clattering into sleep"—that is, by birdsong (however dreadful) translated from mud into dreams, from material substance into pictures. Yet the poet-ephebe knows of the physicist's secret longing and has only to wait for his advances in the "oblique light" of dawn. In the academic world of Princeton, where the poem is set, the physicist may be called "master," yet in the boudoir mastery lies with the poet, whom the physicist desires and embraces. Viewed from the perspective of philosophical materialism, mastery lies with the poet because the lyric poet is the ancient master of metaphor and image, the medium into which the nuclear physicist must translate his calculations of material substance in order to satisfy the demands of realism.

Moss's poem troubles and elaborates the tension between the abstract "secrets" of modern physics and various emblems of domesticity (such as Einstein's bathrobe): "In old slippers, he'd bumble down the stairs. / Genius is human and wants its coffee hot." At the core of this tension is the essential duplicity of any object once it becomes the property of physics or lyric poetry:

I was completely charmed. And fooled.
What a false view of the universe *I* had!
The horsehair sofa, the sagging chairs,
A fire roaring behind the firescreen—
Imagine thinking Princeton was the world!

Somewhat disingenuously, the poet here discounts the world of ordinary perception, corresponding to his youthful fascination with Einstein's domestic and academic circumstance, in favor of the other universe conjured by Einstein's theorems. In reality, the poet believes, "Greenwich and Palomar saw eye to eye"—that is, the poetic experiments associated with Greenwich Village and the astrophysics conducted at the Mount Palomar observatory inhabit the same visionary ("eye to eye") universe. We should therefore be wary of the poet's apparent disavowal or disenchantment of the domestic universe, since the poem's central feature is its elaboration of a personal possession, Einstein's bathrobe. All the same, the old man's bathrobe, in the hands of the poet, is anything but ordinary:

I wove myself of many delicious strands
Of violet islands and sugar balls of thread
So faintly green a small white check between
Balanced the field's wide lawn, a plaid
Gathering in loose folds shaped around him.

Here, in the opening lines of the poem, the poet reveals that *he* is the weaver of Einstein's robe and, more profoundly, that his own poetic text is woven of the same substance as the physicist's robe. And indeed the ethereal substance of Einstein's robe, which evokes the corporeal tunic of atomic vision, defies intuition by its metamorphic and phantasmagorical character. This shimmering garment, composed of "violet islands and sugar balls of thread," calls to mind the "airy semblance" of the radiant species, even as it appears to transform itself and disclose "the field's wide lawn." What's more, Einstein's lawn, appearing for a moment on the screen of his robe, may be also the invisible "field" of wave-theory in physics. And that ambiguity is intrinsic to any object woven of the substance of Einstein's robe.

The image of Einstein's robe in Moss's poem can almost certainly be traced to Wallace Stevens's poetic meteorology, which includes a garment he calls "a robe of rays,"[49] whose radiance is an effect of its meteoric properties:

> This robe of snow and winter stars,
> The devil take it, wear it, too.
> It might become his hole of blue.
>   *("Snow and Stars," 133)*

Snow and stars (and color) combine to make a garment that is almost nothing (it is a "hole"). Elsewhere, the robe retains its blue color, but the weave becomes ever more complex—and moody—in "The Man with the Blue Guitar":

> The color like a thought that grows
> Out of a mood, the tragic robe
>
> Of the actor, half his gesture, half
> His speech, the dress of his meaning, silk
>
> Sodden with his melancholy words,
> The weather of his stage, himself.   *(169–70)*

The robe in this passage mingles thought and gesture, the substance of the actor's trade, his speech, until it cannot be distinguished, as in Moss's poem, from the weather or the artist himself.

The meteoric dissolution (or animation) of the robe reaches its limit in a poem by Stevens called "The Dwarf":

> The web is woven and you have to wear it.
>
> The winter is made and you have to bear it,
> The winter web, the winter woven, wind and wind, . . .

It is the mind that is woven . . .
And tufted in straggling thunder and shattered sun.

It is all that you are, the final dwarf of you,
That is woven and woven and waiting to be worn,

Neither as mark nor as garment but as a being. *(208)*

Composed of "straggling thunder and shattered sun," the substance of the "winter web" can no longer be distinguished from the mind itself. The woven thing is no longer only a mask or a garment: it is "a being." This development fulfills what is implicit in the earlier poems: the robe is a *double* (like the snow man), an image of the "devil" and the "actor"—figures closely related in Stevens's poetry to the "virtuoso." In "The Dwarf," the doubling process takes another turn: the robe becomes "the final dwarf of you," an image resembling a cadaver. In addition, the "dwarf of you" calls to mind the figures of the toy and the automaton, replicas made of the same meteoric substance from which the mind is woven.

A recent poem by David St. John, titled "Merlin," identifies more explicitly the properties of a garment whose phantasmagorical texture coincides with the substance of things:

His chameleon robe, draped casually, hieroglyphics
Passing over it as across a movie screen, odd formulas
Projected endlessly—its elaborate layers of
Embroidery depicting impossible mathematical equations;
Stitched along the hem, the lyrics
Of every song one hears the nightingale sing.[50]

Once again, but with greater relevance to the modern technical media, we encounter the idea of a garment—which is itself essentially a moving picture—whose ambiguous substance not only depicts but embodies "impossible mathematical equations." Merlin's robe also displays, quite literally, the essential proximity of lyric (the nightingale's song) and mathematical hypothesis, as well as the corresponding palimpsest of arcane notational systems obscuring and partially succeeding one another on the screen. In addition, St. John's portrait of Merlin's robe (which functions as a double of Merlin himself) renders more explicitly than Stevens's or Moss's poems the figure of the "virtuoso"—the savant whose investigations pertain to both art and science.[51] The figure of Einstein's or Merlin's robe—the esoteric body—succeeds the archaic figure of the virtuoso of early microscopy, whose virtuosity consisted not in flawless or prodigious technique (as modern usage dictates) but in a talent for looking, for collecting and classifying. The virtuoso is at once curious and erudite, but also visionary, for virtuosity in the microscopist involves discerning the true features of the invisible world, as well as depicting what one sees through the lens. (No one is quite sure, for example, how Leeuwenhoek managed to execute his drawings of transient phenomena and animalcula, which traverse the visual field of the microscope with extreme rapidity.) In the end, Einstein's robe, whether we regard it as a text or a picture or both, reveals itself to be an emblem not only of virtuosity, but also of material substance conceived as an effect of virtuosity.

Howard Moss, as I suggested earlier, is not alone in portraying the physicist as an alter ego of the poet—though in other cases the relation is often more polarized and the hostility more pronounced. Gregory Corso, for example, in his poem "Bomb," refers to the elect of modern physics as "the pimps of indefinite weather"; yet he also discerns in them a sense of estrangement that is not altogether removed from the allure and myth of the Beat poet:

Oppenheimer is seated
in the dark pocket of light
Fermi is dry in Death's Mozambique
Einstein his mythmouth
a barnacled wreath.[52]

Allen Ginsberg, in "Plutonian Ode," also seizes the chance to name names and to bring the person of the physicist—the poet's evil twin—

before us. Further, he describes the radioactive element of plutonium as "a modern epic, detonative, Scientific theme / First penned unmindful by Doctor Seaborg with poisonous hand."[53] Although the poet and the physicist in these lines are both writers in some sense, and hence appear to share a common medium, the physicist inscribes the "new element" with "poisonous hand." In addition to drawing a somewhat ambiguous contrast between poet and physicist, the speaker of the "Plutonian Ode" clearly and repeatedly portrays the "new element" as a "Radioactive Nemesis" to lyric—"a matter that renders Self oblivion!" (702) Yet this antithetical relation is also a contest, and the ode is quite plainly an attempt to *master* the new element:

> Manufactured Spectre
> of human reason! O solidified imago of practitioners in Black
>   Arts
> I dare your Reality, I challenge your very being! I publish your
>   cause and effect.   *(703)*

Because the radioactive element is not only a "spectre" but also an "imago"—that is to say, a *picture*—the poet is prompted to challenge the "poisonous hand" of the physicist and to *reinscribe* in a poem the "imago" of the new element.

The voice of the "Plutonian Ode" repeatedly claims to speak on behalf of the "mute" element: "My oratory advances on your vaunted Mystery! . . . I sing your form at last" (703). Further, the poet declares

> O density! This weightless anthem trumpets transcendent through
>   hidden chambers and breaks through iron doors into the infer-
>   nal room!
> . . . I call your name with hollow vowels, I psalm your fate close
>   by, my breath near deathless ever at your side
> to spell your destiny . . . O doomed Plutonium   *(704)*

Despite the ostensible contrast between the "density" of radioactive matter and the weightlessness of lyric, this confrontation in the reactor's core suggests that the lyric element ("near deathless ever at your side") has somehow assumed the interminable "half-life" of radioactive substance. The "weightless anthem" appears to penetrate the iron doors in a manner that resembles, but also exceeds, the character of radiation. In several other passages, this "epic" confrontation appears to signal the "awakening" of matter and, ultimately, the mingling of the two elements: "Enter my body or not I carol my spirit inside you, Unapproachable Weight, / O heavy heavy Element awakened I vocalize your consciousness" (703). Indeed, belying the superficial antithesis of radioactive and poetic substances, the poet declares to his nemesis: "I enter your secret places with my mind, I speak with your presence" (703). Of course, the history of atomism also concerns the mind's ability to "enter the secret places" of the physical world and to depict the invisibility of matter. Ginsberg's equation of radioactive and poetic substances emphasizes the traumatic (and mysterious) effects of the abstracting power of lyric, thereby recalling Shelley's antithetical determination of poetry as "preserver and destroyer" of life as we know it intuitively. In addition, the destructive implications of a poetics of radiation are plainly at odds with the poet's superficial opposition to the bomb on humanitarian grounds. A poetics of radiant substance, like the corpuscularian doctrine of scientific materialism, thus appears to be implicated in a profoundly antihumanistic, and perhaps essentially theological, vision of the material body. For the lyric body of the radiant species can be visible only to the eyes of God—or to the mechanical and electronic "eyes" of the new media.

Clearly, the poet believes that the metaphysical crisis of the atomic age calls for extreme measures: the poet must give free rein to the "destructive" and metamorphic character of lyric to counteract (through incorporation) the prospect of annihilation inherent in the atom. That is to say, Ginsberg appears to believe that only poetry can challenge the metaphysics of the bomb—by becoming the bomb. Ginsberg's elaboration of what Joseph Conrad called the "destructive element" of literary form reflects the adversarial and critical nature of Beat poetics. In this sense, a poetics of radioactive substance gives new life to the essential negativity of the historical avant-garde.

Although it is important to emphasize the particular contribution of Beat poetry—a belated avant-garde—in the formation of a cultural poetics of radiation, the correspondence of radioactive and lyric substances does not always entail the kind of "epic" confrontation staged by Ginsberg. Indeed, the principle of polarity, which is essential to this correspondence, can be handled in a way that allows the poem to become the medium for a more humanistic—and more tenuous—encounter between incommensurable substances. For example, a poem by C. K. Williams called "Tar" deals with the prospect of radioactive fallout in the aftermath of the Three Mile Island incident in Pennsylvania. In the poem's opening lines, the narrator quickly establishes the purgatorial condition of things (and people) in proximity to the incident: "The first morning of Three Mile Island: those first disquieting, uncertain, mystifying hours."[54] Further, what he calls "the terror of that time, the reflexive disbelief and distancing" (48) stems in part from not knowing what is happening: "After half a night of listening to the news . . . we still know less than nothing" (47).

In this scene of apprehension and distraction (akin, perhaps, to the mystery brewing in the reactor's core in "Plutonian Ode"), the poet's attention fastens on a crew of "roofers" working throughout the day on his house. In his description of this task, which takes up the better part of the poem, the narrator focuses on the roofers' trade, on the material they use (tar), and on the chthonic aspect of their appearance. The speaker remarks "what brutal work it is, how matter-of-factly and harrowingly dangerous" (47), and comments that "the materials are bulky and recalcitrant." Gradually, it becomes evident that the speaker's fascination with the roofers' practice evokes the laborious (and arcane) features of the poet's craft, and that he envisions the workers in a scene charged with imaginative energy: "The enormous sky behind them, the heavy noontime air alive with shimmers and mirages" (48).

Even as the roofers' labor acquires a heroic and sometimes lyrical quality, it also begins to appear in a more sinister and alien light. There is something grotesque about the workers, and this quality stems directly from the material they use:

> In its crucible, the stuff looks bland, like licorice, spill it, though,
>   on your boots or coveralls,
> it sears, and everything is permeated with it . . .
> the men themselves so completely slashed and mucked
>   they seem almost from another realm, like trolls.   *(48)*

As the poet conceives it, tar is an element belonging to an infernal realm. Out of the "little furnace" that boils the tar,

> a dense, malignant smoke shoots up, someone has to fiddle with a
>   cock, hammer it,
> before the gush and stench will deintensify, the dark, Dantean
>   broth wearily subside.   *(48)*

Through the "malignant" qualities of this element, the inferno inhabited by the roofers begins to suggest the nuclear disaster brewing on the speaker's horizon at Three Mile Island. Further, in this sense, the roofers can be seen as poets from hell: inhabitants, but also creators, of an infernal realm that is both like and unlike the speaker's world.

This sense of a world hovering on the brink of transformation— at once entirely mundane and utterly strange—is distilled in the material substance of tar. This enigmatic and hideous substance not only produces the world of "mirages," it holds the secret of its annihilation. In the end, the speaker calls to mind

the men, silvered with glitter from the shingles, clinging like star-
lings beneath the eaves.
Even the leftover carats of tar in the gutter, so black they seemed
to suck the light out of the air.
By nightfall kids had come across them: every sidewalk on the
block was scribbled with obscenities and hearts. *(49)*

In this moment of transformation, the roofers become songbirds (or,
indeed, creatures like angels)—though it is perhaps Hardy's "darkling
thrush," rather than Shelley's skylark, that they most resemble. In
addition, the "carats" of mutable substance are at once precious (like
the silver flecking the roofers' wings) and lethal (like a radioactive
isotope) in their capacity to rob the "air" (the song) of light. Yet from
the darkness created in its own image, the tar provides material for
the scribbling of hearts and obscenities. The tar becomes a material
medium suspended between its magical and lethal effects, between
lyric and radiation.

The metamorphic aspect of Williams's lyric—its discovery of
beauty in the most sinister materials—also characterizes Gregory
Corso's poem "Bomb." Corso orchestrates a related scene of consub-
stantiation—the poem is seduced by radiation (like "Plutonian Ode"),
yet in this case, lyric surrenders to the *charm* of the bomb. In the ludic
device of the bomb—"Impish death Satyr Bomb"—the toy medium
of lyric discovers a reflection of itself.[55] Corso calls the bomb "Toy of
universe" and, in a trope that conflates the atom and the atomic bomb,
a "fairyflake" (65). He also proclaims the bomb's turbulence—its me-
teoric properties—by invoking the "lyric hat of Mister Thunder"; and
he celebrates its antic fatality, calling it "Death's Jubilee" and "a piece
of heaven":

The stars a swarm of bees in thy binging bag
    Stick angels on your jubilee feet. *(66)*

At the same time, drawing on the idea that atomic energy slumbers in the ordinary substance of nature, Corso repeatedly forces the bomb to "frolic zig and zag"—to represent nature in a scene possessed by the history of lyric:

> O Spring Bomb
> Come with thy gown of dynamite green
> unmenace nature's inviolate eye
> Before you the wimpled Past
> behind you the hallooing Future O Bomb
> Bound in the grassy clarion air.   *(66)*

The Green World of the bomb implies, of course, the conjuring presence of the shepherd/poet. If we regard the pastoral scene as artificial, as a toy world, as an extravagant trifle (like Kepler's snowflake), then the artifice of the bomb coincides with an archaic poetic genre that transforms nature into theater. The "grassy clarion air" binds the bomb in antique weather and in the virtuosity of the lyric air.

Ultimately, to no great surprise, the bomb reveals itself to be a monstrous musical swain:

> Battle forth your spangled hyena finger stumps
>   along the brink of Paradise
>   O Bomb O final Pied Piper
> both sun and firefly behind your shock waltz.   *(67)*

Incantation, moreover, is equated with apocalypse:

> You are due and behold you are due
>   and the heavens are with you
> hosannah incalescent glorious liaison
> BOMB O havoc antiphony molten cleft BOOM
>   Bomb mark infinity a sudden furnace.

Corso refers to the bomb's "appellational womb" and regards it as a "liaison" not only to the ancient origins of poetry ("a hymnody feeling of all Troys / yet knowing Homer with a step of grace"), but to the mythological character of ancient physics:

> The temples of ancient times
> > their grand ruin ceased
> Electrons Protons Neutrons
> > gathering Hesperian hair.

With the advent of the bomb, the ancient doctrine of particles (which are no more accessible to intuition than the gods themselves) and the ancient meters of Lucretius cease their long decline into ruin, mingling song with the "carcass elements," to revive the corpuscularian body in a "shock waltz" treading along "the brink of paradise." Further—and this is Corso's way of invoking the problem of ethics—the idea that matter is nothing more than the shadow of the bomb leaves "God abandoned mock-nude." The modern revision of lyrical substance puts God in his grave, and returns God to life as the radiant species of the body.

CHAPTER 7

Ephemera

Unconfusion submits
its confusion to proof; it's
not a Herod's oath that cannot change.
            Marianne Moore, "The Mind is an Enchanting Thing"

Nobody understands quantum mechanics.
            Richard Feynman, The Character of Physical Laws

And new philosophy calls all in doubt,
The element of fire is quite put out;
The sun is lost, and th'earth and no man's wit
Can well direct him where to look for it.
And freely men confess that this world's spent,
When in the planets, and the firmament
They seek so many new; they see that this
Is crumbled out again to his atomies.
'Tis all in pieces, all coherence gone;
All just supply, and all relation.
            John Donne, "The First Anniversary," cited by J. Robert
            Oppenheimer in his final address to the Smithsonian Institute in 1965

PARADOXOLOGY

It is certainly easier to allow for the equation of poetic and radioactive
substances in the context of postwar American lyric than it is to con-

template the "abyss of images" into which our bodies disappear once they become the property of modern physics. Science has become the final arbiter of what constitutes a real body, whereas lyric poetry appears in the public eye to be little more than a toy medium, apparently immune to the obligations of realism. Yet the equation of materiality and invisibility, which precipitates the need for pictures of subliminal bodies, did not disappear with the age of curiosity and early modern science. "Images yet fresh images beget," Yeats observed in a poem about the lyric automaton, and indeed the dolls and meteors of corpuscularian philosophy have now been superseded by "pictures" of material substance that approach, and sometimes exceed, the limits of sensation and analysis.

The "crisis of visualization" related to quantum theory in the 1920s is, in many respects, commensurate with the allegorical lyric of modernity. The poems of Paul Celan, for example, construct and withhold *by degree* the reality of the traumatized body, just as Erwin Schrödinger's wave theory of matter accounts for material substance only by inserting real bodies into an unreal space of indeterminate dimensionality. Marianne Moore liked to think of poems as "imaginary gardens with real toads in them"—scenes in which the reality of a material "species" comes to light only through the alienation of the body from intuition and experience. In poems of this sort, allegory yields, without ever invoking the themes and tropes of the nuclear age, the anamorphic body of modern materialism. In light of these correspondences between physics and poetics, a study that aims to pursue a theory of modern lyric by excavating the relics of materialism would be incomplete without a review of the controversies over the role of "pictures" in quantum mechanics. The brief historical crisis of intuition and analogy in subatomic physics in the 1920s also permits reflection on the prospect of a materialism without pictures, a notion of material substance conceived not in terms of continuity or objectivity but as a constellation of events.

Moritz Schlick, a leading figure in the Vienna Circle of neopositivists in the early 1930s, mounted a ferocious attack on classical atomism and its reliance on intuitive pictures and analogies. In 1949, his lecture "Theories and Pictorial Models" appeared in English. In it he states, "It is only in the most recent phase of the development of physics that the extension to the realm of the invisibly small, of spatio-temporal conditions prevailing in regions of the directly measurable, is no longer regarded as permissible. Accordingly, micro-processes conceived in a visualizable manner and the method of representation by models have been abandoned."[1] In essence, Schlick declares that positivism, represented by several prominent figures in the debate over quantum mechanics, has at last defeated the regime of pictures in scientific materialism.

Schlick's declaration gives no hint of any controversy about the abandonment of pictorial models in physics. Yet in the same year, Richard Feynman, then a young, unknown physicist teaching at Cornell, first published one of his celebrated "diagrams" of subatomic processes.[2] Feynman described his "funny pictures" modestly as "shorthand for the processes I was trying to describe physically and mathematically," but he also offered a more provocative analogy: "In ancient Egypt and Greece the priests and oracles used to look at veins in sheep's livers to forecast the future, and that's the kind of pictures I was drawing to describe physical processes."[3] Though it may seem eccentric to characterize a scientific sketch of invisible phenomena as a form of divination, and even as an oracle, there are distinct precedents in modern physics for Feynman's "shorthand" picture of invisible (and perhaps unknowable) physical phenomena. Most important, the idea of formal pictures divining the future, or the laws of an invisible material world, can be traced to Heinrich Hertz's doctrine of mechanical pictures, which permit us to be "in advance of the facts."[4] Although statistical pictures may be oracular in some fashion, they are also purely formal (and hence frequently counterintuitive), meaning they have no

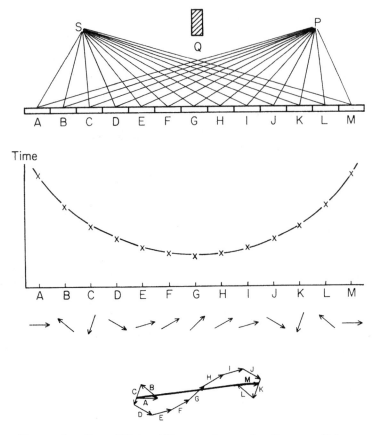

Figure 18.   One of Richard Feynman's oracular diagrams: light goes where the time is least. From Richard Feynman, *QED: The Strange Theory of Light and Matter* (Princeton: Princeton University Press, 1985).

obligation to reproduce the qualities of perceptual experience. Feynman was thus careful to specify that "each diagram signified a mathematical expression."[5] Further, according to James Gleick, "Feynman stressed how free his approach was from customary intuition."[6] To follow Feynman's analogy, just as an oracle must be deciphered to be intelligible—and may remain enigmatic even once it is translated into plain speech—so his "inspired method of picturing," because it is essentially a translation of mathematical functions, has little direct bearing on intuitive experience.[7] As instruments of divination, these pictures are not so much representational as apocalyptic, in the sense that they reveal phenomena that are incompatible not only with prevailing forms of knowledge but also, ostensibly, with basic categories of perception and logic.

In his 1965 Nobel Prize address, Feynman said nothing about the scientific antecedents of his diagrammatic method—and with good reason. The scientific community of physicists remained profoundly suspicious of intuitive or pictorial models after the epistemological crisis of the 1920s: Julian Schwinger, the great mathematician, dismissed Feynman's pictures as "pedagogy, not physics," and pejoratively termed the diagrammatic method a "topology."[8] Today, the pedagogical triumph of Feynman's pictures (which have become standard in physics textbooks) obscures not only the crisis of visualization that produced Schwinger's iconoclasm, but also the revision of the "visual method" *(anschauliche Methode)* by Werner Heisenberg, Wolfgang Pauli, and other physicists who initially opposed any attempt to depict intuitively the physical phenomena formulated by quantum mechanics.

As early as 1922, in his Nobel Prize address, Niels Bohr acknowledged the special constraints placed on representation by quantum analysis: "We are therefore obliged to be modest in our demands and content ourselves with concepts which are formal in the sense that they do not provide a visual picture of the sort one is accustomed to require of the explanations with which natural philosophy deals."[9] With the development in 1926 of Werner Heisenberg's matrix mechanics, which provided the mathematical basis for the new quantum theory, philosophical debate in the scientific community focused on the question of the intuitive content of the new formulations of subatomic phenomena. Was it still possible to depict the invisible foundations of material substance without violating the integrity of the new mathematical models, or did these new formal models defy logical and perceptual categories and hence make visualization impossible? At the center of this extraordinary debate, which suggested that "real" bodies might be composed of "unreal" substance, was the term *Anschaulichkeit*, which pertains to "visual or graphic quality, clearness, vividness, perspicuity." The adjective *anschaulich* can be translated as "visual, graphic, concrete" and also, more generally, as "intuitive, perceptual." Heisenberg vehemently opposed the idea of ordinary pictures of atomic reality, claiming, "The electron and the atom possess not a single degree of the direct physical reality of objects of daily experience";[10] hence "the hypothesis of the atomistic structure of matter is, from the outset, *unanschaulich*."[11] In his 1926 essay "Quantenmechanik" he declares, "The program of quantum mechanics has above all to free itself from these intuitive pictures *[anschauliche Bilder]*"; and further, "the new theory ought above all to give up totally on visualizability *[Anschaulichkeit]*."[12] Understandably, historians of science have regarded the iconoclasm of Bohr, Heisenberg, Pauli, and Paul Dirac (which was generally opposed by the community of German physicists) as a cataclysmic moment in the history of scientific materialism. Sandro Petruccioli summarizes the most extreme interpretation of these developments when he writes, "The loss of visualization brought about by quantum mechanics represented one of the most profound transformations undergone by science since the 17th century."[13]

The suppression, or "transformation," of visual models in the context of quantum mechanics is far more ambiguous than my account suggests. Most important, the idea that quantum mechanics produces an unprecedented rupture between intuition and physical theory should be discounted, since atomism generally is founded on a schism between perception and material substance. The crisis of representation in modern physics cannot be separated from a crisis in modern conceptions of materiality—a reminder of the fundamental equation between pictures and materiality.

To grasp the fundamental ambiguity of iconoclasm in modern phys-
ics, and to determine whether it is more appropriate to speak of a
suppression or a transformation of visual models, it is necessary to
summarize briefly the developments in atomic physics that led to a
crisis of visualization. The historical and technical aspects of my dis-
cussion are extremely modest in scope, since my intention is primarily
to indicate the methodological and sometimes ideological grounds for
the emergence of iconoclasm in modern physics. My dominant con-
cern, as it has done throughout this study, lies with questions of rep-
resentation and simulation, generally speaking, and with the iconog-
raphy or poetics of materialism in particular. I have no intention of
trying to produce an authoritative account of the conceptual founda-
tions of quantum mechanics; the literature on the subject is immense,
and one may consult, for a broader and more technical view of things,
classic works such as Max Jammer's *The Philosophy of Quantum Me-
chanics* and *The Conceptual Development of Quantum Mechanics*, as well
as Bernard d'Espagnat's *Conceptual Foundations of Quantum Mechanics*.
My aim is simply to consider how the "impossible" pictures of quan-
tum mechanics relate to ordinary pictures, and to modern lyric, and
also to take advantage of a moment in cultural and intellectual history
when the equation of materialism and realism was revealed to be
contingent on the viability of ordinary pictures.

Several crucial developments in atomic physics in the early twen-
tieth century converged to produce a fundamental revision of material
substance, as well as the corresponding resistance to pictorial models
associated with quantum mechanics. Increasing evidence of the dual
nature of both light and matter (each exhibiting alternately wave-like
and "granular" qualities) eventually eliminated the basis for any ab-
solute distinction between the two. As a result, the idea of the atom
as a stable, discrete, and unambiguously material particle lost much of
its authority. Following J. J. Thomson's discovery of the electron, a
new hypothesis of atomic structure began to emerge, suggesting that
the atom, formerly regarded as an infinitesimal *object,* was actually a

constellation of electrical charges (called "particles," though no evidence existed that these subatomic phenomena were objects in any conventional sense of the word).

These new theoretical pictures of subatomic reality were based, for the most part, on experiments conducted at the Cavendish Laboratories in Britain beginning in the late nineteenth century, often with the aid of C. T. R. Wilson's cloud chamber device. There, Ernest Rutherford saw in the alpha rays emitted by radioactive substances "a potential 'probe,' with which he might penetrate inside the boundaries of material atoms, and so bring to light something of their substructure. . . . He focused the alpha-rays from a naturally radioactive substance into a beam, and concentrated this beam on to a sheet or film of the substance whose atomic structure he wished to study. He then looked to see how the bombarding alpha-particles were scattered in passing through the film."[14] Wilson's cloud chamber made visible the scattering of subatomic particles and produced the first (and still controversial) photographic evidence of atomic reality. In this respect, the cloud chamber is the most important tool to emerge in the debate over the existence of theoretical entities since the invention of the microscope in the seventeenth century. Peter Galison calls it "the origin of the image tradition" in modern nuclear physics.[15] With these experiments Rutherford achieved the first artificial nuclear transformations, by disturbing the stable structure of the atom in a manner that caused it to emit radioactive phenomena (or particles), thereby revealing evidence of its physical properties. The radioactive traces produced by these interventions constitute the only observable physical evidence of subatomic reality.

By and large, therefore, the empirical evidence on which quantum theory is based pertains to artificially induced phenomena that do not occur in nature. Quantum theory thus emerged as a means of describing and explaining the interaction of radiation and "matter" (a provisional and ambiguous distinction that reasserted itself because of the difficulty of grasping intuitively the nature of subatomic events), induced in order to observe the "untouchable interior" of the atom. Whereas classical atomism, which proceeded under the assumption that atoms are indivisible and hence without any internal parts, addressed the nature of atomic systems (based on relations between atoms), quantum theory pertains ostensibly to the interior of the atom— though the very idea of interiority in this case is contingent on the irredeemably fictional Gestalt of the atom. In addition, one could say that classical mechanics provides the formal basis for a discourse of material *objects,* whereas quantum mechanics calculates a discourse of material transmissions and transformations, in which objects figure only as hypothetical phenomena, if at all. Despite these differences, the mechanism of radiation in quantum theory resembles in crucial respects the *mechanization of air* formulated by corpuscularian philosophers in the context of pneumatics and meteorology. The status of the ordinary object has never been very secure in either classical or quantum mechanics.

Historians of science divide the evolution of quantum physics into two stages: the "old" quantum theory, associated with Niels Bohr's planetary model of the atom in 1913, and the "new" quantum theory, associated with Heisenberg's matrix mechanics in 1925 and Schrödinger's wave mechanics in 1926. Synthesizing various features of the nascent electromagnetic theory of mass, and drawing principally on Rutherford's observation of an atomic nucleus containing the majority of the charged particles of atomic mass, Bohr's research produced a "map" of the arrangement of electrons about the nucleus in a series of concentric orbits. Thus his model of the atom, published in a three-part article in *Philosophical Magazine* in 1913, presented the first unified description of the "mechanism of radiation"—the absorption and emission of energy by electrons in the atom. From his experiments, Bohr concluded that the mechanism of radiation is discontinuous in the sense that it is not only erratic but also fragmentary in nature. More specifically, the emission or absorption of energy by an electron coincides with its transition from one stable state (or orbit) to another within the atom. In addition, since atoms absorb energy only in certain frequencies, rather than indiscriminately, he concluded that electrons can exist only at certain positions in the atom. Bohr's picture of the mechanism of radiation presumed the real existence of electrons in stable states (as well as observable quantities of radiation absorbed or emitted by the atom), thereby depicting the interaction of matter (electrons) and radiation and thus preserving a modified version of the classical atom.

The coherence of Bohr's model was soon undermined, however, by a combination of features intrinsic to its originality and methodological integrity. Because Bohr's calculations implied that electrons exist only in determinate positions, it was impossible to account intuitively for the physical transition that produces the observable radiation emitted by the electron. Thus the electron, in Bohr's model, acts like the Cheshire cat, disappearing from one place only to appear in another, without any plausible explanation for its "quantum leap." The so-called new quantum theory, developed by Bohr, Heisenberg, Pauli, Schrödinger, and others, sought to provide a more precise formal explanation of the mechanism of radiation, without ignoring the paradoxical features of Bohr's model (which were based on sound observation).

The doctrine of positivism, which proscribes the reality of hypothetical objects (entities without directly observable physical evidence of their existence), determined fundamentally the manner in which the "new" quantum theory revised and elaborated Bohr's model. Since electrons do not absorb or emit energy in a stable state, no direct physical evidence of their existence as "objects" exists. Thus, abiding by the implications of positivist criteria, the "new" quantum theorists (above all Wolfgang Pauli) developed their formal models under the assumption that electrons do not exist and that the radiation transmitted by the invisible elements of the atom has no discernible cause. Thus Heisenberg's revolutionary matrix mechanics, adhering strictly to observables, presents a formally coherent picture of an intuitively paradoxical reality. On this basis, atoms too must be judged to be nonexistent, since pictures of hypothetical objects are, of course, inadmissible. Heisenberg thus informed his colleagues in 1926, "In microscopic events, so far we have only relations between experimentally obtained observable quantities, and for the moment we cannot give an immediate intuitive interpretation of the physical events on which they rest."[16] According to these criteria, the subliminal object—the hypothetical cause of observable radiation—can be no more than a set of relations, a constellation of discontinuous events. More radically, Bohr acknowledged that one might conclude, as Schrödinger did, that "the essential characteristic of matrix mechanics was the final recognition of the impossibility of ascribing a physical reality to a single stationary state."[17] What's more, the traces of radiation from which we might infer the existence of the electron in a steady state derive from a process in which the stable identity of the subliminal object dissolves in an exchange of energy. The electron is observable only when it is *between* stable states, only in the midst of transformation—in essence, when it is no longer identical to itself and has thus ceased to be an object. In terms of quantum mechanics, therefore, scientific materialism reveals itself to be truly, in Agamben's phrase, a "science without object."

The epistemological crisis of quantum physics does not end with the displacement of the material *object* by a material transmission (or material event). As Sandro Petruccioli explains, "Atoms are unobservable objects when in a definite, stable state. In observing them, we have to interact with them through another physical object—radiation—and thus irreversibly modify their state."[18] Not only is the materiality of subliminal objects to be described solely in terms of radiation and transmission, but the observability of the atom is contingent on the observer's intervention and alteration of the invisible "object." What we observe is not the "object" in its natural state (which is unobservable), but an artifact of the conditions of observation, a measurable disturbance that is fundamentally discontinuous, in the sense that it does not exist until the observer produces it, and then it disappears almost as soon as it appears. Thus Bohr contends, "The unavoidable interaction between the objects and the measuring instruments sets an absolute limit to the possibility of speaking of a behavior of atomic objects which is independent of the means of observation."[19] In a paper delivered in 1927, Bohr explains,

> Our usual description of physical phenomena is based entirely on the idea that the phenomena concerned may be observed without disturbing them appreciably.... Now, the quantum postulate implies that any observation of atomic phenomena will involve an interaction with the agency of observation not to be neglected. Accordingly, *an independent reality in the ordinary physical sense can neither be ascribed to the phenomena nor to the agencies of observation.* ... This situation has far-reaching consequences. On one hand, the definition of the state of a physical system, as ordinarily understood, claims the elimination of all external disturbances. But in that case, according to the quantum postulate, any observation will be impossible.... On the other hand, if in order to make observation possible, we permit certain interactions with suitable agencies of measurement, not belonging to the physical system, an unambiguous definition of the state of the system is naturally no longer possible, and there can be no question of causality in the ordinary sense.[20]

In Bohr's view, the specific properties of the subliminal "object," as well as its very existence, are effects of the observer's intervention and the "agency of measurement": "No elementary phenomenon is a phenomenon until it is a registered (observed) phenomenon."[21] Each intervention produces not a picture of a stable and enduring entity but a *different phenomenon*. On this point Bohr's position is identical to Heisenberg's: "The trajectory of an electron comes into existence only when we observe it."[22] Thus, it is not simply that observation, and therefore representation, *produce* quantum materiality, but that material substance necessarily reflects the *ephemerality* of observation and representation. When observation ceases, the physical phenomenon of atomic reality ceases to exist. The foundation of corporeality is therefore essentially discontinuous.

Bertrand Russell, whose philosophy of logical atomism anticipated the essential features of quantum materiality, explains the significance of these developments in physics:

> Matter, for common sense, is something which persists in time and moves in space. But for modern relativity-physics this view is no longer tenable. A piece of matter has become, not a persistent thing with varying states, but a system of interrelated events. The old solidity is gone, and with it the characteristics that, to the materialist, made matter seem more real than fleeting thoughts. Nothing is permanent, nothing endures; the prejudice that the real is permanent must be abandoned.[23]

The idea that "fleeting thoughts" are no less substantial than what we had taken to be material objects first emerged as a feature of Russell's logical philosophy, which resembled Ernst Mach's empirio-criticism in its theory of objects. In Russell's view, "What I can know is that there are a certain series of appearances linked together, and the series of these appearances I shall define as being a desk. In that way the desk is reduced to a logical fiction, because a series is a logical fiction. In that way the objects of ordinary life are extruded from the world of what there is."[24] Just as quantum materiality consists solely of the ephemeral and discontinuous "particles" transmitted by a hypothetical electron, so the ordinary desk, conceived as an object, is a fiction constituted by a "series" of discrete sense data or "appearances."

Russell goes on, in more vivid terms, to explain the significance of his views for our assumptions concerning the reality of material objects, and the unreality of ephemeral matters: "I have talked so far about the unreality of things we think real. I want to speak with equal emphasis about the reality of things we think unreal, such as phantoms and hallucinations. Phantoms and hallucinations, considered in themselves, are on exactly the same level as ordinary sense data. . . . They have the most complete and absolute and perfect reality that anything could have."[25] Let us not, however, misunderstand Russell's point. The "phantoms" and "hallucinations" of which he speaks are *material* phenomena: the fleeting sensory impressions that constitute, like the ephemeral traces of quantum materiality, the only observable and hence authentic physical reality. Thus he concludes, "The real things that we know by experience last for a very short time, one tenth or one half a second, or whatever it may be. Phantoms and hallucinations are among those, among the ultimate constituents of the world" (145). These material ghosts serve as the analytic foundation for determining the logical atoms of physical reality—the "ultimate constituents of the world." Any *relation* between these discontinuous elements is hypothetical, and any object, whether mundane or subliminal, based on such relations is irredeemably fictional.

The most radical implication of quantum mechanics is not so much the equation of corporeality and radiation as the *discontinuity* of matter. The so-called individuality of quantum phenomena stems in part from the irresolvable paradox of the "quantum leap," but also from the unavoidable convergence of representation and material substance, of mental and physical realities, in quantum physics. In the context of the history of materialism, this convergence of inner and outer worlds spells the end of the "mechanical hypothesis," the end of the reign of the automaton in physics: "Nature at the quantum level is not a machine that goes its inexorable way. Instead, the answer we get depends on the question we put, the experiment we arrange, the registering device we choose. We are inescapably involved in bringing about that which appears to be happening."[26] From this standpoint, Bohr's insistence on the scientist's role in *producing* the observable phenomena of atomic reality amounts to a revival of Bishop Berkeley's immaterialism *(esse est percipi)*: matter, as such, does not exist, and what does exist physically cannot be distinguished from our ideas, or pictures, of it. Thus, in Sandro Petruccioli's view, Bohr grants "an uneliminable role to metaphysics in the most daring and creative phases of scientific endeavor."[27]

We might assume that the eclipse of the figure of the automaton (the demechanization of the world picture) coincides with a general collapse of the pictorial method in atomic physics. And indeed we have seen how a group of "anti-imagists," convinced of the essential discontinuity of quantum phenomena, cultivated a powerful and enduring resistance to intuitive or pictorial models. Yet the iconoclasm of Heisenberg and others was by no means absolute, and the initial rejection of pictorial models quickly developed into a more qualified *revision* of the concept of *Anschaulichkeit*. In addition, it is impossible to isolate the crisis of visualization in quantum physics, and the larger question of the value of intuitive experience, from the social turbulence of the Weimar period (in which quantum mechanics was born) and the emerging ideology of National Socialism.

The resistance to depicting a material "object" at the quantum level stemmed in part from the impossibility of determining an unambiguous cause of the observable phenomena. For a picture of a subliminal object is by conventional definition a picture of the *cause* of phenomenal reality. If, however, the observer has a fundamental role in producing the measurable phenomena of quantum reality, then it is entirely inappropriate to depict a stable (and hypothetical) object as the sole cause of such phenomena. The correlation of visuality and causality in this context led some prominent physicists in the German community to support an *acausal* interpretation of quantum mechanics and, more significant, to declare that the epistemological questions raised by quantum theory implied a crisis of causality in a more general sense. The breach of causality in the context of scientific materialism was highly compatible, ideologically, with the irrationalism and ahistoricism of National Socialism, and indeed it becomes difficult to discern whether the attacks on causality and visuality in the context of physics were primarily scientific or ideological developments. Bohr, for example, in his 1927 Como paper (in which he introduced the complementarity principle) stresses the "inherent irrationality" of the quantum postulate, thereby intimating the grounds of an *irrational science*—an idea easily exploited in the context of fascist ideology. Certainly, the abrogation of causality, which Oswald Spengler labeled a "Baroque phenomenon" and "an artificial possession," lies at the core of fascist historiography, and it is entirely possible that attacks on pictorial or mechanical models, insofar as they were regarded as emblems of causality and rationalism, were influenced by the ideology of National Socialism. Indeed, an important essay by Paul Forman on Weimar culture and the development of quantum theory argues that a rejection of causality is by no means an implicit or necessary feature of quantum mechanics, and that "extrinsic influences led physicists to ardently hope for, and actively search for, and willingly embrace, an acausal quantum mechanics."[28]

Whatever one may conclude about the ideological content of the conflicts over pictorial models of material substance, the iconography of materialism, even when it takes the form of iconoclasm, cannot be isolated from its historical and cultural milieu. Forman contends, for example, that "the demand for *Anschaulichkeit* was very closely connected with the predilections and antipathies characteristic of the Weimar intellectual environment."[29] More specifically, he notes, the word *Anschaulichkeit* was one of the emblematic terms of *Lebensphilosophie,* the celebration of "life," intuition, and unanalyzed experience that played such a prominent role in fascist ideology.[30] Thus any assessment of Heisenberg's iconoclasm, or the intense debate over visualization among many other prominent quantum theorists, should not ignore these cultural and political influences. Heisenberg's rejection of pictorial models was initially absolute and unequivocal. Yet the essay in which he articulated the iconoclastic implications of his matrix mechanics ("Quantenmechanik" of 1926) remained captive to the prevailing vocabulary of visual experience. In that essay, Forman indicates, "Heisenberg used *Anschauung, anschaulich,* or some other form of this root, once in every 250 words, sixteen times in all, concluding that 'thus far there is still some essential feature missing in our picture.' "[31] In fact, Heisenberg's famous paper on the indeterminacy principle, written shortly after the quantum mechanics paper, abandons his unequivocal opposition and seeks to articulate a revision of *Anschaulichkeit* compatible with his formal principles (but also compatible with the ideological pressures of fascist *Lebensphilosophie*). The indeterminacy paper, published in 1927, is titled "On the Intuitive *[anschaulich]* Content of Quantum Theoretical Kinematics and Mechanics."

Significant debate over the viability of intuitive pictures of quantum materiality occurred between 1918 and 1935. It reached a climax in 1926 and 1927, when decisive confrontations took place among Bohr, Heisenberg, Einstein, and Schrödinger. The apocalyptic tenor of the debate stemmed in part from the nature of the dilemma: on one hand, most participants in the debate agreed that the very existence of quantum phenomena is to some degree contingent on the event of representation, yet this event yields physical data that permit counterintuitive or paradoxical notions of the phenomenon observed. Hence the reality of material substance depends on pictures that are sometimes unintelligible; representation becomes at once constitutive and impossible.

The debate over pictures and *Anschaulichkeit* pertained, however, only to *interpretations* of formal systems. The great clashes between Heisenberg and Schrödinger, for example, did not concern any significant formal differences between matrix and wave mechanics (the mathematical basis of the "new" quantum theory), but rather disputed the admissibility of drawing intuitive conclusions from these mathematical functions. By 1927, Pascual Jordan and Paul Dirac had developed the "transformation" functions that demonstrated conclusively the formal equivalence and convertibility of matrix and wave mechanics. Thus it was not application but interpretation, not the mathematical integrity of quantum theory but the possibility of ascribing intuitive reality to quantum materiality, that were at stake in the debate over pictures. Further, much of what the general public knows today about quantum mechanics stems from the debate about pictures, including Bohr's model of complementarity and Heisenberg's famous indeterminacy principle, both of which constitute theories of imagery. In essence, the debate about pictures in quantum physics was a philosophical rather than scientific argument, much as the "corpuscularian hypothesis" of the seventeenth century, regarded as a symptom of natural philosophy, moved well beyond (and perhaps in opposition to) science. We should recall that the problematic reliance of materialism on pictures, in its Baroque manifestation, could not easily be distinguished from a "philosophy" of pleasure and machines or from certain highly unstable formations of "curiosity" and "virtuosity."

For philosophical and ideological reasons that remain obscure (yet disclose the historical imperative for the equivalence of materialism and realism), Heisenberg retreated from an absolute prohibition of intuitive pictures of quantum phenomena. Thus the crisis of visualization in physics was not so much a conflict between advocating or rejecting intuitive pictures, in any absolute sense, as a heated philosophical debate about what *kind* of pictures were appropriate. Further, none of the intuitive models that emerged from this debate were intended as representations of the *physical* reality of subatomic processes. Edward MacKinnon, commenting on the generation of physicists working immediately prior to the evolution of the "new" quantum theory, observes, "Following Hertz, Helmholtz, and Planck, and under the direct influence of Kant, physicists began to insist that physics should supply a coherent picture of reality, but that such pictures need not be interpreted as representations of reality as it exists objectively."[32] Thus quantum theorists' rejection of mimesis as a function of intuitive pictures followed the precedent of an earlier generation by sustaining the powerful tendency toward abstraction exhibited generally by atomism.

The images of material substance composed (sometimes reluctantly) by quantum theorists are not reproductions, then, but *tools,* or as Erwin Schrödinger called them, *allegories.* The abandonment of the mimetic function of pictures suggests a retreat from the premises of objective realism, but it also allows us to consider how pictures might be used to maintain the principle, or possibility, of realism, divorced from any intuitive content. Heisenberg's indeterminacy principle, which is essentially an iconology of matter (a theory of pictures), is based on a principle of *translation,* or should I say *faulty* translation, since it offers a means of calculating precisely the intuitive *limitations* of our grasp of subliminal material reality—limits that do not pertain to mathematical models. Indeed, it was Jordan and Dirac's transformation theory (demonstrating the formal equivalence of matrix and wave mechanics) that served as the original model for Heisenberg's notion of intuitive "translations" of formal principles.

Yet Heisenberg's revision of *Anschaulichkeit* modifies his basic iconoclasm only slightly, since these intuitive "translations" bore no relation, as far as Heisenberg was concerned, to physical reality. Indeed, as Edward MacKinnon notes, Heisenberg's intuitive pictures were no more than decoys or probes: "Heisenberg used models of the atom which he knew to be unrealistic to suggest new mathematical formulations"; and, further, he "was quite willing to introduce models which were both inherently implausible and also inconsistent with established physics provided they supplied a basis for solving particular problems."[33] Thus Heisenberg's pictures engage in a "poetics" of *abusive translation,* in the sense that fidelity to mathematical reality—to the equation—can be achieved only through catachresis and improbable correspondences. In addition, such "translations" may reveal formal solutions to new problems not evident in the "original" model, suggesting an *apocalyptic* mode of translation in which revelation coincides with interpretive violence. This helps to explain why some historians of science have found in Heisenberg's revision of *Anschaulichkeit* a precedent for Feynman's "inspired method of picturing."[34] But Heisenberg's iconoclasm, which underlies his apocalyptic mode of translation, is evidence of a profound commitment to *realism:* he disdained intuitive pictures because he regarded them as incommensurable with the reality encrypted in the equation. Thus his resistance to intuitive pictures betrays a fundamental belief in the objective reality of quantum phenomena, in contrast to Bohr's immaterialism, which regards subliminal materiality as an effect of representation.

Heisenberg's indeterminacy paper, written in February 1926, developed a means of calculating the formal determinants of intuitive uncertainty about the electron's physical reality. This unavoidable uncertainty stems from the impossibility of determining precisely and *simultaneously* all of the physical variables (such as momentum and location) pertaining to the reality of the electron. These constraints constitute the main feature of the "paradoxology" of quantum mechanics. Thus, at the level of intuitive representation, relations between physical variables are, in Heisenberg's view, essentially *contradictory*. More precisely, the physical reality and its mathematical calculation are unambiguous, whereas our intuitive grasp of material reality at the atomic level is indeterminate: although nature is formally coherent, our intuitive picture of it is out of focus. Heisenberg's pictures of material substance are therefore only marginally coherent from an intuitive perspective, since the calculation of one variable necessarily precludes determination of the others. Something is always missing from the picture (but not from the equation, or in reality).

In September 1927, at the International Congress of Physics at Lake Como, Bohr introduced his complementarity principle, which revised Heisenberg's uncertainty relations according to Bohr's insistence on the uneliminable role of the observer in producing quantum phenomena. Against Heisenberg's realism, which implies that much of what exists and how it exists cannot be represented, Bohr proposed a doctrine of quantum pictures based on the most rigorous standards of positivism: what is not observed, or even what cannot be observed, does not exist. If representation is constitutive of quantum materiality, then the picture is the physical reality; no other reality extrinsic to the picture based on observable data, whether it be coherent or not, can be said to exist. Hence, in Bohr's opinion, relations between variables are not contradictory, but *complementary*. One aspect of the picture determines, for example, a causal reference, calculating exclusively the energy associated with a stationary state of the electron, while a different aspect determines, once again exclusively, the "behavior" of the electron induced by the observer—its spatio-temporal coordinates. Likewise, pictures of both light and matter as particles or waves are not contradictory but complementary. To be more precise, individual pictures are not really different aspects of a single phenomenon, but pictures of disparate phenomena and *different realities*. Bohr's concept of complementarity bears some relation to Hertz's doctrine of logical pictures, which allows for multiple pictures of reality. Hertz writes, "Various images of the same objects are possible. . . . One image may be more suitable for one purpose, another for another"; and, further, "By varying the choice of the propositions which we take as fundamental, we can give various representations of the principles of mechanics. Hence we can thus obtain various images of things."[35] Bohr radicalizes this thesis by contending that different pictures describe different realities and that every picture refers to a different reality. Though Bohr alluded several times to the analogy of cubism, we must be careful not to infer from this comparison that Bohr's pictures of materiality are intuitively ambiguous: although relations between aspects of subliminal materiality are exclusive, each aspect of the overall picture is intuitively coherent, and relations between the aspects of reality are determinate and complementary.

Bohr's commitment to intuitive pictures of nonintuitive realities derived from his belief that the perceptual categories embedded in ordinary language are intrinsic to the conditions of observation and representation. Hence the physical effects of representation, such as quantum materiality, are susceptible, by definition, to intuition. In a discussion of the intuitive foundation of complementarity, Bohr observes, "The difficulties of quantum theory are connected with the concepts, or rather with the words, that are used in the customary description of nature, which all have their origin in classical theories."[36]

In the Como paper, Bohr insists, "Every word in the language refers to our ordinary perception," and he warns against "adapting our modes of perception borrowed from the sensations to the gradually deepening knowledge of the laws of Nature"—against the notion implicit in Heisenberg's "pictures" that perception can be revised in accordance with mathematical models.[37] In a later essay, Bohr confirmed his belief in the necessary correspondence between knowledge, discourse, and the intuitive pictures embedded in ordinary language: "The aim of every physical experiment—to gain knowledge under reproducible and communicable conditions—leaves us no choice but to use everyday concepts."[38]

Bohr's reference to the categories of ordinary language provides a rationale for his views about the philosophical necessity of intuitive pictures of quantum phenomena, yet it does not explain what scientific function these pictures might have, or indeed whether they are compatible with the ends of science. With Heisenberg, aside from the conservative ideological demands for a return to visual models in physics (which placed the iconoclasts in a position resembling the avant-garde),[39] it is difficult to discern a clear scientific motivation for his reconciliation with the tradition of *anschauliche Bilder*. Indeed the rapprochement is perplexing because he rejected Bohr's thesis that the perceptual categories of ordinary language constitute the limits of scientific knowledge. As far as Heisenberg was concerned, mathematics can provide an unambiguous account of a physical reality that exceeds the laws of intuition. Why, therefore, submit to the need for misleading pictures? Part of his response to this question, as I indicated earlier, concerns the notion that realistic pictures can be used as decoys or "probes" of nonintuitive physical environments. A more satisfactory response to this question, which challenges the basic iconicity of materialism, can be found in the views of the most prominent and reliable intuitionists, such as Einstein, Schrödinger, and Max Planck. Their defense of intuitive pictures is not so much an apology for naive or objective realism as it is an attempt to salvage the *pretense* to realism on which physics is based, even if it must be stripped of empirical content. Thus, as Edward MacKinnon observes, "Even Planck did not hold that the pictures given by scientific theories depict the world as it exists objectively. His argument, rather, was that a unified picture of reality is necessary for the coherence of physical science."[40] From this standpoint, the equation of science and realism (the claim that science is realistic) rests on the viability of ordinary pictures, regardless of whether they depict something that exists. In this sense, a picture of the atom is no longer a picture of anything, but simply the last picture before the abyss of a purely mathematical and hence *unimaginable* system of material reality—a picture emerging from a tension between reason and the imagination, which recalls Kant's conception of the sublime.

WILD KINGDOM

Although no one, at first glance, is likely to associate atomism with realism, the crisis of visualization in quantum theory was essentially a crisis of realism and, more specifically, a crisis of the equation of materialism and realism. Generally speaking, in the context of atomism, the impossibility of direct observation, coupled with social and imaginative impulses to depict what cannot be seen, always places a given system of representation at risk, and this was especially true of quantum mechanics. Further, realism, according to Ian Hacking, presumes the act of representation: "First there is representation, and then there is 'real.' First there is a representation and much later there is a creating of concepts in terms of which we can describe this or that respect in which we have similarity."[41] Hacking therefore regards "the real as an attribute of representations" (137). Hence, without pictures, there can be no realism or claim to reality. More specifically, with respect to the emergence of quantum mechanics, "New theories are new representations. They represent in different ways and so there are new kinds of reality" (139). Although new pictures may produce new realities in ways that initially defy comprehension, *some* kind of picture must prefigure the new reality. Thus as long as quantum mechanics failed to provide pictures of an invisible material world, it failed to constitute a new reality. Further, the crisis of representation in quantum physics exposed the most troubling implication of atomist doctrine (which has always been an open secret): *materialism is not inherently realistic.* The equation of materialism and realism depends on the production of ordinary pictures—though these pictures may refer to physical phenomena that defy ordinary experience. The function of pictures in this context therefore had little or nothing to do with the analytic integrity or success of scientific practice. Certainly it was not "the equation" that required Heisenberg to draw back from the abyss of immaterialism and to begin toying with "implausible" translations of material substance. It appears, then, that questions of language and pleasure—the determining features of Agamben's "science without object"—played a decisive role in the evolution of quantum theory.

In the great controversy over pictures in modern physics, Erwin Schrödinger would be considered an iconophile, though hardly an advocate of naive realism. It was his so-called wave function that served as the principal icon of visuality opposing the imageless truth of Heisenberg's matrix mechanics. Though both models, as I indicated earlier, are formally equivalent, Heisenberg initially labeled as "crap" Schrödinger's wave interpretation of the electron.[42] As a picture of material substance, however, the figure of the wave is by no means compatible with objective realism—even at the quantum level—since, to achieve his calculation, Schrödinger was obliged to configure the object (the electron) in non-Euclidean space. Hence the wave function presents a "real" object in "unreal" space. Further, the wave function is not a representation; in Schrödinger's view, the picture is primarily a tool, "suitable for guiding us to just what measurements can in principle be made on the relevant natural object."[43] MacKinnon explains, "For Schrödinger such pictures cannot be taken as representations of physical reality as it exists objectively; he considered physical reality a collective construct. The real function of such pictures is to supply a ground for intuition and a test for consistency."[44] A picture, according to Schrödinger, functions as a governor on the engine of formal speculation, a failsafe against the elaboration of impossible realities (physical realities), as a guide rail in the dark.

Schrödinger's understanding of the iconology of materialism, as well as his unique sensibility, offers an ideal platform from which to sound the correspondences between quantum physics and modern lyric. The conclusions to be drawn from Schrödinger's materialism, however, are not at all what we might expect. For although Schrödinger called his wave function "an unintelligible transformation of an incomprehensible transition,"[45] his rendering of material substance, while not representational, is intuitive in the most ordinary sense of the word. Schrödinger thought hard about the role of pictures in the history of materialism, and one of his most famous papers supplies an analogy that illustrates not only the crisis of *Anschaulichkeit* in quantum physics but also the greater pictorial logic of atomism. The cat paradox, as it is called, is a hyper-icon: it presents at once a picture of quantum materiality and a picture of the pictorial method by which we grasp the intuitive content of quantum mechanics. In its reflexivity and its multiple frames of reference, the cat paradox functions very much like the figure of the automaton in corpuscularian philosophy. It is a picture that tells us something about the nature of corporeality, and also about the nature of pictures in the context of materialism.

Schrödinger offers the cat paradox as a means of clarifying, conceptually, a technical summary of Heisenberg's indeterminacy principle, but it also functions as a critique of Heisenberg's philosophical assumptions and as an illustration of Schrödinger's own wave interpretation (the ψ-function). In essence, the scene Schrödinger depicts is a parable of the intrinsic uncertainty of material substance:

> One can even construct cases which are almost burlesque. A cat is
> penned up in a steel chamber, along with the following diabolical

device (which one must keep out of the cat's reach): in a Geiger counter there is a tiny bit of radioactive substance, so little that in the course of an hour *perhaps* one atom of it disintegrates, but also with equal probability not even one; if it does happen, the counter responds and through a relay activates a hammer that shatters a little flask of prussic acid. If one has left this entire system to itself for an hour, one would say that the cat still lives *if* no atom has decayed. The first atomic decay would have poisoned it. The ψ-function of the entire system would express this by having the living and the dead cat (pardon the expression) mixed or smeared out in equal parts.

It is typical of such cases that an indeterminacy originally restricted to the atomic domain becomes transformed into macroscopic indeterminacy, which can then be resolved by direct observation. This prevents us from accepting in a naïve way a "blurred model" as an image of reality. In itself it would not embody anything unclear or contradictory. There is a difference between a shaky or out-of-focus photograph and a snapshot of clouds and fog banks.[46]

The first thing I want to emphasize about Schrödinger's "method" is his willingness to employ what he calls a "burlesque" image to depict a mathematical function, to concoct a mundane and even "vulgar" illustration of the "blurred" features of quantum materiality, that is, to establish a correspondence between intuitive and abstract knowledge. Schrödinger called this kind of representation of quantum materiality "an allegorical picture of the situation"[47]—a conception that has a distinct bearing, as we shall discover, on the character of modern lyric.

The signal feature of Schrödinger's model is the complete inaccessibility of the physical phenomenon under consideration. Whether the cat (which stands for the electron) is alive or dead, existent or nonexistent, cannot be determined exactly by the observer. In ordinary, "macroscopic" reality, this uncertainty could be resolved immediately by simply opening the chamber and observing the cat—though he points out that there is nothing inherently "unclear or contradictory" about a "blurred model" of reality. At the level of quantum reality, however, direct observation is impossible, so the cat (i.e., the electron) can only be determined to be *either* dead or alive (or *both,* in Schrödinger's view). Furthermore, the unobservable phenomenon (the cat's fate) is entirely the effect, as it is in the case of quantum physics, of the agency of measurement. Whether the cat exists or not depends on the "diabolical device" installed by the observer: the event to be observed, which cannot be observed, is precipitated by the observer and yet eludes formal comprehension—though sometimes an "inspired method" of picturing can divine the occult reality of matter.

In terms of Heisenberg's uncertainty principle, our knowledge of the physical variables in this scenario is *contradictory;* hence the cat is *either* dead or alive, without any prospect of our determining which. Heisenberg would say that it is not the cat, but our picture of the invisible cat, which is indeterminate, blurred, or out of focus. Bohr, by contrast, adhering to the most radical criteria of positivism, would say that the cat is *neither* dead nor alive until a human observer opens the box and makes that determination. Thus Heisenberg's realism contends that the cat is real but cannot be represented precisely, whereas Bohr's immaterialism contends that, since the cat cannot be observed, it does not exist (though certain isolated phenomena—a meow, perhaps—could be acknowledged as real). Schrödinger's wave function, however, allows him to reject both Heisenberg's belief that the cat is real and Bohr's contention that it is unreal, to formulate "a blurred reality"—"the living and the dead cat . . . mixed or smeared out in equal parts." The blurred reality of the cat (which is *both* dead and alive) reflects the intuitive qualities of a wave (its continuity), and hence this new image of matter is neither "unclear nor contradictory." Thus, in Schrödinger's view, it is not our picture of quantum materiality but the phenomenon itself that is blurred—a position that recalls Marx's Epicurean phenomenology. Schrödinger is careful to emphasize, however, that the "fundamental properties of *new* classes of characteristics" (such as a blurred physical reality) are permissible only in the context of microscopic or subliminal environments (though such characteristics are not inconceivable even in a "macroscopic" world). The wave function, which formulates a paradoxical physical reality, does not apply pragmatically (though it could theoretically) to macroscopic conditions; indeed, its viability depends on the invisibility of quantum phenomena. Because there is no condition in ordinary experience corresponding to microscopic indeterminacy, we must rely on allegorical pictures (such as the cat paradox) to convey the anomalous features of quantum materiality.

Schrödinger's cat paradox yields insight into the hermetic theater of quantum mechanics, but it also displays the relationship of quantum theory to the greater iconography of atomist doctrine. The principal object—an invisible object—of Schrödinger's burlesque is an *animal,* the paradigmatic *living machine* of corpuscularian philosophy. In the eyes of Descartes and other mechanical philosophers, the animal without mind or soul is a *natural automaton.* Hence the figure occupying center stage in Schrödinger's quantum theater, a picture of automatism, is the very emblem of mechanical philosophy. And, indeed, since quantum theory spells the end of the regime of the automaton, we are given to witness the unobservable death of the animal-machine (and perhaps the man-machine as well), a death precipitated by, yet also concealed from, the quantum observer. So the automaton in this traumatic scene is either living or dead (or both), and this blurred reality is itself the uncertain effect of another machine—the "diabolical" apparatus standing in for the observer. Yet the violent or "poisonous" act is not restricted to quantum theatrics, for the abstraction worked upon the body by the doctrine of atomism, and the blurred reality of configured space, are inherently traumatic and fatal to experience. Just as quantum materiality consists solely of ephemeral traces issuing from the "bombardment" and alteration of the electron, so the animal body must be "mixed or smeared out in equal parts" to become intelligible in the allegorical space of quantum physics. In the end, however, the mechanism of radiation preserves the philosophy of meteors, for Schrödinger's wave function offers a snapshot of "clouds and fog-banks"—a picture of the weather. The fictitious interior of the atom conspires with the lyrical body of air, like a meteor in a cloud chamber.

Allegory, the representation of the invisible by the visible, is the dominant modality of quantum pictures (with the exception of Hei-senberg's "translations," which never really transcend his basic icono-clasm). And it is precisely the allegorical nature of quantum represen-tation that allows a more detailed comparison with the essential qualities of modern lyric. The reality of the subliminal material world may be a blur, as Schrödinger contends, or discontinuous and ephem-eral, in Bohr's opinion, yet the *pictures* supplied by the wave function or by complementarity are perfectly intelligible (though Bohr's com-plementarity does entail a significant degree of formal innovation). Thus the poetic function most compatible with quantum representa-tion is not abstraction or extreme formalism, but a symbolic mode in which literal images of ordinary experience betray, but do not repre-sent, an invisible world of impossible bodies and events. The unreal, material world is depicted in this case by what it is not, by the intuitive features of ordinary things. Hence the allegorical picture is best un-derstood, in this sense, as a *map,* referring, by convention, to a world which is fundamentally alien to the terms of the picture. Precise re-alism, in Paul de Man's view, is an indispensable feature of the refer-ential instability characteristic not only of modern lyric but also of the profound unreality of allegorical pictures.[48]

Allegorical lyric customarily alludes to an invisible world equated with ideas or immutable forms, yet in quantum representation and modern poetry the realm of the invisible is a *material* world, and the poetry of experience (*Erlebnislyrik,* to use Emil Staiger's term) therefore renews its meditation on uncertainty and ambiguity by alluding to the "blurred reality" of the body. We must remember, however, that we have intimations of the discontinuous and indeterminate nature of material substance—its unreality—only through pictures that are intelligible, yet which allude to a world that defies intuition. Allegorical lyric betrays a poetics of the supernatural detail and a discourse of virtuosity comprehending the features of an invisible material world. And it frequently ends in *obscurity*—the elemental substance of lyric and the defining feature of a poet whose "studies" of nature grow less intelligible as they become more precise. One could argue, then, that allegorical lyric presumes the metaphysical crisis of the radioactive body to be the general condition of all bodies at all times.

To consider more fully the nature of allegorical lyric and its correlation to quantum theory, I want to return to the work of Marianne Moore, whose antipathy to "poetry" may be understood as a feature of the poetics of allegory.[49] William Carlos Williams once introduced Marianne Moore's poetry by imagining a reader "shocked and bewildered" by its effects:

> If one come with Miss Moore's work to some wary friend and say, 'Everything is worthless but the best and this is the best,' adding, 'only with difficulty discerned,' will he see anything, if he be at all well read, but destruction? From my experience he will be shocked and bewildered. He will perceive absolutely nothing except that his whole preconceived scheme of values has been ruined. And this is exactly what he should see.... It is this that one means when he says destruction and creation are simultaneous.[50]

Williams is alluding to Shelley's definition of lyric poetry as "preserver and destroyer" of the world possessed by intuition, and indeed Moore's poetry can be described as allegorical insofar as it plays on the dialectic of preservation and destruction. We should also recall Kant's thesis that poetry excels as a means of apprehending nature precisely because of its estrangement from nature. Poetry places "illusion" in the service of understanding, devising impossible pictures of nature that bring us closer to the substance of nature than "mere imitations."[51] Yet the destruction of the intuitive world contrived in Moore's poems stems, in part, from close observation of nature and a "prismatic" sense of detail. She emphasized repeatedly her commitment to literalism, to recording what is explicit or manifest in the world. One of her essays is titled "A Burning Desire to Be Explicit," and she claims, in another essay, to be possessed of "a mania for straight writing."[52] Yet precision, in Moore's work, serves more than the ends of naturalism or realism.

In a review of the work of the painter Robert Andrew Parker, Moore describes his images in a way that clearly evokes the allegorical qualities of her own poetry: "Parker is one of the most accurate and at the same time most unliteral of painters. He combines the mystical and the actual, working both in an abstract and in a realistic way."[53] In particular, Moore mentions a drawing of a school of fish, which she describes as an instance of "private calligraphy," composing "a signature or family cipher." Wallace Stevens, whose tastes run toward the "finical phraseology" of Moore's poetry, describes her own work in a similar way. In an essay on one of her animal poems, "He 'Digesteth Harde Yron,'" Stevens observes, "This poem has an extraordinarily factual appearance. But it is, after all, an abstraction."[54] And in his conclusion he remarks, "As it happens, she has the faculty of digesting the 'harde yron' of appearance" (103). This judgment evokes Moore's famous comment in which she praises poets who are "literalists of the imagination" and who compose poems resembling "imaginary gardens with real toads in them."[55] The allegorist reveals and exploits the "harde yron" of appearance by encrypting nature in a picture that is unassailably realistic in its particulars but estranged as a whole from intuitive experience.

Moore's revival of the allegorical lyric coincides historically with Schrödinger's use of the term *allegory* to indicate the essential nature of quantum pictures and with Walter Benjamin's study of Baroque allegory as a means of elucidating modern lyric (Baudelaire's poetry in particular). These disparate formulations, all developed in the 1920s, suggest that a powerful and wide-ranging revision of the principle of allegory must be counted as a significant feature of the discourse of high modernism. Comments made by Winifred Ellerman (Bryher) allude more specifically to the allegorical properties of Moore's work: "Her eyes are different from ours, instead of a flashing whole, her mind sees first and they obey its orders in microscopic detail, while she seems to lie perched on a rock above a warm and shallow lake, surveying an earlier globe."[56] Bryher's description of Moore's poetics calls to mind qualities associated with the Epicurean virtuoso: most important, the poet's attention to "microscopic detail," which coincides with a form of vision originating in the mind; her remoteness from experience, and her attraction to an "earlier globe," a world estranged from ordinary perception by its archaism and its microscopic character. Indeed, the poet's eyes envision a world others do not see, which is nevertheless composed, or contrived, from the ingredients of intuitive experience.

Considering the natural philosophy of the Baroque virtuoso, we should not be surprised that Moore recognized in the doctrine of atomism a metaphysics and an intellectual style compatible with the poetics of allegory. In an article on the artist E. McKnight Kauffer, Moore states, "Kauffer is a parable of uncompromise—a master of illusion—verifying Democritus' axiom, 'Compression is the first grace of style.' What is to be feared more than death? the man asked; the sage replied, 'Disillusion.' Here, actually, we have a product in which unfalsified impulse safeguards illusion."[57] Moore sees "disillusion," therefore, as the antithesis of atomist doctrine, suggesting that poet and physicist alike are masters of illusion and compression.

The virtuoso is not an idle figure of comparison or comprehension in relation to Moore's poetry; nor is it restricted to the profile of the Baroque virtuoso. For Moore is one of the central figures in a modern constellation of lyric virtuosity that includes Wallace Stevens. She herself alludes to the premises of virtuosity and applies the term to her favorite modern poets. A 1948 review of T. S. Eliot's *Old Possum's Book of Practical Cats* is titled "A Virtuoso of Make-Believe"—echoing perhaps Moore's notion of the atomist as a "master of illusion."[58] She also published a piece titled "A Bold Virtuoso," an appreciation of Wallace Stevens, whom she compares to Jean de La Fontaine, the seventeenth-century writer of animal fables.[59] The figure of the Baroque virtuoso, who was a collector of "curiosities" as well as a philosopher, a microscopist, and an illustrator, even crops up in Moore's assessment of her own poetry: "My writing is, if not a cabinet of fossils, a kind of collection of flies in amber."[60] We should not overlook, moreover, the correlation in Moore's mind between virtuosity and the representation of animals—especially with respect to La Fontaine, whose animal fables Moore translated in their entirety. La Fontaine (1621–1695) published his first volumes of animal fables in 1668, during the heyday of mechanical and corpuscularian philosophy, when the leading minds of the age regarded animals as natural automata.

In addition to her translations of La Fontaine, Moore followed quite literally her own advice to write poems about "imaginary gardens with real toads in them" by writing a number of celebrated poems about animals. Just as La Fontaine's fables subtly probe the new "philosophy" of animated machines, and as Schrödinger's cat paradox depicts the traumatic (and uncertain) demise of the animal-machine, so, too, must we regard Moore's animal poems as a lyrical discourse on the *transformation* of the automaton (a project related to Hans Bellmer's anatomy of the doll). In addition, as an episode in the poetics of materialism, Moore's poems anticipate the scenes of metamorphosis conjured by lyric poetry in the shadow of the atomic bomb. Further, her poetry reveals that the *thematics* of material transformation associated with the bomb rests on the more fundamental poetic principle of lyric substance (which has no thematic identity). Her poems help to restore the correspondences between natural philosophy and lyric poetry by subtly portraying animals as machines or toys, sometimes explicitly so. In "The Pangolin," for example, she observes the

machine-like
form and frictionless creep of a thing
made graceful by adversities

and then reveals what kind of "machine" she has in mind:

A sailboat
was the first machine. Pangolins, made
for moving quietly also, are models of exactness.[61]

Another poem, "The Jerboa," is set among the ancient Egyptians:

These people liked small things;
they gave to boys little paired playthings such as
nests of eggs, ichneumon and snake, paddle
and raft, badger and camel;

and made toys for them-
selves: the royal totem.   *(11)*

The jerboa, "a small desert rat," counts among the "dwarfs" which
lent

a fantasy
and a verisimilitude that were
right to those with, everywhere,
power over the poor.   *(12)*

The jerboa is thus one of Pharaoh's toys (recalling Yeats's Byzantium poems)—an instance of what the poet calls "too much" (the subtitle of the first section of the poem).

Moore's animal fables are the measure of the poet's virtuosity, a talent for seeing things that is characterized by a "destructive" element. Here, for example, is a descriptive passage from one of her most celebrated animal poems:

All
external
    marks of abuse are present on this
    defiant edifice—
    all the physical features of

ac-
cident—lack
    of cornice, dynamite grooves, burns, and
    hatchet strokes, these things stand
    out on it; the chasm-side is

dead.
Repeated
    evidence has proved that it can live
    on what can not revive
        its youth.

                    ("The Fish," 32–33)

Two things about this passage (aside from its great beauty) are signif-
icant: first, the reader is deprived of any reference indicating that the
phenomenon described so vividly and concretely is an animal, much
less a fish. The virtuosity of Moore's observation decomposes the in-
tuitive coherence of objects. Second, like Schrödinger's cat—though
much more explicitly—the "defiant edifice," whose mesmerizing fa-
çade defies the reader's comprehension, swims in the element of ad-
versity, thereby betraying a world of mortal danger: the animal is, to
be more precise, a picture of "accident" and "abuse"—a ruin. Indeed,
half of it is gone ("the chasm-side is dead"), though "it can live" on
other living things. Again, like Schrödinger's cat, the creature in this
traumatic (though somehow neutral) milieu is *both* dead and alive,
"mixed or smeared out in equal parts."

Despite the wealth of visual and sensory evidence, Moore's poem
does not represent a fish-object; instead, it depicts a "blurred reality,"
or complementary aspects of it, that resist integration into a coherent
or determinate picture of physical reality. The ruined creature of

Moore's virtuosity is poised between the visible and the invisible, a picture of ephemerality; yet it is also a cipher, like Bellmer's doll, a corporeal anagram combining social, imaginative, and material realities. In all of Moore's fables, however, the animal-cipher is born from the meticulous observations of the naturalist:

> Floating on spread ribs,
>   the boat-like body settles on the
> clamshell-tinted spray sprung from the nut-meg tree
>   —minute legs
> trailing half akimbo—the true divinity
> of Malay.
>
> ("*The Plumet Basilisk*," *20–21*)

Under the gaze of the virtuoso, the animal body (or a part of the body) appears with unmistakable clarity and yet remains inscrutable:

> And the
> defenseless human thing sleeps as sound as if
>
> incised with hard wrinkles, embossed with wide ears,
> invincibly tusked, made safe by magic hairs!
> As if, as if, it is all as ifs; we are at
> much unease. But magic's masterpiece is theirs—
>
> Houdini's serenity quelling his fears.
>
> ("*Elephants*," *128*)

The world conjured by the virtuoso—Houdini's world—"is all as ifs," and for this reason we sense the mortal danger in which the conjurer and the animal, or its separate parts, exist. But the conjurer pulls off her trick (an escape) and safeguards illusion; so, too, the poet's dream of the animal limb (a "defenseless human thing") is "made safe by magic hairs"—by the objective details of imaginary bodies. Houdini's stunt—the cause of "much unease"—is a virtuoso performance but also, in its simulation of trauma and superhuman dexterity, a displacement of the animal-cipher.

In the poem I have just been considering, "Elephants," the allusion to Houdini, which springs from the parable of the slumbering elephant's trunk, suggests a functional relation between the magician and the animal-cipher. (Houdini took his name from the nineteenth-century French maker of automata, Robert-Houdin.) Moore develops the relation between sorcerer and animal more explicitly in "Snakes, Mongooses, Snake-Charmers, and the Like," in which the elephant's trunk becomes a snake and Houdini a snake-charmer. Concerning the "exotic asp," the poet observes,

> One is compelled to look at it as at the shadows
>   of the alps
> imprisoning in their folds like flies in amber,
>   the rhythms of the skating-rink. . . .
>
> For what was it invented?
> To show that when intelligence in its pure form
> has embarked on a train of thought which is
>   unproductive, it will come back?
> We do not know.   *(58)*

The observer, bewitched, gazes at the snake as into a shadow, seeing only the circular rhythms of the skating-rink imprisoned, "like flies in amber," in the folds of the Alps. This peculiar analogy recalls Moore's comparison of her poetry to "a kind of collection of flies in amber" and suggests an equation between abstract vision and the cabinet of curiosities. Further, the abstract gaze of the virtuoso resembles that of the snake-charmer, who bewitches the animal but is also himself bewitched: "Engrossed in this distinguished worm nearly as wild and as fierce as the day it was caught, / he gazes as if incapable of looking at anything with a view to analysis." Indeed, we could say that the virtuoso *conjures* "the plastic animal all of a piece," since the snake is "invented" and therefore expresses the uncertain rhythm of "intelligence in its pure form," which is at once circular and unproductive.

The cryptic and ephemeral nature of Moore's animals also finds expression through metamorphosis. She notes the "quicksilver ferocity" of the basilisk (24), which she compares to a "living firework"— a meteoric body (20). Thus, she describes a

> dragon that as you look begins to be a
> nervous naked sword on little feet, with three-fold
> separate flame above the hilt, inhabiting
> fire eating into air. *(24)*

The jerboa, too, is a minor spectacle of shifting "contours" and "blurred" identity:

> strange detail of the simplified creature,
> fish-shaped and silvered to steel by the force
> of the large desert moon. *(14)*

A moment later, this "fish-shaped" rat

> hops like the fawn-breast, but has
> chipmunk contours—perceived as
> it turns its bird head.

Moore's talent for seizing the momentary aspects of the beast is part of her virtuosity; she calls the ostrich a "camel-sparrow," adding

> He is swifter than a horse; he has a foot hard
> as a hoof; the leopard
> is not more suspicious.
> *("He 'Digesteth Harde Yron,'" 99)*

The figure of metamorphosis in Moore's animal fables achieves its finest expression in the poet's elaboration of a gesture: the leap, the "as if" bridging visible and invisible realities. Here is the jerboa's staggered flight:

> The translucent mistake
> of the desert, does not make

hardship for one who
can rest and then do
the opposite—launching
as if on wings, from its match-thin hind legs, in
    daytime or at night; with the tail as a weight,
    undulated out by speed, straight.

("The Jerboa," 13–14)

Climbing through "steps of air," the weightless creature is "Part terrestrial / and part celestial"—one of the "air angels" (13). Indeed, in this moment of transformation, the angelic animal (already counted among Pharaoh's toys) joins the discourse of angels and dolls (and meteors) that once captivated mechanical philosophy and now possesses modern lyric.

Moore figures the rhythmic qualities of the jerboa's leap in a manner that points directly to the lyric identity of the animal-cipher:

By fifths and sevenths,
in leaps of two lengths,
    like uneven notes
of the Bedouin flute, it stops its gleaning
    on little wheel castors, and makes fern-seed
    footprints with kangaroo speed.

Its leaps should be set
to the flageolet.   *(14–15)*

In these lines, the poet equates metamorphosis, the leap "as if on wings" between terrestrial and celestial identities, with the art of lyric (a scene recalling the antigravitational dance of Kleist's marionette). Indeed, the trope of the lyric leap captures in a single gesture the diverse implications of Moore's sense of the ephemerality of the animal machine (and its lyric substance). In "The Plumet Basilisk," the connection between the leap and lyric identity becomes even more explicit as Moore emphasizes the metamorphic aspect of the leap:

a scared frog, screaming like a bird, leaps out
   from the weeds in which
it could have hid, with the curves of the meteorite . . .

the basilisk portrays
mythology's wish
to be interchangeably man and fish—

traveling rapidly upward, as
spider-clawed fingers can twang the
bass strings of the harp, and with steps
as articulate, make their way
back to retirement on strings that
vibrate till claws are spread flat.

   Among tightened wires,
minute noises swell
and change, as in the woods' acoustic shell

they will with trees as avenues of steel to veil

as from black opal emerald opal emerald—
scale which Swinburne called in prose, the
noiseless music that hangs about
the serpent when it stirs or springs.   *(22–23)*

In this daring passage, the leap coincides with the basilisk's transfor-
mation from "screaming frog" to bird (a lyrical beast unlike the "anon-
ymous nightingale"), from man to fish, and back to the figure of the
"serpent" (recalling the "plastic animal" conjured by the snake-
charmer). Ultimately, the lizard becomes the body of the lyre from
which "minute noises swell"—also the "noiseless music" heard by
Swinburne when the serpent "stirs or springs" in prose. What's more,
this rhapsodic progression describes a parabolic figure, as it follows
"the curves of the meteorite"—that is, the tropes of the meteoric body.

   In her poem on the ostrich, Moore declares, "The power of the
visible / is the invisible,"[62] and it is quite evident that this principle,
which defines the essence of allegorical lyric, offers a key to the most

extraordinary effects of her animal poems. Through the figure of the leap, the evanescent body of the animal-machine depicts the engine of lyric virtuosity: the ephemeral body becomes indistinguishable from lyric substance. For the leap, as Moore describes it, is an *impossible* gesture, a parabolic figure modulating visible and invisible identities through a body that has no stable form. The lyric leap of the jerboa or the basilisk is profoundly estranged from intuitive experience, and it therefore resembles the "quantum leap" identified by Bohr as the key to the mechanism of radiation. Further, just as the electron's enigmatic "leap" precipitated in atomic physics a fundamental revision of material substance, so in Moore's animal poems the leap is at once a challenge to the intuitive coherence of the body and a *picture* of the animal-machine transformed by Moore's lyric virtuosity. Understood as a *gesture,* the ephemeral body corresponds to the "blurred reality" of Schrödinger's wave interpretation of matter and also to the figure of *anamorphosis,* which Paul de Man ascribes to "the path of the dancer's soul" (and to allegory in general). In quantum physics, the wave and the leap are both figures of continuity founded on a material reality that is essentially discontinuous; the same is true of Moore's elaboration of the lyric leap. These figures are anamorphic pictures, representational distortions of a material world that happens to be invisible. Finally, we must regard the allegorical scenes composed by Schrödinger and Moore as probes or decoys, as images of a material and imaginative reality that can be represented only by what it is not.

Conclusion

Take away number in all things and all things perish. Take calculation from the world and all is enveloped in dark ignorance, nor can he who does not know the way to reckon be distinguished from the rest of the animals.

Saint Isidore of Seville

Intoxication is a number.

Charles Baudelaire, "Fuses"

What are we to make finally of the correspondences between poetics and materialism? I have presented evidence from diverse historical periods demonstrating a problematic—but apparently unavoidable— lyric dimension of scientific and philosophical theories of matter. In addition, I have tried to show how poetry and atomic physics often converge, especially in the context of modernism, in their *representations* of material substance and the nature of corporeality. This is not to say, of course, that lyric poetry and quantum mechanics produce the same kind of knowledge. There is no mystery about what separates science from poetry: it is mathematics. The authority of modern physics rests on its capacity to quantify and calculate material substance. With science, true knowledge of the material world cannot be isolated from mathematics, and so reality is understood to be essentially mathematical. Yet numbers, which are entirely devoid of quality, can provide only the most tenuous approximation of intuitive experience. Indeed, as Heisenberg and other quantum theorists discovered, the mathematical realism of modern physics falls short of constituting a new "reality" that conforms to intuitive categories. To salvage the equation of materialism and realism, and to produce an intelligible doctrine of material substance, something more than calculation was required.

Public and scholarly opinion concerning the relation between science and poetry (or materialism and poetics) has long been dominated by views stressing the incommensurability of these two kinds of knowledge. This perspective, exemplified in the humanities by the theories of T. S. Eliot and Martin Heidegger, assumes not only that the worlds envisioned by lyric poetry and scientific materialism are essentially different, but also that overcoming this cultural schism implies either a reformation of poetry in the image of science or a fundamental assault on scientific method. The evidence I have gathered suggests that these views are mistaken, with regard to both the nature of intuitive experience and the particular character of philosophical materialism. First, with regard to a model of intuition, the pictures of material substance conjured by lyric poetry and by modern physics are equally remote from experience. In addition, to hold that poetry and modern materialism yield incompatible conceptions of material substance would require us to ignore, as Heidegger does, the constitutive role of intuitive "pictures" in the doctrine of atomism. Only if scientific materialism were reduced to a purely mathematical science—a development that would deprive physics of any claim to realism—could we say that poetics and physics are antithetical phenomena. The leading theorists of quantum physics, when confronted with the prospect of imageless substance, found it impossible to renounce the regime of pictures in materialism.

Heidegger contends that man's calculation of the "world picture" is antithetical to the "open place" of poetry, where "man is the one who is looked upon by that which is."[1] Given, however, the irreducible lyricism of scientific theories of matter (which Heidegger ignores), we must conclude that the animation of nature (and the disappearance of "man") that he associates with poetry are already intrinsic to atomic physics. Could it be that the radiant or invisible body that emerges repeatedly in the history of materialism is an effect of man being "looked upon by that which is"? Whatever the correlation between atomic physics and non-eidetic Being, we can be sure that the problem of materiality functions in Heidegger's philosophy as a site for negotiating the relation between bodies and pictures, being and nonbeing, the visible and the invisible. By equating atomic physics and the world picture, Heidegger inadvertently betrays the phantasmagorical materialism recovered by Marx from the Alexandrian "system" of Epicurus.

If physics, the most rigorous form of materialism, possesses an irreducible lyric dimension, then what are we to make of materialist criticism in the humanities? In terms of pure intuition (if such a thing exists), we have no trouble determining what constitutes a body and what does not. Intuitive certainty vanishes, however, as soon as we try to determine what we know to be true, universally, about the material substance of bodies. Only mathematics can provide authoritative knowledge of material substance, yet the pictures it supplies are alien to experience. Thus, the authority of materialism, as a theoretical perspective, depends on knowledge that is either purely intuitive (the goal of empiricism) or purely mathematical. Quite obviously, materialist criticism in the humanities (in the study of literature, for example) is neither purely empirical nor purely mathematical. As a result, the integrity of material evidence has no authoritative foundation in historicist criticism.

This is not to say, of course, that we should not practice historical criticism, but only that its claims to authenticity, as against a more philosophical approach to the object, should be tempered in light of the inescapably lyrical—and even phantasmagorical—nature of materiality. It is precisely in this respect that we must reassess the role we grant to lyric poetry in public discourse. For, if we discount forms of knowledge that are purely mathematical or purely intuitive, lyric poetry emerges not merely as the object of literary criticism but as a *model* of materialist criticism in its most searching and original form. Lyric poetry, according to Giorgio Agamben, is the very model of a "science without object," which we must now equate with materialist or historical criticism in its most authentic—that is to say, philosophical—mode. For lyric substance—the "sense" of materiality supplied to us by poets like Wallace Stevens and Marianne Moore—constitutes a world whose inaccessibility is legitimized by the principles of scientific materialism. Indeed, science beholds its future—as a cultural practice—in the nexus of its Baroque formulation, in the heterogeneity and iconophilia of natural philosophy, but also in the "wit" of Metaphysical poetry. Thus the significance of poetics for the history of materialism offers an important precedent for current debates about the reciprocity of literary criticism and the emerging discipline of cultural studies. For if we acknowledge that materialism possesses an inherently lyrical dimension, then we can also assume that the history of poetics contains a viable model for the study of material culture in the humanities. That is to say, rather than exceeding or displacing the field of literature, cultural criticism may, in its best moments, display a greater degree of lyricism in method and style, an orientation rooted in a more productive and lyrical conception of materiality.

To propose that lyric poetry might serve as a model for materialist criticism—for criticism that carries some weight in public discourse—is a gesture that possesses a certain charm. Yet what could possibly legitimize or substantiate such a proposal? Is there anything about lyric poetry that might allow it to speak with authority on the question of what is real, or, let us say, on the prospect of reality as something that is socially and imaginatively constructed? Lyric poetry and materialism coincide in their dependence on pictures and in the priority assigned to representation as a means of establishing the intuitive coherence of a world (whether real or imagined). Yet the value or significance as-

signed to pictures in the context of physics is utterly different from
the assumptions we make about the imagery of lyric poetry. For, as
we discovered in reviewing the crisis of visualization in quantum me-
chanics, pictures preserve the equation of materialism and realism;
indeed, pictures constitute the last vestige of realism in modern ma-
terialism. In poetry, however, quite the reverse is true: pictures and
analogies that function in the same way as the allegories of quantum
theory are judged to be the essence of *unreality*, even though the imag-
inative coherence of this unreality relies on forms of mediation that it
shares with the "objective" world conjured by science. The substance
of reality in physics is the substance of illusion in poetry. Theoretically
speaking, the only thing that prevents us from regarding the imagery
of lyric as the currency of realism is the authority of mathematical
calculation intrinsic to modern materialism. Yet mathematics guar-
antees only the authority of the real, not its intelligibility. The substance
of lyric therefore remains an essential element in the fabrication of the
real.

Despite the opposing values commonly associated with the uses of
imagery in poetry and science, it is no longer possible to ignore the
role of mediation in science or to isolate the scientific imagination from
the function of images in poetry (or the arts in general). Both science
and lyric poetry, compelled and confounded by the world as we ex-
perience it, make claims about invisible bodies that require some form
of mediation—often an image or a trope—to become intelligible and
to ensure, theoretically, their coexistence with visible bodies (or the
visible aspect of invisible bodies). In poetry, as in science, the image is
never merely imitative, never superfluous; rather it is indispensable to
the appearance of the phenomenon it depicts. To say this about poetry
is hardly surprising, but the productive character of mediation in sci-
ence (practice, instrument, representation, inscription) is just beginning
to emerge as a topic of public and scholarly debate. Ultimately, Bruno
Latour contends, "By concentrating on the trivial aspects of the cook-
ing of science, we may also end up accounting for its vanishing points,

res and *cogito.*"[2] Poetry, of course, excels at "cooking" the data, to the extent that "subject" and "object" are likely to dissolve in the field of lyric "mediation"—a process now threatening to engulf the mind and the object of science. This shift toward the middle ground (between the mind and the world "out there") is the pretext for Giorgio Agamben's nomination of poetry and criticism as the proper agents of a "science without object"—the culmination of the training of the scientific gaze on invisible material phenomena.[3] Further, Latour suggests that the methodology of historians and philosophers of science (and even science itself) could benefit from the example of disciplines that are adept at "multiplying the mediators."[4] Latour has in mind recent materialist scholarship in art history, but he also alludes to the prospect that art itself may provide the ultimate model, the telos, of scientific practice—insofar as science coincides with realism. For as long as materialism sees fit to maintain the pose of realism and, at the same time, insist that material substance is invisible, then the ingenuity and "thickness" of lyric "culture" (of reality as poetry inscribes it) must serve as the unattainable standard of representational practice for science.

Although it is essential, from a philosophical standpoint, to establish the iconography and the means shared by science and poetry, my claim is not that science will become poetry (or vice versa), but rather that lyric poetry might serve as a model for materialist criticism in the *humanities*. Philosophical materialism, as I hope I have demonstrated, veers historically between empiricism and the theoretical gaze of natural philosophy and deductive physics (the legacy of atomism). These perspectives yield different (and often incompatible) views of material bodies: one intuitive and experiential, the other abstract and figurative. Since the philosophy of Epicurus, however, materialism has repeatedly combined these irreconcilable positions in a single doctrine, the most important modern example of this syncretism (for the humanities) being Marx's theory of dialectical materialism. The chief emblem of Marx's Epicurean phenomenology is his conception of the commodity fetish, an "object" characterized by its *Doppelcharakter,* its duality. For Marx repeatedly insists that commodities are "sensuous things which are at the same time suprasensible" *(sinnliche übersinnliches).*[5] A fetish is a body that is both material and immaterial, perceptible and theoretical, at the same time. Thus we have Marx's famous remark about the latency of the fetish: "A commodity appears at first sight an extremely obvious, trivial thing. But its analysis brings out that it is a very strange thing, abounding in metaphysical subtleties and theological niceties."[6] We should not, however, understand the duplicity of the fetish to be an aberration of materialism; on the contrary, the fetish revives for modernity the enigma of the Epicurean body, even as it illustrates the schismatic nature of scientific materialism. The double vision of philosophical materialism, embodied in the *Doppelcharakter* of the fetish, therefore yields a conception of the body that is at once intuitive and abstract, mundane and phantasmagorical, real and unreal.

Materialism finds its true voice (or a reflection of itself) in the apparatus of lyric poetry, which, according to Paul de Man, exploits "the ambivalence of a language that is representational and nonrepresentational at the same time."[7] Poetry's vision of things (and of material substance) displays the same combination of empiricism and unbridled speculation that produces the impossible bodies of modern materialism. Furthermore, the duplicity of lyric finds complete expression in what de Man calls allegory, since "allegorical poetry must contain a representational element that invites and allows for understanding, only to discover that the understanding it reaches is necessarily in error."[8] From this perspective, de Man's theory of allegory reproduces in remarkable ways the scandalous features of materialist doctrine, as if allegory were the key to the representational practice of modern materialism (a thesis confirmed by the importance of Kleist's marionette to de Man's theory of allegory). Ultimately, the provisional realism of allegorical lyric corresponds to the provisional empiricism of materialist doctrine. In both cases, the practice of imitation defers to (though it is not displaced by) a language that is no longer solely mimetic, that renounces, imperfectly, the task of modeling objective reality.

Taking into account these correspondences between lyric poetry and materialist doctrine, we could say that the discourse of lyric, suspended between empiricism and speculation, between representation and rhetoric, offers the most authentic model for materialist criticism in the humanities. For the double vision of lyric (and allegory in particular) is the key to its modernity, to its special significance for modern sensibility. Lyric poetry is *inherently* modern—in a theoretical rather than a historical sense—because lyric discourse embodied the dichotomy of modern consciousness long before that sensibility became a pervasive, historical phenomenon. The world has always been modern in the eyes of lyric. The same could be said for the gaze of materialism, since Marx judged the syncretism and incoherence of Epicurean phenomenology to be the essence of its appeal to modernity. That contemporary cultural criticism, especially when it is truly dialectical, has already assimilated many of the features of lyric discourse should therefore not be surprising. In its attraction to the surface of things—but also in its profound suspicion of manifest content—and in its emphasis on historical, ideological, and imaginary constructions of social reality, materialist criticism today already adheres, as poetry does, to a model of provisional realism. Lyric poetry and materialist criticism in its most authentic form thus both maintain a realism without authority, based on the powers of persuasion and divination inherent in pictures. A body composed of pictures is little more than the substance of history and the imagination. As long as things appear to us in this way, and as long as matter remains a problem, poetry will be an indispensable guide to reality.

NOTES

INTRODUCTION

1. Materialist criticism today tends to ignore, for example, the degree to which Marxian principles derive from specific sources in ancient materialism, or the manner in which Georges Bataille's concept of heterogeneity—to cite another salient feature of contemporary materialism—recuperates certain rhetorical postures long associated with materialism. The effects of missing materialism are also implicated in the fate of deconstruction. An exception to this general trend can be found in the work of Yve-Alain Bois and Rosalind E. Krauss, whose book *Formless: A User's Guide* (New York: Zone, 1997), gives serious attention, from the perspective of art history, to configurations of materiality in modernism.

2. Bruno Latour, "How to Be Iconophilic in Art, Science, and Religion?" in *Picturing Science, Producing Art*, ed. Caroline A. Jones and Peter Galison (New York: Routledge, 1998), 422.

3. Giambattista Vico, *The New Science,* trans. Thomas Goddard Bergin and Max Harold Frisch (Ithaca: Cornell University Press, 1970), 75. On the poetic derivation of the sciences, see 72.

CHAPTER 1

1. T. S. Eliot, "The Metaphysical Poets" (1921), in *Selected Prose of T. S. Eliot*, ed. Frank Kermode (New York: Harcourt Brace, 1975), 64.

2. Martin Heidegger, "The Age of the World Picture," in *The Question Concerning Technology and Other Essays*, trans. William Lovitt (New York: Harper, 1975), 118–19, 127.

3. Marianne Moore, "Poetry," *The Complete Poems of Marianne Moore* (New York: Viking, 1967), 36. The version of this poem Moore chose to publish in her *Complete Poems* consists of only three lines, shortened considerably from the original version of thirty-eight lines (published in 1919 in the journal *Others*). The complete text of the short version is as follows:

> I, too, dislike it.
> Reading it, however, with a perfect contempt for it, one discovers
> in it, after all, a place for the genuine.

The earlier version can be found in the author's notes to the *Complete Poems*, 266–67. Perhaps we should regard the poem's contraction as evidence of Moore's uneasiness about "poetry."

4. Samuel Johnson, "Lives of the Poets," in *Selected Poetry and Prose,* ed. Frank Brady and W. K. Wimsatt (Berkeley: University of California Press, 1977), 348.

5. William Butler Yeats, "Sailing to Byzantium," in *The Poems*, ed. Richard Finneran (New York: Macmillan, 1983), 193.

6. Yeats made this comment in a BBC lecture prepared in 1931, cited in A. Norman Jeffares, *A New Commentary on the Poems of W. B. Yeats* (Stanford: Stanford University Press, 1984), 213 (emphasis added).

7. Thomas Whitaker typifies this idealist interpretation when he describes the mechanical bird of "Sailing to Byzantium" as "set apart from the flux of time." *Swan and Shadow* (Chapel Hill: University of North Carolina Press, 1964), 277.

8. Yeats, "Byzantium," in *Poems*, 248.

9. The "scorn" reserved by the automaton for "common bird or petal / And all complexities of mire or blood" echoes an earlier poem by Yeats. In "The Dolls" (1914), the newborn child of a dollmaker and his wife is denounced by a group of animated dolls as "an insult to us" and "a noisy and

filthy thing." Even the infant's mother refers to it, apologetically, as an "accident." Yeats, *Poems*, 126–27.

10. On the history of the topos of the animate image, see David Freedberg, *The Power of Images*, especially his chapter "Live Images" (Chicago: University of Chicago Press, 1989).

11. Paul Virilio, *The Vision Machine*, trans. Julie Rose (Bloomington: Indiana University Press, 1994), 12.

12. *October* 77 (Summer 1996), 25.

13. W. J. T. Mitchell, "What Do Pictures *Really* Want?" *October* 77 (Summer 1996), 81.

14. E. F. Peters, *Greek Philosophical Terms* (New York: New York University Press, 1967), 8, 13, 15. Peters does not note, however, that αισθάνομαι (to see, to perceive) derives from αίσθω (to breathe in, to gasp). This derivation suggests that aesthetic experience may be associated, at its origin, with the *effect* of a startling perception (and with breath in particular).

15. Peters, *Greek Philosophical Terms*, 162.

16. To be precise, Aristotle calls plot "the first principle and, as it were, the soul of tragedy." *Poetics* (1450a80), trans. James Hutton (New York: Norton, 1982), 51.

17. Richard McKeon, "Rhetoric and Poetic in the Philosophy of Aristotle," in *Aristotle's Poetics and English Literature*, ed. Elder Olson (Chicago: University of Chicago Press, 1965), 233.

18. Aristotle discusses the souls of plants in *De anima*, i.5.411^{b}25.

19. On the superiority of poetry in the hierarchy of the fine arts, and its relation to the "figural" in contemporary aesthetics, see D. N. Rodowick, "Impure Mimesis, or the Ends of the Aesthetic," in *Deconstruction and the Visual Arts*, ed. Peter Brunette and David Wills (Cambridge: Cambridge University Press, 1993), 106–9.

20. G. E. Lessing, *Laocoön: An Essay on the Limits of Painting and Poetry*, trans. Edward Allen McCormick (Baltimore: Johns Hopkins University Press, 1984), 88.

21. Lessing discusses at some length poetry's ability (and painting's inability) to evoke the Homeric "cloud" of invisibility. *Laocoön*, 68–70.

22. Immanuel Kant, *Critique of Judgment*, trans. Werner S. Pluhar, (Indianapolis: Hackett, 1987), part 1, book 2, section 53, 196.

23. Kant, *Critique of Judgment*, 196–97. Hence Kant contends, "*Poetry is*

the art of conducting a free play of the imagination as a task of understanding" (part 1, book 2, section 51, 190).

24. Kant, *Critique of Judgment*, part 1, book 2, section 49, 183.

25. Martin Heidegger, "The Origin of the Work of Art," *Poetry, Language, Thought*, trans. Albert Hofstadter (New York: Harper, 1971), 75, 73. At times, for the sake of clarity, I have drawn on Hofstadter's earlier translation of Heidegger's essay, printed in *Philosophies of Art and Beauty*, ed. Albert Hofstadter and Richard Kuhns (Chicago: University of Chicago Press, 1986). All page numbers in parentheses refer to the Harper edition.

26. Heidegger, "The Origin of the Work of Art," 72. Heidegger develops the concept of "the Open" more extensively in relation to Rilke's poetry in the essay "What Are Poets For?" (1936), in *Poetry, Language, Thought*.

27. Bertrand Russell, *A Critical Exposition of the Philosophy of Leibniz* (Cambridge, U.K.: The University Press, 1900), 75.

28. Gianni Vattimo, "Au-delà de la matière et du texte," *Matière et philosophie*, ed. Arnauld Pontier (Paris: Editions du Centre Pompidou, 1988), 50 (my translation).

CHAPTER 2

1. Daston and Galison collaborated in an essay on photography and mechanical objectivity, "The Image of Objectivity," *Representations* 80 (Fall 1992), 81–128. Among Daston's other publications, see her recent book with Katherine Park, *Wonders and the Order of Nature* (New York: Zone Books, 1998), and her essay "Baconian Facts, Academic Civility, and the Prehistory of Objectivity," in *Rethinking Objectivity*, ed. Allan Megill (Durham: Duke University Press, 1994). Additional work by Galison and Daston can be found in a collection of essays titled *Picturing Science, Producing Art*, ed. Caroline A. Jones and Peter Galison (New York: Routledge, 1998).

2. On the problem of depicting the invisible in modern physics, see Peter Galison's magisterial work *Image and Logic: A Material Culture of Microphysics* (Chicago: University of Chicago Press, 1997), which concerns images of material substance produced by machines and the genealogy of these devices.

3. Bruno Latour, "How to Be Iconophilic in Art, Science, and Religion?" in Jones and Galison, *Picturing Science, Producing Art*, 421.

4. Giambattista Vico, *On the Study Methods of Our Time* (1709), trans. Elio Gianturco (Indianapolis: Bobbs-Merrill, 1965), 43–44.

5. Many translations of "The Sandman" into English are available; my citation is from E. T. A. Hoffmann, *Tales of Hoffmann*, trans. R. J. Hollingdale (Harmondsworth: Penguin, 1982), 121, 98. I should say that Spalanzani is the *principal* creator, since Olympia is jointly fabricated by Spalanzani, who furnishes the clockwork and the voice, and by Coppelius, a purveyor of optical devices, who furnishes the eyes. The automaton is therefore the offspring of two men—a detail that is worth bearing in mind.

6. E. T. A Hoffmann, "The Automaton," *The Best Tales of Hoffmann*, trans. E. F. Bleiler (New York: Dover, 1967).

7. Hoffmann, "The Sandman," 113.

8. An editor to whom Hoffmann sent his story extracted this lengthy passage on the mechanical reproduction of "nature's music" from the narrative of "The Automaton" and published it separately in 1814 (prior to publication of the story itself) in a musicological journal, *Allgemeine Musikalische Zeitung*.

9. The figure of the "Talking Turk" in Hoffmann's story is based on the famous "Chess Player" automaton constructed by Baron von Kempelen in 1770 and exhibited throughout Europe in a series of challenge matches with heads of state (including Catherine the Great and Napoleon, who lost his match to the android). The Chess Player, costumed to resemble a Turkish sultan, was revealed—with the help of an exposé written by Edgar Allan Poe—to be a false automaton. For a more detailed account of the escapades of the Chess Player, see Alfred Chapuis and Edmond Droz, *Les automates* (Neuchâtel: Griffon, 1949), 371–73. Von Kempelen's chess player is also the source for the chess automaton—"the puppet called 'historical materialism'"—described by Walter Benjamin at the beginning of his last completed text, "Theses on the Philosophy of History," published in *Illuminations*, trans. Harry Zohn (New York: Schocken Books, 1969), 253.

10. On the history of mechanical divines and magicians, see Chapuis and Droz, *Les automates*, 251–70.

11. In the natural philosophy of the Middle Ages, it is not uncommon, according to Silvio Bedini, to find anecdotes about scientists (including Albertus Magnus, Robert Grosseteste, and Roger Bacon) constructing automata as part of their philosophical enterprise. Silvio Bedini, "The Role of Automata

in the History of Technology," *Technology and Culture* 5, no. 1 (Winter 1964), 31. The first biological automaton (in human form) is thought to have been built by Hans Bullman in Nuremberg about 1525.

12. These comments by a M. Poisson in 1619 are reported by Derek J. de Solla Price in his article "Automata and the Origins of Mechanism and Mechanistic Philosophy," *Technology and Culture* 5, no. 1 (Winter 1964), 12. Descartes's interest in automata is symptomatic of a broader "modern" fascination with such devices. Montaigne, for example, in his *Journal de voyage* of 1581, expressed keen interest in the development of waterworks and musical automata in Italy and Germany.

13. In addition to his designs for a calculating machine and a clock, Leibniz devised improvements in "distance-reckoning, barometry, the design of lenses, carriages, windmills, suction pumps, gearing mechanisms, and many other devices." Roger Ariew, "G. W. Leibniz, Life and Works," in *The Cambridge Companion to Leibniz*, ed. Nicholas Jolley (Cambridge: Cambridge University Press, 1995), 26.

14. Georges Canguilhem, "Machine and Organism," in *Incorporations*, ed. Jonathan Crary and Sanford Kwinter (New York: Zone Books, 1992), 66.

15. A. G. Drachmann reviews the available evidence for the water-clock and automata of Ktesibios in *Ktesibios, Philon, and Heron: A Study in Ancient Pneumatics* (Copenhagen: E. Munksgaard, 1948), 3, 114. The so-called Heronic tradition of technics and pneumatic philosophy, which played a decisive role in the emergence of early modern technology, derived from the work of Ktesibios and two other Hellenistic philosophers: Philo of Byzantium and the most influential of the three, Hero of Alexandria (first century A.D.). Hero's influence can be explained in part by the survival of the complete text of his *Pneumatics*, whereas the works of Ktesibios and Philo survive only in citation or from Arabic sources.

16. Price, "Automata," 15. Silvio Bedini makes a similar point: "The greatest advances in the development of biological automata, of astronomical models, and of fine mechanisms, were probably simultaneous in point of time and derivation." Bedini, "The Role of Automata," 19.

17. Price, "Automata," 15. Among the seventy or so devices described by Hero in his *Pneumatics* are "a bird made to whistle by flowing water"; "a trumpet, in the hands of an automaton, sounded by compressed air"; "figures made to dance by fire on an altar"; and "an automaton, the head of which

continues to be attached to the body, after a knife has entered the neck at one side, passed completely through it and out the other." *The Pneumatics of Hero of Alexandria* (a facsimile of the 1851 Woodcroft edition), introduction by Marie Boas Hall (London: Macdonald, 1971), 29, 71, 95, 109.

18. Some years ago, Jacques Derrida, with typical ingenuity and melodrama, insinuated the *parergon* into the exclusive core of Kantian aesthetics, arguing that "the entire frame of the analytic of the beautiful functions, with respect to that which determines content or internal structure, like a parergon." Derrida, "The Parergon," trans. Craig Owens, *October* 9 (Summer 1979), 33. Though Derrida's equation of aesthetic philosophy and the so-called logic of the *parergon* is essentially correct (as the ambiguity of the automaton confirms), he diminishes the scope and appeal of his argument, in my opinion, by considering the *parergon* exclusively as an effect of the frame.

19. Regarding Vitruvius's description of the inaugural water-clock of Ktesibios, Drachmann observes, "There is here no mention at all of any scale of hours or pointer; that comes afterwards. It seems reasonable to conclude that the first clock had no scale of hours at all, but only made signals to be seen and heard at the end of each hour." Drachmann, *Ktesibios, Philon, and Heron*, 19.

20. Price, "Automata," 13.

21. We can ignore, for the moment, the uncertain bearing of the Stoic doctrine of *pneuma* (breath or soul) on pneumatic technology, since the correlation of soul and toy remains only imperfectly articulated (in La Mettrie's *L'homme-machine,* for example) until Baudelaire's *aesthetique du joujou* in the mid-nineteenth century.

22. Democritus (460?–357 B.C.E.), the founder of atomist doctrine, states, "By convention are sweet and bitter, hot and cold, by convention is color; in truth are atoms and the void." Fragment 589 in *The Pre-Socratic Philosophers*, trans. and ed. G. S. Kirk and J. E. Raven (Cambridge: Cambridge University Press, 1957), 422.

23. Ernst Mach, *Popular Scientific Lectures*, trans. Thomas J. McCormack (LaSalle: Open Court, 1943), 187.

24. Karl Marx presented his dissertation, *On the Difference between the Democritean and Epicurean Philosophies of Nature*, at Jena in 1841. A thorough review of this work reveals the degree to which Marx's theory of fetishism, which he developed in the mid-1840s, derives its fundamental philosophical

orientation from his earlier critique of ancient atomism. I offer a reading of this critique in chapter 5.

25. Marie Boas makes this point in her article "Hero's *Pneumatics*: A Study of its Transmission and Influence," *Isis* 40 (1949), 38.

26. The most substantial work of Epicurean philosophy from antiquity, Lucretius's *On the Nature of Things,* was first printed in Basel (in Latin) in 1473. The writings of Epicurus himself survive only in citation from Book X of *Lives and Opinions of Eminent Philosophers* by Diogenes Laertius, a work printed for the first time in 1523. Democritus, whose physical doctrine of atoms was adopted almost without revision by Epicurus, does not figure prominently in the modern revival of atomism only because so little of his writing survives directly or in citation.

27. According to the *Oxford English Dictionary,* the term *epicure* in English was employed in the sixteenth and seventeenth centuries as a synonym for a profligate and an atheist.

28. Marie Boas, "Hero's *Pneumatics*," 48. Excerpts from Hero's text were first printed by Giorgio Valla in 1501; the full text was printed in Latin in 1575 and in Italian in 1589.

29. Boas, "Hero's *Pneumatics*," 47.

30. Boas, "Hero's *Pneumatics*," 39, 43.

31. Boas, "Hero's *Pneumatics*," 39.

32. Boas, "Hero's *Pneumatics*," 43. Hero's interest in the technology of illusion extended to the so-called science of mirrors, a subject on which he produced a treatise called the *Catoptrica*. In the Heronic tradition, then, the pneumatic "philosophy" of the automaton is never far removed from the science of optics.

33. In *Coryat's Crudities* (1611), Thomas Coryat refers to the mechanized figure as "a vice which the Grecians call αυτοματον."

34. Daniel Garber, "Leibniz and the Foundations of Physics," *The Natural Philosophy of Leibniz*, ed. Kathleen Okruhlik and James Robert Brown (Dordrecht: Reidel, 1985), 92.

35. Catherine Wilson, *The Invisible World: Early Modern Philosophy and the Invention of the Microscope* (Princeton: Princeton University Press, 1995), 11.

36. René Descartes, *Philosophical Writings of Descartes*, vol. 1, trans. John Cottingham, Robert Stoothoff, and Dugald Murdoch (Cambridge: Cam-

bridge University Press, 1984–1985), 99. Descartes goes on, in considerable detail, to compare the body to "the grottoes and fountains in the royal gardens" at Saint-Germain-en-Laye (100–101). One of these creations, the Grotto of Orpheus, designed by Salomon de Caus, has statues of animals moving in concert with the lyre music of a mechanical Orpheus. Here once again we find confirmation of the symbolic relation between pneumatic technology and a personification of lyric poetry.

37. Descartes, *Philosophical Writings*, vol. 1, 329–30.

38. Descartes, "Principles of Philosophy," in *Philosophical Writings*, vol. 1, 279.

39. Descartes, *Philosophical Writings*, vol. 2, 405.

40. G. W. Leibniz, "Principles of Nature and Grace," in *Philosophical Essays*, ed. and trans. Roger Ariew and Daniel Garber (Indianapolis: Hackett, 1989), 207.

41. On the correlation of atom and automaton, Jean-Claude Beaune notes, "The living machine meets its mirror image, *live matter* . . . the atom of concentrated mechanicity inside the object." Jean-Claude Beaune, "The Classical Age of the Automaton: An Impressionistic Survey," in *Fragments for a History of the Human Body*, part 1, ed. Michel Feher, Ramona Naddaff, and Nadia Tazi (New York: Zone Books, 1989), 434.

42. Michel Serres, *Le système de Leibniz et ses modèles mathématiques*, vol. 1 (Paris: Presses Universitaires, 1968), 363 (my translation).

43. G. W. Leibniz, *The Monadology and Other Philosophical Writings*, trans. Robert Latta (Oxford: Oxford University Press, 1968), 331–32, 333.

44. Wilson, *Invisible World*, 8.

45. Laurens Laudan, "The Clock Metaphor and Probabilism: The Impact of Descartes on English Methodological Thought," *Annals of Science* 22, no. 29 (June 1966), 89. Laudan indicates that the clock was commonly used as a figure for method by English natural philosophers, including Robert Boyle, Joseph Glanvill, Henry Power, and John Locke.

46. Laudan, "The Clock Metaphor," 80.

47. Laudan, "The Clock Metaphor," 80.

48. On the radical exteriorization of the body in mechanical philosophy, Michel Serres observes, "The mechanical model is such that exteriority devours interiority." *Le système de Leibniz*, vol. 1, 337 (my translation).

49. G. W. Leibniz, "On the Method of Arriving at a True Analysis of

Bodies and the Causes of Natural Things," *Philosophical Papers and Letters*, trans. Leroy E. Loemker (Dordrecht: Reidel, 1976), 173.

50. Silvio Bedini, "The Role of Automata," 29–30.

51. Leibniz, "On the Method of Arriving at a True Analysis," 173.

52. The correlation between angelic intelligence and mathematical physics appears in a letter from Leibniz to Herman Conring (1678): "Suppose that some angel wishes to explain the nature of color to me distinctly. He will accomplish nothing by chattering about forms and faculties." Nevertheless, Leibniz concludes, if the angel "explains everything in such a way that it is clear that it could not happen otherwise, then at least he will have increased my knowledge, since he has treated physics mathematically." *Philosophical Papers and Letters*, 219.

53. Robert E. Butts, "Leibniz on the Side of Angels," in Okruhlik and Brown, *The Natural Philosophy of Leibniz*, 210, 220. In essence, Butts contends, "The methodological angel would, I think, urge upon us *the doing of science*" (209). On the genealogy of methodological angels in nineteenth-century science (in Charles Darwin and James Clerk Maxwell, specifically), see Silvan S. Schweber, "Demons, Angels and Probability," in *Physics as Natural Philosophy*, ed. Abner Shimony and Herman Feshbach (Cambridge: MIT Press, 1982).

54. Price, "Automata," 17.

55. Loosely translated into English (but not by machine):

A young child driven by passion
Seeks the prize of your good favor.
And don't be surprised if he obtains it:
A desire to please you brought this prodigy to life.

The one poem in English composed by the toy tends, however, toward toy doggerel:

Unerring is my hand the small
May I not add with truth
I do my best to please you all.
Encourage then my youth.

These texts (in the flowery hand of the toy) can be found in Chapuis and Droz, *Les Automates*, 316.

56. Julien Offray de la Mettrie, *Man a Machine*, trans. Richard A. Watson and Maya Rybalka (Indianapolis: Hackett, 1994), 30.

57. La Mettrie, *Man a Machine*, 69, 32. In another passage, we find that his conception of the man-machine also retains the seventeenth-century fascination with toys and popular culture: "Man is but an animal, or a contraption of springs, each of which activates the next without our being able to tell which one nature used to start the merry-go-round of human society." (65).

58. John Locke, "Essay Concerning Human Understanding" (Oxford: The Clarendon Press, 1894), book IV, chapter 10.

59. Aram Vartanian, *La Mettrie's 'L'Homme-Machine': A Study in the Origins of an Idea* (Princeton: Princeton University Press, 1960), 32.

60. One of the most prominent features of La Mettrie's treatise is his belief in spermatic doctrine, a vitalist offshoot of atomism, which regards *spermata* (seeds) as irreducible particles of organic life.

61. Donna Haraway, "A Manifesto for Cyborgs," *Socialist Review* 15, no. 2 (March–April 1985), 60. It is remarkable that Haraway makes no reference to La Mettrie's essay or to any other documents of mechanical philosophy (with the exception of a dismissive reference to "Foucault's biopolitics"). One would think, from Haraway's treatment of it, that the cyborg appears historically for the first time on the horizon of postmodern feminism.

CHAPTER 3

1. Roman Paska, "The Inanimate Incarnate," in *Fragments for a History of the Human Body*, part 1, ed. Michel Feher, Ramona Naddaff, and Nadia Tazi (New York: Zone Books, 1989), 412.

2. E. T. A. Hoffmann, "The Sandman," *Tales of Hoffmann*, trans. R. J. Hollingdale (Harmondsworth: Penguin, 1982), 116, 120.

3. Heinrich von Kleist, "Über das Marionettentheater," *Sämtliche Werke und Briefe*, ed. Helmut Sembdner (Munich: Hanser, 1961), vol. 2, 338–45. Two translations of Kleist's essay are available in English. My references are to Roman Paska's translation, "On the Marionette Theater," in Feher, Naddaff, and Tazi, *Fragments for a History of the Human Body*, 415. Another English translation of Kleist's text is available in *Essays on Dolls*, trans. Idris Parry (London: Penguin/Syrens, 1994). This petite volume also contains, conveniently, writings by Rilke and Baudelaire.

4. Paul de Man, "Aesthetic Formalization: Kleist's *Über das Marionetten-theater*," in *The Rhetoric of Romanticism* (New York: Columbia University Press, 1984), 314, 266, 270.

5. Kleist, "On the Marionette Theater," 418.

6. De Man's reference is to Rilke's angel in the *Duino Elegies*, though it would not be inappropriate to call on the Baroque angel of method to explain the marionette's defiance of gravity ("Aesthetic Formalization," 287).

7. Paska, "The Inanimate Incarnate," 411.

8. Jean-Pierre Vernant, "Dim Bodies, Dazzling Bodies," trans. Anne M. Wilson, in Feher, Naddaff, and Tazi, *Fragments for a History of the Human Body*, 23, 34.

9. Charles Baudelaire, "Morale du joujou," *Curiosités esthétiques, l'art romantique, et autres oeuvres critiques* (Paris: Garnier, 1983), 204, 206. An English translation of this essay appears as "The Philosophy of Toys" in *Essays on Dolls*. My renderings of Baudelaire's text depart occasionally from Parry's for the sake of clarity.

10. Theodor W. Adorno, "On Lyric Poetry and Society," *Notes to Literature*, vol. 1, trans. Shierry Weber Nicholsen, ed. Rolf Tiedeman (New York: Columbia University Press, 1991), 37.

11. Adorno, "On Lyric Poetry," 38, 40.

12. W. R. Johnson, *The Idea of Lyric* (Berkeley: University of California Press, 1982), 13. On the correlation of image and lyric, see also Andrew Welsh, *Roots of Lyric: Primitive Poetry and Modern Poetics* (Princeton: Princeton University Press, 1978), 67–99. Welsh regards the image as one of the "fundamental powers that form the language and direct the meanings of poetry" (21).

13. Hugo Friedrich, *The Structure of Modern Poetry*, trans. Joachim Neugroschel (Evanston: Northwestern University Press, 1975), 53.

14. Friedrich, *Structure of Modern Poetry,* 53, 20–21.

15. Paul de Man, "Lyric and Modernity," in *Blindness and Insight* (Minneapolis: University of Minnesota Press, 1983), 168, 186.

16. T. S. Eliot, "The Metaphysical Poets," in *Selected Essays*, ed. Frank Kermode (New York: Harcourt Brace, 1960), 247.

17. As an indication of just how far he is willing to go in the strategic recuperation of the mimetic aspect of lyric, de Man contends, "Mallarmé

remains a representational poet as he remained in fact a poet of the self" ("Lyric and Modernity," 182).

18. De Man, "Aesthetic Formalization," 274.

19. Baudelaire, "Philosophy of Toys," 16.

20. This statement appears in an editorial note of the Garnier edition of Baudelaire's prose. *Curiosités esthétiques*, 207.

21. Indeed, the incongruity of terms in the essay's title, "Morale du jou-jou," subtly evokes the ambiguity of the lyrical toy. *Morale*, in the context of Baudelaire's reflections, is most appropriately translated as "moral philosophy," or simply "philosophy," a term that leads us to expect a work of some intellectual gravity. Yet the term *joujou*, unlike its synonym *jouet*, does not lend itself to conceptual or figurative elaborations. (A *joujou* is just a toy and not, by extension, the "toy" of destiny.) Thus the "toy" Baudelaire seems to have in mind is *antithetical*—at once philosophical and inimical to reflection, ideal and concrete. In this respect, Baudelaire's "philosophy" of the toy participates in the dialectics of materiality with which the automaton has been so prominently associated in the history of philosophy and poetics.

22. Baudelaire, "Philosophy of Toys," 17.

23. This segment of Baudelaire's essay appeared as a separate prose poem, "Le joujou du pauvre" (The Poor Boy's Toy) in *Petits poèmes en prose* (1862).

24. Rainer Maria Rilke, *Puppen*, in *Sämtliche Werke* (Frankfurt: Insel Verlag, 1966), vol. 6, 1063–74. Two translations of Rilke's essay are available in English. My references are to "Some Reflections on Dolls," in *Where Silence Begins: Selected Prose by Rainer Maria Rilke*, trans. G. Craig Houston (New York: New Directions, 1978), 43. An English translation is also available in *Essays on Dolls*.

25. Rainer Maria Rilke, "The Angels," *Selected Poems*, trans. C. F. MacIntyre (Berkeley: University of California Press, 1940), 27.

26. Rainer Maria Rilke, *New Poems*, trans. J. B. Leishman (New York: New Directions Books, 1964), 75.

27. Rainer Maria Rilke, *The Duino Elegies*, trans. Leslie Norris and Alan Keele (Columbia, S.C.: Camden House, 1993), 9.

28. Rilke, "Some Reflections on Dolls," 48.

29. The "Ka" in ancient Egypt was a guardian spirit that accompanied a person throughout life and survived bodily death, taking up residence in the

tomb (where it was nourished on imaginary or toy food passed to it through an aperture in the sepulchre).

30. De Man, "Lyric and Modernity," 179.

31. One could make a strong case for regarding the commodity fetish, which Marx describes as a "chrysalis," as the social exemplar of the metamorphic object. Marx repeatedly emphasizes the *Doppelcharakter* of commodities, which are "at once sensuous and suprasensible things." The *dialectical* materiality of the fetish is the key to the spell it exerts over the modern consumer. Karl Marx, *Capital: A Critique of Political Economy*, vol. 1, trans. Ben Fowkes (Harmondsworth: Penguin, 1976), 159, 165.

32. Rilke, *The Duino Elegies*, 21.

33. Rainer Maria Rilke, *Letters of Rainer Maria Rilke*, trans. Jane Bannard and M. D. Herter Norton (New York: Norton, 1969), vol. 2, 375–76.

34. Walter Benjamin, "Moscow Diary," trans. Richard Sieburth, *October* 35 (Winter 1985), 18, 20, 75, 83, 84, 91.

35. Walter Benjamin, "Russian Toys," trans. Richard Sieburth, *October* 35 (Winter 1985), 123.

36. Walter Benjamin, "Spielzeug und Spielen" (1928), in *Gesammelte Schriften*, vol. 3, ed. Hella Tiedemann-Bartels (Frankfurt: Suhrkamp Verlag, 1972), 131 (my translation).

37. Benjamin's conception of the monadic image is essential to his theory of allegory and hence figures prominently in the prologue to his *Trauerspiel* book. Walter Benjamin, *The Origin of German Tragic Drama*, trans. John Osborne (London: Verso, 1985), 47–48.

38. Jacques Lacan, *The Four Fundamental Concepts of Psychoanalysis*, ed. Jacques-Alain Miller, trans. Alan Sheridan (New York: Norton, 1981), 53.

39. Lacan, *Four Fundamental Concepts*, 53, 55–56. Lacan treats the figure of the automaton in his sessions on "The Network of Signifiers"; "*Tuchè* and Automaton"; and "The Split Between the Eye and the Gaze."

40. Rosalind E. Krauss, *The Optical Unconscious* (Cambridge: MIT Press, 1993), 71–72, 88.

41. Lacan, *Four Fundamental Concepts*, 67.

42. Roger Caillois, *The Necessity of the Mind*, trans. Michael Syrotinski (Venice, Calif.: Lapis Press, 1990), 1, 4, 23.

43. Caillois, *Necessity of the Mind*, 83, 84. Caillois speculates that the pleasure principle may be the source of the automatism of the female mantis; he

wonders "whether the mantis's goal in decapitating the male before mating is not to obtain, through the ablation of the inhibitory centers of the brain, a better and longer execution of the spasmodic movements of coitus. So that in the final analysis it would be for the female the pleasure principle that would dictate the murder of her lover, whose body, moreover, she begins to eat during the very act of making love" (81–82). The automatism of the male, once decapitated, is equally astonishing: "There are hardly any reactions that it is not able to perform when decapitated, that is, in the absence of any central point of representation or voluntary activity. In this condition, it can walk, regain its balance, move one of its threatened limbs autonomously, assume the spectral position, mate, lay eggs, build an ootheca, and quite astoundingly, fall down into a corpse-like immobility when confronted by danger . . . when dead, the mantis can simulate death" (83). Caillois also relates the mantis, by analogy, to one of the most celebrated automata of the eighteenth century; he refers, in one of the dreams that constitute the "analytic" of lyrical thinking, to "Baron von Kempelen's false automaton chess player" (28)—the device that inspired the "Talking Turk" of Hoffmann's tale "The Automaton." Furthermore, Caillois links the "chess delirium" constituted by the automaton to the "femme fatale"—to the mantis (55).

44. Caillois, *Necessity of the Mind*, 114. Caillois goes so far as to offer detailed mathematical formulas and calculations in support of some of the more unlikely effects of "lyrical synthesis": 30, 88–89, 110–11.

45. Caillois explicitly rejects the surrealist practice of "automatic writing," precisely because of its "literary" character, in favor of what he calls "automatic thinking." The distinction as Caillois presents it, however, is never entirely clear. *Necessity of the Mind*, 25–26.

46. A fuller explication of Caillois's notion of the poetic ideogram would include consideration of Ezra Pound's "ideogrammic method" (based on the poetics of imagism) and of Walter Benjamin's construction of *Denkbilder* (thought-pictures) after the example of Chinese calligraphy. All three conceptions (formulated in the early 1930s) betray the influence of Leibniz's monadology. See Caillois on Leibniz, *Necessity of the Mind*, 32, 53; and Benjamin on calligraphy, "Peintures chinoises à la Bibliothèque Nationale," *Écrits français*, ed. Jean-Maurice Monnoyer (Paris: Gallimard, 1991). Pound's thoughts about the ideogram (and about Leibniz) can be found, most substantially, in *ABC of Reading* (New York: New Directions Books, 1960) and

Guide to Kulchur (New York: New Directions Books, 1970). Both books were originally published in 1934, the same year Caillois wrote *The Necessity of the Mind.*

47. Peter Webb (with Robert Short), *Hans Bellmer* (London: Quartet Books, 1985), 26.

48. Fritz Bellmer was an engineer (like his father) who had "designed and patented a flying machine whose wings could move like those of a bird." Webb, *Hans Bellmer*, 27.

49. Webb, *Hans Bellmer*, 24. Rilke's essay is subtitled "On the Wax Dolls of Lotte Pritzel." Pritzel, a well-known theatrical designer of the period, created provocative *Vitrinenpupen* (display dolls), often with erotic characteristics. Her influence extended to Oskar Kokoschka, who asked her in 1918 to make him a life-size doll (in the likeness of Alma Mahler, following the breakup of Kokoschka's relationship with her). She declined his request. Kokoschka had the doll made by Hermine Moos and published a series of letters addressed to it ("Liebes Fraülein M.") in a volume titled *The Fetish* (1926). Kokoschka made some twenty drawings of the doll as well as two paintings: "Woman in Blue" (1919) and "Self-Portrait with Doll" (1919). He destroyed the doll in the mid-1920s (presumably because it didn't answer his letters). On yet another shore of the surrealist infatuation with dolls and automata, one finds Paul Klee producing a painting titled *Zwitschermaschine* (Twittering Machine) in 1922, a few years before the mechanical singing bird made its appearance in Yeats's poetry.

50. Hans Bellmer, "Notes au sujet de la jointure à boule" (Notes on the Subject of the Ball Joint), in *Les jeux de la poupée* (Paris: Editions Premières, 1949), 7.

51. Bellmer, cited in Webb, *Hans Bellmer*, 30.

52. Webb, *Hans Bellmer*, 30. In the preface to his photographs of the first doll, published in *Die Puppe* in 1934, Bellmer alludes to this mechanism: "Fit joint to joint, testing the ball-joints by turning them to their maximum position in a childish pose; gingerly follow the hollows, sampling the pleasures of curves, losing oneself in the labyrinth of the ear; make everything pretty and liberally spill the salt of deformation. Further, don't stop short of the interior mechanism: Lay bare the thoughts retained of little girls, so that the ground on which they stand is revealed, ideally through the navel, visible as a colorful panorama electrically illuminated deep within the stomach." Hans

Bellmer, "Memories of the Doll Theme," trans. Peter Chametzsky, Susan Felleman, and Jochen Schindler, *Sulfur* 26 (1990), 33.

53. Bellmer, "Notes au sujet de la jointure à boule," 10 (my translation).

54. Hans Bellmer, with Georges Hugnet, *Oeillades ciselées en branches* (Glances Cut on the Branch) (Paris: Jeanne Bucher, 1939).

55. Hans Bellmer, "Preface to *Hexentexte*," trans. Pierre Joris, *Sulfur* 29 (Fall 1991), 85.

56. Bellmer, "Notes au sujet de la jointure à boule," 12.

57. Hans Bellmer, *Petite anatomie de l'inconscient physique, ou l'anatomie de l'image* (Paris: Terrain Vague, 1957), 38 (my translation).

58. Bellmer, cited in Webb, *Hans Bellmer*, 38.

59. Bellmer, "Notes au sujet de la jointure à boule," 16.

60. Bellmer, "Notes au sujet de la jointure à boule," 16.

61. Gianni Vattimo, "Au-delà de la matière et du texte," *Matière et philosophie*, ed. Arnauld Pontier (Paris: Editions du Centre Pompidou, 1988), 49 (my translation).

CHAPTER 4

1. Stephen Toulmin and June Goodfield, *The Architecture of Matter* (Chicago: University of Chicago Press, 1962), 176.

2. On the relation between atomism and "incorporeal substances" in Boyle's experiments, see Steven Shapin and Simon Schaffer, *Leviathan and the Air-Pump: Hobbes, Boyle, and the Experimental Life* (Princeton: Princeton University Press, 1985), 19, 87.

3. Pierre de la Primaudaye, cited in S. K. Heninger Jr., *A Handbook of Renaissance Meteorology* (Durham, N.C.: Duke University Press, 1960), 5. My account of the term's history depends on Heninger's well-documented summary.

4. Johannes Kepler, *The Six-Cornered Snowflake: A New Year's Gift* (1611), trans. Colin Hardie (Oxford: Clarendon Press, 1966), 3.

5. The analogy occurs in book II, lines 688–99:

Notice that scattered throughout these very verses
Are many letters common to many words,
But still you must confess, each word and verse

Has different letters for its elements;
It's not that only a few run common to all,
Or that two words are made from the same letters—
All words are not alike in all respects.
So, although various things possess a mix
Of atoms shared by many other things,
The constituted wholes may be unlike,
And it is right to say that different atoms
Make up mankind and grains and the glad orchards.

Lucretius, *On the Nature of Things*, ed. and trans. Anthony M. Esolen (Baltimore: Johns Hopkins University Press, 1995), 76–77.

6. Michel Serres, *La naissance de la physique dans le texte de Lucrèce* (Paris: Editions de Minuit, 1977), 176 (my translation). On the hermeneutic dimension of atomism and its relation to deconstruction, see Jacques Derrida, "My Chances/*Mes Chances*: A Rendezvous with Some Epicurean Stereophonies," trans. Irene Harvey and Avital Ronell, in *Taking Chances: Derrida, Psychoanalysis, and Literature*, ed. Joseph H. Smith and William Kerrigan (Baltimore: Johns Hopkins University Press, 1984).

7. Lancelot Law Whyte, "Kepler's Unsolved Problem and the *Facultas Formatrix*," in Kepler, *The Six-Cornered Snowflake*, 62.

8. Heninger, *Handbook of Renaissance Meteorology*, 4–5.

9. Serres, *La naissance de la physique*, 108 (my translation).

10. Arden Reed, *Romantic Weather: The Climates of Coleridge and Baudelaire* (Hanover, N.H.: University Press of New England, 1983), 8–9.

11. The other essential classical source for the philosophy of meteors is Aristotle's *Meteorologica*, trans. H. D. Lee (Cambridge: Harvard University Press, 1952).

12. Serres, *La naissance de la physique*, 107–8.

13. Serres, *La traduction* (Paris: Editions de Minuit, 1974), 234, 237. Cited in Reed, *Romantic Weather,* 55. Jeffrey Mehlman, also under the influence of Serres, performs a Lucretian anatomy of Diderot and assimilates the "the stochastic irregularity of meteorology" to the principles of atomism. Mehlman finds at the core of Diderot's conception of vision "a stochastic chaos, a suspended fog, out of which things and times in their plurality are precipitated." Mehlman, *Cataract: A Study in Diderot* (Middletown: Wesleyan University Press, 1979), 5, 8.

14. Mehlman's reading of meteorology is predicated on the same division: "The 'utopian mechanism' we have seen Diderot undermining from the inception of our study is the clock of classical mechanics. . . . Meteorology, in its very unpredictability, opens up a margin of aleatory freedom in the controlled environment." Mehlman, *Cataract*, 98.

15. Serres, *La naissance de la physique*, 85. The French word *temps* means both "time" and "weather," so that each time Serres speaks of the weather, he invokes the inherent temporality of the meteoric phenomenon.

16. On Descartes's knowledge of Kepler's essay, see Whyte, "Kepler's Unsolved Problem," 60. The other two appendixes to the *Discourse* are the *Optics* and the *Geometry*.

17. René Descartes, *Discourse on Method, Optics, Geometry, and Meteorology*, trans. Paul J. Olscamp (Indianapolis: Bobbs-Merrill, 1965), 332.

18. In a letter to de Volder in 1674, for example, Leibniz claims, "Matter or extended mass is nothing but a phenomenon grounded in things, like the rainbow." Leibniz, *Philosophical Papers and Letters*, trans. and ed. Leroy E. Loemker (Dordrecht: Reidel, 1970), 536.

19. Descartes's comment about optics can be found in his *Oeuvres philosophiques* (Paris: Garnier, 1988), vol. 1, 760.

20. Primary sources on fireworks from the Baroque period (and later) include John Babington, *Pyrotechnia: Or a Discourse of Artificiall Fire-works* (London, 1635); Jean Appier Hanzelet, *La Pyrotechnie de Hanzalet de Lorrain, où sont representez les plus rares et plus appreuvez secrets des machines et des feux artificiels* (Pont-à-Mousson: Gaspard Bernard, 1630); and articles by Diderot on fireworks in the *Encyclopédie* (1761–1765). Secondary sources include Alan St. Hill Brock, *A History of Fireworks* (London: Harrap, 1949); Arthur Lotz, *Das Feuerwerk: Seine Geschichte und Bibliographie* (Zurich: Olms, 1978); *Fetes, Fireworks, and Other Festivities* (New York: Metropolitan Museum of Art, 1971); and Kevin Salatino, *Incendiary Art: The Representation of Fireworks in Early Modern Europe* (Los Angeles: Getty Research Institute, 1997). This last source, from which I have drawn the other bibliographic materials, is richly illustrated.

21. In "Adagia," Stevens writes, "Weather is a sense of nature. Poetry is a sense." *Opus Posthumous*, ed. Samuel French Morse (New York: Alfred Knopf, 1957), 161. Vico's influence on modern literature is best known through the work of James Joyce, but Yeats as well makes reference to Vico.

22. The most prominent example of this type of unexamined allusion occurs in the title of Harold Bloom's book *Wallace Stevens: The Poems of Our Climate* (Ithaca: Cornell University Press, 1976). Despite the title, Bloom never explores in any detail the trope of weather in Stevens's poems. Even an essay that purports to address the trope more carefully (by inverting the sense of Bloom's title) understands the term "climate" only in the loosest sense: see Joseph N. Riddell, "The Climate of Our Poems," *Wallace Stevens Journal* 7 (Fall 1983), 59–75.

23. Stevens, "Adagia," *Opus Posthumous*, 159.

24. Wallace Stevens, "The Bouquet," *The Collected Poems* (New York: Random House, 1982), 449. Stevens makes reference to the doctrine of "elements" in a number of other poems, including "Wild Ducks, People and Distances" and "Two Versions of the Same Poem." All page references to Stevens's poems in my text refer hereafter to *The Collected Poems*.

25. Giambattista Vico, *The New Science,* trans. Thomas Goddard Bergin and Max Harold Frisch (Ithaca: Cornell University Press, 1970), 26–27, 76. The "giants of sense" possess a distinct meteorological dimension, in that they were said to have come into existence "when the heavens thundered for the first time" (31). Vico and one of his modern disciples, James Joyce, both suffered from a pathological fear of thunderstorms (hence the significance of the recurrent thunderclap in *Finnegans Wake*).

26. Concerning the language of the age of giants, Vico states, "That first language, spoken by the theological poets, was not a language in accord with the nature of the things it dealt with . . . but was a fantastic speech making use of physical substances endowed with life and most of them imagined to be divine" (86).

27. Stevens, "Adagia," *Opus Posthumous*, 170.

28. Margaret Russett has written a superb essay on the concept of meter in Romantic poetics and its role in the historical and juridical determination of literary property. Russett's discussion of the court's theorization of lyric "substance" suggests that the ambiguous materiality of meter as a literary (or legal) concept pertains directly to the nebulous form, and also to the technics, of the meteoric body. Margaret Russett, "On the Prehistory of Poetic Voice: Coleridge, *Christabel*, and Copyright," lecture delivered at the 1996 meeting of the North American Society for the Study of Romanticism.

29. Catherine Wilson, *The Invisible World: Early Modern Philosophy and*

the Invention of the Microscope (Princeton: Princeton University Press, 1995), 40.

30. Descartes, *Discourse on Method,* 264, 336.

31. Descartes, "Treatise on Man," *Philosophical Writings of Descartes*, trans. John Cottingham, Robert Stoothoff, and Dugald Murdoch (Cambridge: Cambridge University Press, 1985), vol. 1, 100.

32. Descartes, *Passions of the Soul*, in *Philosophical Writings*, vol. 1, 331–32.

33. Newton, cited in Robert Darnton, *Mesmerism and the End of the Enlightenment in France* (Cambridge: Harvard University Press, 1968), 11.

34. Isaac Newton, *Opticks*, reprinted from the fourth edition, foreword by Albert Einstein (New York: McGraw-Hill, 1931), 349, 353–54.

35. Robert Darnton, *Mesmerism*, 10.

36. My account of Mesmer's training and development in Vienna follows Maria M. Tatar, *Spellbound: Studies on Mesmerism and Literature* (Princeton: Princeton University Press, 1978), 8–9, 11.

37. Tatar, *Spellbound*, 15. In a brief discussion of the medical history of "vapors," Henri Ellenberger cites several eighteenth-century treatises on the subject: Joseph Raulin, *Traitè des affections vaporeuses du sexe* (Paris 1759); and Pierre Pomme, *Traitè des affections vaporeuses des deux sexes, ou maladies nerveuses* (Paris, 1760). Henri F. Ellenberger, *The Discovery of the Unconscious* (New York: Basic Books, 1970), 246.

38. Robert Darnton, *Mesmerism*, 107.

39. Cited in French in Tatar, *Spellbound*, 273–75 (my translation). An English translation is available in Franz Anton Mesmer, *Mesmerism: A Translation of the Original Scientific and Medical Writings of F. A. Mesmer* (Los Altos: W. Kaufman, 1980).

40. In *Cataract*, Jeffrey Mehlman develops a reading of Diderot's meteorology around the figure of the cataract (21–22).

41. A harbinger of these developments can be found in the work of Robert Macnish (1802–1837), especially his *Philosophy of Sleep*. The translation of mesmerism into modern medical discourse during this period is just beginning to receive scholarly attention. A fine article by Jonathan Miller, "Going Unconscious," appeared in the *New York Review of Books* (10 April 1995). One may also consult Alison Winter, *Mesmerized: Powers of Mind in Victorian Britain* (Chicago: University of Chicago Press, 1998).

42. William B. Carpenter, *Mesmerism, Spiritualism, Historically and Scientifically Considered* (New York: Appleton, 1887), 15.

43. Charles Darwin, *The Expression of the Emotions in Man and Animals* (Chicago: University of Chicago Press, 1965), 9.

44. Marina Warner, "Waxworks and Wonderlands," in *Visual Display*, ed. Lynn Cooke and Peter Wollen (Seattle: Bay Press, 1995), 199.

45. Darnton, *Mesmerism*, 3.

46. Martin Green, *Mountain of Truth*: *The Counterculture Begins, Ascona 1900–1920* (Hanover, N.H.: University Press of New England, 1986).

47. The most obvious expressions of the Asconan idea in post–World War II culture are the alternative communities that developed in Big Sur and Carmel in California, the emergence of the so-called Woodstock generation, and the development of the politics of the New Left, especially the radical Weather Underground faction of the Students for a Democratic Society (SDS). The initial manifesto of the Weather Underground, titled "You Don't Need a Weatherman to Know Which Way the Wind Blows" (from Bob Dylan's song "Subterranean Homesick Blues"), appeared in the SDS publication *New Left Notes*, 18 June 1969.

48. Hans Fischer, in a review of 1928, contends, "Wigman stands at once as the decidedly greatest and last solo dancer and as the first master of group dance." Cited in Susan A. Manning, *Ecstasy and the Demon: Feminism and Nationalism in the Dances of Mary Wigman* (Berkeley: University of California Press, 1994), 85.

49. On eurythmics and the concept of "animated plastic art" (which calls to mind the figure of the automaton), see Manning, *Ecstasy and the Demon*, 53.

50. Laban, cited in Green, *Mountain of Truth*, 109.

51. From a review cited by Green, *Mountain of Truth*, 193.

52. Wigman, cited in Green, *Mountain of Truth*, 100.

53. Lincoln Kirstein, cited in Manning, *Ecstasy and the Demon*, 22.

54. A detail noted by Green, *Mountain of Truth*, 169.

55. Carpenter, *Mesmerism*, 4.

56. Laban, cited in Green, *Mountain of Truth*, 93.

57. Manning, *Ecstasy and the Demon,* 2, 7.

58. Green, *Mountain of Truth*, 109, 113.

59. Manning, *Ecstasy and the Demon*, 1, 3.

60. Manning, *Ecstasy and the Demon*, 68.

61. Cited in Manning, *Ecstasy and the Demon*, 68–69.

62. The combination of dance and "philosophy" in Wigman's modernist innovations is confirmed, at least in terms of an ideological critique, by comments made by Joseph Goebbels in 1937. Rejecting what he called "the philosophical dance of Wigman," Goebbels declared that "dance must be buoyant and must show beautiful women's bodies." Cited in Manning, *Ecstasy and the Demon*, 202. Goebbels's comment followed a lengthy period of collaboration between Wigman and the Nazi Ministry of Culture.

63. Laban, cited in Green, *Mountain of Truth*, 97.

64. Laban's integration of the idea of festival into avant-garde practice antedates by some twenty years the elaboration of this idea in the context of surrealism in Paris at the meetings of the Collège de Sociologie. Roger Caillois, whose preoccupation with the problem of automatism I have already discussed, delivered an influential lecture on the topic of festival to the College of Sociology. Denis Hollier has remarked, "Of all the lectures given at the College, no doubt the one of May 2, 1939, had the greatest impact." That was the session in which Caillois presented his theory of 'Festival.' " *The College of Sociology*, ed. Denis Hollier, trans. Betsy Wing (Minneapolis: University of Minnesota, 1988), xxvi. The text of Caillois's lecture appeared in his book *L'homme et le sacré* (1940). In relation to the dance practice of Laban and Wigman, see in particular his "Expenditure and Paroxysm," in *College of Sociology*, 301–2.

65. On the relations between Wigman's modern dance and fascist mass spectacle, see Peter Wollen, "Tales of Total Art and Dreams of the Total Museum," in Cooke and Wollen, *Visual Display*.

66. Peter Galison, *Image and Logic: A Material Culture of Microphysics* (Chicago: University of Chicago Press, 1997), 74. My remarks on the cloud chamber follow Galison's account of its development.

67. Galison provides a fine, brief account of the "aesthetic, popular, and scientific fascination with clouds in Victorian times" in *Image and Logic*, 73–81.

68. Heinrich von Kleist, "On the Marionette Theater," trans. Roman Paska, *Fragments for a History of the Human Body*, part 1, ed. Michel Feher, Ramona Nadoff, and Nadia Tazi (New York: Zone Books, 1989), 416.

69. Paul de Man, "Aesthetic Formalization: Kleist's *Über das Marionetten-*

theater," in *The Rhetoric of Romanticism* (New York: Columbia University Press, 1984), 288, 290.

CHAPTER 5

1. The third chapter of Bachelard's book *Les intuitions atomistiques* is titled "La metaphysique de la poussière." Originally published in 1933, in the wake of the great debates about quantum mechanics, the work was reissued by J. Vrin in Paris in 1975.

2. Michel Serres, *La naissance de la physique dans le texte de Lucrèce* (Paris: Editions de Minuit, 1977), 117 (my translation).

3. Catherine Wilson, *The Invisible World: Early Modern Philosophy and the Invention of the Microscope* (Princeton: Princeton University Press, 1995), 37–38.

4. Giorgio Agamben, *Stanzas: Word and Phantasm in Western Culture*, trans. Ronald L. Martinez (Minneapolis: University of Minnesota Press, 1993), xvi. Agamben makes no explicit reference to Vico, perhaps because the debt is so transparent.

5. Bertrand Russell, *The Philosophy of Logical Atomism* (1918), ed. David Pears (La Salle, Ill.: Open Court Press, 1985), 154.

6. Edward MacKinnon, *Scientific Explanation and Atomic Physics* (Chicago: University of Chicago Press, 1982), 86.

7. Wilson, *Invisible World*, 27.

8. Ian Hacking, *Representing and Intervening* (Cambridge: Cambridge University Press, 1983), 142.

9. J. A. Crowther, "The Atom Again," *Nature* 118, no. 2967 (11 September 1926), 365.

10. Bachelard, *Les intuitions atomistiques*, 3 (my translation).

11. Stanley Fish, "How the Right Hijacked the Magic Words," *New York Times*, 13 August 1995, 15.

12. Hacking, *Representing and Intervening*, 141.

13. Heinrich Hertz, *The Principles of Mechanics,* trans. D. E. Jones and J. T. Walley (New York: Dover, 1956), 25.

14. In his introduction to F. A. Lange's *A History of Materialism* (a work originally published in 1865), Russell observes, "The two dogmas that con-

stitute the essence of materialism are: first, the sole reality of matter; secondly, the reign of law." Russell, "Materialism, Past and Present," in *The Basic Writings of Bertrand Russell* (New York: Touchstone, 1961), 241.

15. Russell, *Philosophy of Logical Atomism*, 37.

16. Wilson, *Invisible World*, 38; Fontenelle cited 219.

17. Hacking, *Representing and Intervening*, 140.

18. On the conflict between Democritean physics and empiricism, Edward MacKinnon observes, "Epicurus and Lucretius insisted on the primacy of sensation as the source of knowledge. Yet the doctrine that only atoms and the void are real leads to the conclusion that sensed qualities lack physical reality. . . . The reasoning supporting atomism seems to contradict its evidential base." *Scientific Explanation*, 15.

19. Karl Marx, *On the Difference between the Democritean and Epicurean Philosophy of Nature*, in *Collected Works* (New York: International Publishers, 1975), vol. 1, 34.

20. Wilson, *Invisible World*, 229.

21. Hacking, *Representing and Intervening*, 217, 218.

22. MacKinnon, *Scientific Explanation*, 14.

23. It is significant that Ludwig Boltzmann (Hertz's teacher), who was instrumental in establishing the usage of the term *picture* in modern physics, was known to have held in high esteem the creations of eighteenth-century automaton makers such as Vaucanson and Jaquet-Droz. Thus it would not be misleading to regard the logical picture as an immaterial automaton. On Boltzmann and automata, see Silvio Bedini, "The Role of Automata in the History of Technology," *Technology and Culture* 5, no. 1 (Winter 1964), 40–41.

24. George Berkeley, *The Principles of Human Knowledge* (1720), in *The Works of George Berkeley* (Edinburgh: Thomas Nelson, 1948–1957), vol. 2, Section 47.

25. Moritz Schlick, "Theories and Pictorial Models," in *Philosophy of Nature*, trans. Amethe von Zeppelin (New York: Philosophical Library, 1949), 28, 29.

26. MacKinnon, *Scientific Explanation*, 267–68.

27. Despite his antipathy to atomism, Moritz Schlick acknowledges the epistemological advantage of abstraction: "This theory of the atom had one advantage, from the standpoint of epistemology, which cannot be too highly

estimated: it yielded a world picture devoid of all qualitative differences." Schlick, "The Concept of the Atom," *Philosophy of Nature*, 96.

28. La Mettrie declared, "Because everything depends absolutely on the diversity of *organization,* a well-put-together animal to whom one has taught astronomy can predict an eclipse, just as he can predict the recovery or death of a patient after he has studied in the school of Hippocrates." *Man a Machine*, trans. Richard A. Watson and Maya Rybalka (Indianapolis: Hackett, 1995), 75 (my emphasis).

29. Hertz, *Principles of Mechanics*, 1.

30. Martin Heidegger, "The Age of the World Picture" (1937), in *The Question Concerning Technology and Other Essays*, ed. and trans. William Lovitt (New York: Harper, 1975), 119.

31. Merleau-Ponty, for example, insists on the realist orientation of modern particle physics: "The design of ontological realism is always present in theoretical physics, even in its most abstract formulations; physics, in my opinion, is inseparable from realism." J. Merleau-Ponty, *Leçons sur la genèse des théories physiques* (Paris: J. Vrin, 1975), 9 (my translation). Ian Hacking takes a similar position on the "phenomenological" realism of modern physics. See especially his discussion of the divergent usages of the term *phenomenon* in philosophy and physics. *Representing and Intervening*, 220–23.

32. I have benefited from illuminating discussions of the terms *Vorstellung* and *Darstellung* in Hacking, *Representing and Intervening* (130–34), and Allen Janik and Stephen Toulmin, *Wittgenstein's Vienna* (New York: Simon and Schuster, 1973), 132–48. Toulmin's analysis, in particular, outlines the broader philosophical context of the terms, beginning with Kant.

33. Hacking, *Representing and Intervening*, 130.

34. Derek J. de Solla Price discusses the historical correspondence between the development of automata and new optical devices and effects in his essay "Automata and the Origins of Mechanism and Mechanistic Philosophy," *Technology and Culture* 5, no. 1 (Winter 1964), 21. In a similar vein, Silvio Bedini notes the "talking heads claimed to have been constructed by Albertus Magnus, Roger Bacon, and Robert Grosseteste"—all leading figures in the emerging science of optics. Bedini, "The Role of Automata," 31.

35. Wilson, *Invisible World*, 255.

36. Cited in Wilson, *Invisible World*, 65.

37. Marx, *On the Difference*, 36.

38. David Hume, *Enquiries Concerning Human Understanding and Concerning the Principles of Morals,* ed. L. A. Selby-Bigge (Oxford: Clarendon Press, 1902), sec. VIII, part 1, 65.

39. Hooke and Berkeley, cited in Wilson, *Invisible World,* 244.

40. Hooke, cited in Wilson, *Invisible World,* 38.

41. Gustave Bergman, "Outline of an Empiricist Philosophy of Physics," cited in Hacking, *Representing and Intervening,* 187–88.

42. Lisa Cartwright, *Screening the Body: Tracing Medicine's Visual Culture* (Minneapolis: University of Minnesota Press, 1995), 82.

43. Wilson, *Invisible World,* 235.

44. Cited in Wilson, *Invisible World,* 223.

45. Cited in Wilson, *Invisible World,* 89.

46. Wilson, *Invisible World,* 212.

47. Hooke, *Discourse Concerning Telescopes and Microscopes,* cited in Wilson, *Invisible World,* 226.

CHAPTER 6

1. David C. Lindberg, *Theories of Vision from Al-Kindi to Kepler* (Chicago: University of Chicago Press, 1976), 116. The theory of visual intromission may, as Richard Onians contends, be implicated in the etymology of our term "aesthetic." The Greek root of *aesthetic* (αισθάνομαι) means "to see, to perceive," but also to "breathe in"—as if vision were a form of inhalation. See Richard Onians, *The Origins of European Thought* (New York: Arno Press, 1973), 75.

2. Epicurus, "Letter to Herodotus," in *Letters, Principal Doctrines, and Vatican Sayings,* ed. and trans. Russell M. Geer (Indianapolis: Bobbs-Merrill, 1964), 14.

3. Lucretius, *The Way Things Are [De rerum natura],* trans. Rolfe Humphries (Bloomington: Indiana University Press, 1968), 120–21. All page references to Lucretius hereafter refer to this edition.

4. In English, *species* has the root meaning "visible form" or "mental image," derived from Latin *species,* "a sight, hence outward form or shape, hence a sort or kind" (from the Latin verb *specio,* "I look, I see"). Moreover, the word *species* in English is embedded in a matrix of cognate terms that refer

not only to a range of visual experience but also to the illegitimacy, or corruption, of vision: *specimen, aspect, perspective, spectacle, specter, suspect, spy, specious,* and, unexpectedly, *spice* (from a Latin usage denoting "wares," or "articles of merchandise," especially spices and aromatics). Many of the aspects of visuality expressed by these terms are, indeed, inherent in the history of the English usage of the word *species.* In addition to the basic sense of "appearance, outward form," the *Oxford English Dictionary* records the following meanings for *species:* (1) "The image of something as cast upon, or reflected from, a surface; a reflection"; (2) "A thing seen; a spectacle, *esp.* an unreal or imaginary object of sight; a phantom or illusion"; (3) "A supposed emission or emanation from outward things, forming the direct object of cognition for the various senses or for the understanding"; (4) "A mental impression: an idea"; (5) "The essential quality or specific properties of a thing"; (6) "A distinct, class, sort, or kind"; (7) "The separate materials or ingredients used in compounding a perfume, drug, or similar preparation" (hence a simple substance, or primary element); (8) "Metal (gold or silver) used for coinage; a particular kind or sort of coin or money" (i.e., *visible* payment); (9) "Sorts of provisions or produce." The significance of the word *species* therefore ranges from the constellation of image, phantom, or spectacle to notions associated with atomism (simple substance), numismatics, and commodity fetishism (wares or merchandise). The conjunction of phantasm, atomism, and fetishism is of singular importance in modern formulations of visuality.

5. Roger Bacon, *Roger Bacon's Philosophy of Nature,* ed. and trans. David C. Lindberg (Oxford: Clarendon Press, 1983), 93; Lindberg, *Theories of Vision,* 109. Robert Grosseteste describes the "multiplication of species" in the following manner: "A natural agent multiplies its power from itself to the recipient, whether it acts on sense or on matter. This power is sometimes called species, sometimes a likeness." Cited in Lindberg, *Theories of Vision,* 98.

6. Bacon, *Roger Bacon's Philosophy of Nature,* lxiii.

7. David C. Lindberg, "Introduction," in *Roger Bacon's Philosophy of Nature,* lxvi.

8. S. K. Heninger Jr. writes, "In the thirteenth century, the study of meteors had an offshoot: optics, or perspectives. This line of investigation, which began with Aristotle's attempts in the *Meteorologica* to explain atmospheric phenomena of reflection (such as rainbows and lunar halos), developed through Robert Grosseteste, Roger Bacon, and John Pecham in England." *A*

Handbook of Renaissance Meteorology (Durham, N.C.: Duke University Press, 1960), 14.

9. Lindberg discusses Kepler's debts to medieval perspectivism and to corpuscularian theories of vision: *Theories of Vision*, 188–90, 202–8. Kepler's interest in optics was precipitated by the "enigma" of a solar eclipse.

10. Michel Serres, *La naissance de la physique dans le texte de Lucrèce* (Paris: Editions de Minuit, 1977), 114 (my translation).

11. William Butler Yeats, "Byzantium," in *The Poems*, ed. Richard J. Finneran (New York: Macmillan, 1983), 249.

12. Stephen Toulmin and June Goodfield, *The Architecture of Matter* (Chicago: University of Chicago Press, 1962), 217.

13. Erwin Schrödinger, the principal architect of wave mechanics, cited by Edward MacKinnon, *Scientific Explanation and Atomic Physics* (Chicago: University of Chicago Press, 1982), 233.

14. Sandro Petruccioli, *Atoms, Metaphors, and Paradoxes: Niels Bohr and the Construction of a New Physics*, trans. Ian McGilvray (Cambridge: Cambridge University Press, 1993), 23.

15. Isaac Newton, *Opticks*, fourth edition, foreword by Albert Einstein (New York: McGraw-Hill, 1931), 370, 389.

16. Newton, *Opticks*, 261. Newton's corpuscular theory of light led him to a similar conclusion about the passage of light through a prism. According to A. I. Sabra, "Newton was an atomist who believed that matter is composed of hard and permanent particles which are endowed with various properties from the beginning of creation. From this point of view, the dispersion of light in a prism could be readily explained: the prism simply separates the mixed corpuscles and, as a result, colors appear." A. I. Sabra, *Theories of Light from Descartes to Newton* (London: Oldbourne, 1967), 296.

17. David Lindberg discusses the correlation in Bacon's work between the "philosophy of light" and the doctrine of *species*. *Theories of Vision*, 97, 113.

18. Lindberg, *Theories of Vision*, x.

19. Lindberg, *Theories of Vision*, 95.

20. MacKinnon, *Scientific Explanation*, 87.

21. Isaac Newton, like many early commentators on microscopy, observed that matter loses its color and opacity under the microscope: "The least parts of almost all natural Bodies are in some measure transparent: And the Opacity of these Bodies ariseth from the multitude of Reflections caused in their

internal Parts." *Opticks*, book II, part III, proposition 2. The transparency of matter explains the need for aniline dyes to restore visibility to the microscopic (or radiographic) body.

22. Lisa Cartwright characterizes radiography as "a technique that renders its viewing subject an object of a pervasive disciplinary gaze—a truly radiant gaze—that threatens to perform a quite literal disintegration of the body." *Screening the Body: Tracing Medicine's Visual Culture* (Minneapolis: University of Minnesota Press, 1995), 108.

23. Alexander Hammond, "Rescripting the Nuclear Threat in 1953: *The Beast from 20,000 Fathoms*," in *Warnings: An Anthology on the Nuclear Peril,* ed. John Witte (Portland: Northwest Review Books, 1984), 192–93.

24. Robert Penn Warren, "New Dawn," in *New and Selected Poems, 1923– 1985* (New York: Random House, 1985), 35.

25. Cathy Caruth, "Introduction," *American Imago* 48, no. 1 (1991), 3.

26. Hammond, "Rescripting the Nuclear Threat," 189.

27. *United States Civil Defense in Action* (1954), a U.S. government informational film on survival tactics in the event of nuclear war.

28. W. H. Auden, "For the Time Being," in *The Collected Poetry of W. H. Auden* (New York: Random House, 1945), 410.

29. Galway Kinnell, "The Fundamental Project of Technology," in *The Past* (Boston: Houghton Mifflin, 1985), 48.

30. *Los Angeles Times*, 28 October 1945.

31. Voiceover narration from *Let's Face It* (1954), informational film produced by the U.S. Air Force and the National Civil Defense Administration.

32. *Operation Cue* (1954), informational film produced by the National Civil Defense Administration.

33. *United States Civil Defense in Action.*

34. *Let's Face It.* The spokesman for *United States Civil Defense in Action* makes a similar point, characterizing "a mass atomic attack" as "an event we must be prepared to face"—that is, to visualize.

35. *United States Civil Defense in Action.*

36. *United States Civil Defense in Action.*

37. *Let's Face It.*

38. *Let's Face It.*

39. William Stafford, "At the Bomb Testing Site," in *Stories That Could Be True: New and Selected Poems* (New York: Harper and Row, 1977), 41.

40. Kinnell, "The Fundamental Project of Technology," 48.

41. William Dickey, "Armageddon," in *Writing in a Nuclear Age*, ed. Jim Schley (Hanover, N.H.: University Press of New England, 1983), 42.

42. Dickey, "Armageddon," 42–43.

43. Hans Magnus Enzenberger, "The Doctrine of Categories," trans. Felix Pollak and Reinhold Grim, in *Warnings*, 65.

44. Richard Wilbur, "Advice to a Prophet," in *Advice to a Prophet and Other Poems* (New York: Harcourt Brace, 1961), 6.

45. Gary Snyder, "Strategic Air Command," in *Axe Handles* (San Francisco: North Point Press, 1983), 37.

46. Gary Snyder, "Vapor Trails," in *The Back Country* (New York: New Directions, 1968), 37.

47. Snyder, "Vapor Trails," 37.

48. Howard Moss, "Einstein's Robe," in *New Selected Poems* (New York: Atheneum, 1985), 295–96.

49. Wallace Stevens, "An Ordinary Evening in New Haven," in *The Collected Poems* (New York: Random House, 1982), 477. All page references to Stevens's poems hereafter refer to *The Collected Poems*.

50. David St. John, "Merlin," in *Study for the World's Body: New and Selected Poems* (New York: Harper Collins, 1994), 126.

51. As I note in chapter 5, the earliest usage of the term *virtuoso* emerges in seventeenth-century natural philosophy, in which context, according to the *Oxford English Dictionary*, it denotes "a learned person; a scientist, savant, or scholar." Secondarily, but rooted in the same historical and intellectual context, *virtuoso* refers to "a collector of antiquities, curiosities, or rarities."

52. Gregory Corso, "Bomb," in *Mindfields: New and Selected Poems* (New York: Thunder's Mouth Press, 1989), 68–69.

53. Allen Ginsberg, "Plutonian Ode," in *Collected Poems, 1947–1980* (New York: Harper and Row, 1984), 702.

54. C. K. Williams, "Tar," in *Tar* (New York: Vintage Books, 1983), 47–49.

55. Corso, "Bomb," 65.

CHAPTER 7

1. Moritz Schlick, "Theories and Pictorial Models," in *Philosophy of Nature*, trans. Amethe von Zeppelin (New York: Philosophical Library, 1949), 29.

2. Feynman first introduced his diagrammatic method in an article titled "Space-Time Approach to Non-relativistic Quantum Mechanics," which appeared in *Reviews of Modern Physics* in 1949.

3. Richard Feynman, cited in Jagdish Mehra, *The Beat of a Different Drum: The Life and Science of Richard Feynman* (Oxford: Clarendon Press, 1994), 291.

4. Heinrich Hertz, *The Principles of Mechanics,* trans. D. E. Jones and J. T. Walley (New York: Dover, 1956), 1.

5. Feynman, cited in Mehra, *The Beat of a Different Drum*, 291.

6. James Gleick, *Genius: The Life and Science of Richard Feynman* (New York: Pantheon, 1992), 273.

7. Feynman, cited in Gleick, *Genius*, 245.

8. Julian Schwinger, cited in Gleick, *Genius*, 276.

9. Niels Bohr, *Collected Works*, ed. L. Rosenthal et al. (Amsterdam: North-Holland, 1972), vol. 3, 432.

10. Werner Heisenberg, "Quantenmechanik," cited in Arthur I. Miller, *Imagery in Scientific Thought* (Boston: Burkhauser, 1984), 148.

11. Heisenberg, cited in Paul Forman, "The Reception of an Acausal Quantum Mechanics in Germany and Britain," in *The Reception of Unconventional Science*, ed. Seymour H. Mauskopf (Boulder: Westview, 1979), 22.

12. Heisenberg, "Quantenmechanik," cited in Miller, 148.

13. Sandro Petruccioli, *Atoms, Metaphors, and Paradoxes* (Cambridge: Cambridge University Press, 1993), 33 n. Petruccioli's comment summarizes the views of J. Hendry, "The History of Complementarity: Niels Bohr and the Problem of Visualization," in Proceedings of the International Symposium on Niels Bohr, *Revista di Storia della Scienza* 2 (1985), 391–407.

14. Stephen Toulmin and June Goodfield, *The Architecture of Matter* (Chicago: University of Chicago, 1982), 277. My knowledge of the history of quantum physics is indebted to this account as well as to Petruccioli, *Atoms, Metaphors, and Paradoxes,* and Edward MacKinnon, *Scientific Explanation and Atomic Physics* (Chicago: University of Chicago Press, 1982).

15. Peter Galison, *Image and Logic: A Material Culture of Microphysics* (Chicago: University of Chicago Press, 1997), 73. My remarks on the cloud chamber follow Galison's account of this extraordinary device.

16. Werner Heisenberg, "Quantenmechanik" (1926), cited in Petruccioli, *Atoms, Metaphors, and Paradoxes*, 155.

17. Niels Bohr, letter to Ralph Fowler, 26 October 1926, cited in Petruccioli, *Atoms, Metaphors, and Paradoxes*, 165.

18. Petruccioli, *Atoms, Metaphors, and Paradoxes*, 69.

19. Niels Bohr, "Natural Philosophy and Human Cultures," in *Philosophical Writings of Niels Bohr* (Woodbridge, Conn.: Ox Bow Press, 1987), vol. 2, 25.

20. Niels Bohr, "The Quantum Postulate and the Recent Development of Atomic Theory" (1928), in *Philosophical Writings of Niels Bohr*, vol. 1, 53–54 (my emphasis).

21. Niels Bohr, cited in *Quantum Theory and Measurement*, ed. John Archibald Wheeler and Wojciech H. Zurek (Princeton: Princeton University Press, 1983), 184.

22. Werner Heisenberg, letter to Wolfgang Pauli, 27 February 1927, cited in Petruccioli, *Atoms, Metaphors, and Paradoxes*, 170.

23. Bertrand Russell, "Materialism, Past and Present," introduction to F. A. Lange, *A History of Materialism* (London: Lund Humphries, 1925). Reprinted in *The Basic Writings of Bertrand Russell* (New York: Touchstone, 1961), 241. Russell's essay was published in the same year that Heisenberg developed his matrix mechanics.

24. Bertrand Russell, *The Philosophy of Logical Atomism,* ed. David Pears (La Salle, Ill.: Open Court Press, 1985), 144.

25. Russell, *Philosophy of Logical Atomism*, 144–45.

26. John Wheeler, "Law without Law," in Wheeler and Zurek, *Quantum Theory and Measurement*, 185.

27. Petruccioli, *Atoms, Metaphors, and Paradoxes*, 6.

28. Paul Forman, "Weimar Culture, Causality, and Quantum Theory, 1918–1927," in *Historical Studies in the Physical Sciences*, ed. Russell McCormmach (Philadelphia: University of Pennsylvania Press, 1971), 3. Forman insists on "the rise of a will to believe that causality does not obtain at the atomic level *before* the invention of an acausal quantum mechanics" (100).

29. Forman, "Weimar Culture," 64.

30. Forman, "The Reception of an Acausal Quantum Mechanics," 13.

31. Forman, "The Reception of an Acausal Quantum Mechanics," 22.

32. Edward MacKinnon, *Scientific Explanation,* 6.

33. MacKinnon, *Scientific Explanation*, 7, 196.

34. Arthur I. Miller, for example, contends that "Heisenberg's notion of *Anschaulichkeit* set the stage for Feynman's diagrammatic method." Miller, *Imagery in Scientific Thought,* 174.

35. Heinrich Hertz, *Principles of Mechanics*, 2, 3, 4.

36. Niels Bohr, letter to Albert Einstein, 13 April 1927, cited in Petruccioli, *Atoms, Metaphors, and Paradoxes*, 90.

37. Bohr, "The Quantum Postulate," 248.

38. Bohr, "Natural Philosophy," 26.

39. As for the ideological profile of the iconoclasts (and those who placed causality in doubt), Paul Forman observes, "Correlations might be anticipated between a physicist's position on the causality issue and his general intellectual-political orientation. And, in fact, those physicists who were readiest and earliest to repudiate causality had either distinctly 'progressive' political views by the standards of their social class and the German academic world, and/or had an unusually close interest in, or contact with, contemporary literature." The conservatives (Planck, Einstein, et al.), by contrast, "kept their knowledge of Greek well polished." Forman, "Weimar Culture," 113.

40. MacKinnon, *Scientific Explanation*, 191–92.

41. Ian Hacking, *Representing and Intervening* (Cambridge: Cambridge University Press, 1983), 139.

42. Heisenberg, letter to Wolfgang Pauli, 8 June 1926, cited in MacKinnon, *Scientific Explanation*, 238.

43. Erwin Schrödinger, "The Present Situation in Quantum Mechanics," trans. John D. Trimmer, in Wheeler and Zurek, *Quantum Theory and Measurement*, 154.

44. MacKinnon, *Scientific Explanation*, 222.

45. Erwin Schrödinger, *Collected Papers on Wave Mechanics*, trans. J. Shearer and W. Deans (London: Blackie, 1927), 13.

46. Schrödinger, "The Present Situation," 157. I have slightly modified Trimmer's translation for the sake of clarity. The original essay in German,

"Die gegenwärtige Situation in der Quantenmechanik," was published in a three-part article in *Naturwissenschaften* 23 (1935): 807–12, 823–28, 844–49.

47. Erwin Schrödinger, *My View of the World*, trans. C. Hastings (Cambridge: Cambridge University Press, 1964), 19. The essay containing Schrödinger's remark about allegorical pictures is prefaced by an epigraph from Goethe: "And thy spirit's highest fiery flight / Is satisfied with likeness and with image."

48. I discuss Paul de Man's conception of allegorical lyric in chapter 3, but his views are worth repeating in this context. Modern lyric, according to de Man, exploits "the ambivalence of a language that is representational and nonrepresentational at the same time. All representational poetry is always also allegorical, whether it be aware of it or not, and the allegorical power of the language undermines the specific literal meaning of a representation open to understanding. But all allegorical poetry must contain a representational element that invites and allows for understanding only to discover that the understanding it reaches is necessarily in error." By taking this "discovery"—the moment of awakening to "error"—as its subject, modern lyric discloses what de Man calls "the enigma of language." Paul de Man, "Modernity and Lyric," in *Blindness and Insight* (Minneapolis: University of Minnesota Press, 1983), 185.

49. Moore's denunciation of poetry appears in her poem "Poetry," in *The Complete Poems of Marianne Moore* (New York: Viking, 1967), 36. See chapter 1 of the present study for discussion of this poem.

50. William Carlos Williams, "Marianne Moore: A Novelette and Other Prose, 1921–1931," in *Selected Essays of William Carlos Williams* (New York: Random House, 1954), 12.

51. A passage from Kant's *Critique of Judgment* that I cited in chapter 1 helps to illuminate the "destructive element" in Marianne Moore's poetry (as well as the allegorical qualities of quantum theory). Kant writes,

Poetry fortifies the mind: for it lets the mind feel its ability—free, spontaneous, and independent of natural determination—to contemplate and judge phenomenal nature as having aspects that nature does not on its own offer in experience either to sense or to the understanding, and hence poetry lets the mind feel its ability to use nature on behalf of and, as it were, as a schema of the suprasensible. Poetry plays with illusion, which it produces at will, and yet without using illusion to deceive us.

Thus, Kant contends, "poetry is the art of conducting a free play of the imagination as a task of understanding." Kant, *Critique of Judgment*, trans. Werner S. Pluhar (Indianapolis: Hackett, 1987), 196–97, 190.

52. Marianne Moore, "A Burning Desire to Be Explicit," in *Tell Me, Tell Me* (New York: Viking Press, 1967). The latter statement occurs in Moore's essay "Idiosyncrasy and Technique," in *A Marianne Moore Reader* (New York: Viking Press, 1961), 172.

53. Marianne Moore, "Robert Andrew Parker," in *A Marianne Moore Reader*, 205.

54. Wallace Stevens, "About One of Marianne Moore's Poems," in *The Necessary Angel: Essays on Reality and the Imagination* (New York: Random House, 1951), 95.

55. Moore, "Poetry," 267.

56. Bryher, *The Heart to Artemis*, cited in Charles Molesworth, *Marianne Moore: A Literary Life* (New York: Atheneum, 1990), 153.

57. Marianne Moore, from an article in *The Dial*, cited in Darlene Williams Erickson, *Illusion Is More Precise than Precision* (Tuscaloosa: University of Alabama, 1992), 70.

58. Marianne Moore, "A Virtuoso of Make-Believe," in *The Complete Prose of Marianne Moore*, ed. Patricia C. Willis (New York: Viking, 1986), 416.

59. Marianne Moore, "A Bold Virtuoso," in *Complete Prose*, 446. In another article published the same year, Moore states, "Wallace Stevens is the La Fontaine of our day" (430).

60. Moore, "Foreword," *A Marianne Moore Reader*, xv.

61. Moore, "The Pangolin," *Complete Poems*, 118–19. All parenthetical references to Moore's poems in the text hereafter are to this edition.

62. Moore, "He 'Digesteth Harde Yron,'" 100.

CONCLUSION

1. Martin Heidegger, "The Age of the World Picture," trans. William Lovitt, in *The Question Concerning Technology and Other Essays* (New York: Harper, 1975), 131.

2. Bruno Latour, "How to Be Iconophilic in Art, Science, and Religion?" in *Picturing Science, Producing Art*, ed. Caroline A. Jones and Peter Galison (New York: Routledge, 1997), 427.

3. Giorgio Agamben, *Stanzas: Word and Phantasm in Western Culture*, trans. Ronald L. Martinez (Minneapolis: University of Minnesota Press, 1993), xvi.

4. Bruno Latour, "How to Be Iconophilic," 422.

5. Karl Marx, *Capital: A Critique of Political Economy*, vol. 1, trans. Ben Fowkes (Harmondsworth: Penguin, 1976), 165.

6. Marx, *Capital*, 163.

7. Paul de Man, "Lyric and Modernity," in *Blindness and Insight* (Minneapolis: University of Minnesota Press, 1983), 185.

8. De Man, "Lyric and Modernity," 185.

INDEX

abstraction, 111, 132, 133, 181–82, 218, 239, 319n.27

"abyss of images," 246

Adorno, Theodor, 68–69, 71

aesthetic(s), 6, 24, 64, 72; aesthetic experience, 297n.14; aesthetic pleasure, 64; discourse of, 24; genealogy, 6, 15–16, 27; in modern culture, 23; nature of, viewed through history of materiality, 16; philosophy, 25, 27, 28; role, 40

Agamben, Giorgio, 159–62, 255, 268, 290, 292

"age of the world picture," 13

air, 96, 97, 104, 105, 107, 117, 127, 132; lyric, 113; mechanization, 253. *See also* breath; wind

"airy semblances," 204

aisthēsis, 24

Alexandrian philosophy, 171, 289

alienation, 174

allegory, 262, 273–76, 291; allegorical image(s), 73, 262, 273; allegorical lyric, 246, 273, 275, 284, 293, 329n.48; allegorical object, 73; allegorical poetry, 71, 293, 329n.48; automata as problem of, 71; Baroque, 275; Benjamin's theory of, 308n.37; de Man's theory of, 293; monadological theory of, 81

amalgam, 92–93

anachronism, 129, 172

anagrams, 91; anagrammatic dolls, 91–93

analogy(ies), 4, 6, 15, 85, 86, 92, 159; atomism's reliance on, 175, 187; mechanistic, 106; role in shaping knowledge of material substance, 2–3

analysis, 165, 168, 169

"analytic" verse, 17

anamorphosis, 66–67, 157, 193, 285

androids, 56, 61

angel(s), 54–55, 67, 75, 99; angelic animal, 283; angelic intelligence, 304n.52; angelic mind, 80; and animalcula, 195–98; anomalous body, 24; automata and, 54, 55; dolls and, 77, 79, 80; in Duino elegies, 75–77, 79–80; figure, 78; "mechanical" and clairvoyant mind, 76; as medium, 76; methodological, 304n.53; souls and, 76; virtue, 115–16; and the weather, 115–16

animal-machine, 135, 272, 277, 285

animal magnetism, 139–44, 212, 227

Williams, C. K., 240, 242; "Tar,"
    325n.54
Williams, William Carlos, 274
Wilson, C. T. R., 153–54, 162, 169,
    170, 252
Wilson, Catherine, 51, 135, 159, 175,
    185, 188, 195, 197, 314n.29
wind, 107, 114, 116, 119, 129–31, 136,
    137, 229, 235. *See also* breath
Winter, Alison, 315n.41
Wittgenstein, Ludwig, 168, 175, 183,
    213

Wollen, Peter, 317n.65
wonder, 64
word, naming power of the, 30
World War II, 216–17

X ray, 210, 214

Yeats, William Butler, 17–22, 27, 68, 71,
    74, 204–5, 310n.49, 313n.21; "Byzan-
    tium," 17, 20–21, 41, 111, 205, 278;
    "The Dolls," 296n.9; "Sailing to By-
    zantium," 17–20, 41, 111, 278

Compositor:	Binghamton Valley Composition
Text:	11/15 Granjon
Display:	Granjon
Printer and Binder:	Data Reproductions